Foreword by Bill G

D0607950

12-11-21

the world's best
brunches
where to find them
& how to make them

lonely planet

Melbourne ✶ London ✶ Oakland

Contents

Drinks & condiments

✶ ✶ ✶ ✶ ✶

Foreword

*****

By Bill Granger

When I opened my first bills café in Darlinghurst, Sydney, in 1992, I can honestly say that I wasn't intentionally setting out to make serving all-day brunch my 'concept'. Restricted by the fact that the local council would only allow me to trade between 7.30am and 4pm, I decided that it would make sense to take a leaf out of the classic brasserie's book and serve unfussy offerings throughout the day with no particular division between breakfast and lunch. At the time there was no one I knew of in Sydney doing what I was doing, so I guess that's why brunch-style dishes became my signature repertoire. And they still are to this day, over 20 years later, at all my restaurants in four different continents. I guess that's testament to the appeal of brunch!

As far back as 1895 author Guy Beringer wrote an article entitled 'Brunch: a plea' for the UK's *Hunter's Weekly*. An extract from it reads: 'Why not a new meal, served around noon that starts with tea or coffee, marmalade and other breakfast fixtures before moving along to the heavier fare? By eliminating the need to get up early on Sunday, brunch would make life brighter for Saturday night carousers.' It makes perfect sense. Whether you've been out late the night before or awoken early by your beloved little larks, a substantial late-breakfast-come-early-lunch fits the bill like nothing else.

My own early adult experiences of brunch were catching up with my friends at about 2pm, after a big night out in hedonistic, late Eighties Sydney (is 5pm the reasonable cut off for brunch?). However, my true indoctrination was when I had children. I still smile at the irony of the fact that the same relaxed meal is just as appealing to sleep-deprived young parents keen to share their highs and woes with sympathetic sorts, as it is to nocturnal rabble rousers.

So what constitutes brunch? We know *when* you eat it, but what type of dishes are best suited to and most commonly consumed during this particular time slot? The answer is, these days, a pretty wide range of things. For me, the important parts are good, fresh ingredients put together in a simple and pleasing way – and coffee. Always coffee.

For a long time those American favourites: pancakes, eggs (every which way), crispy bacon and all the rest were considered 'classic brunch fayre'. But these days the options have become a lot more diverse and 'New World'. In the Granger household it might be eggs Benedict one weekend, shakshuka or nasi goreng another or organic sourdough toast with avocado or buffalo mozzarella and fresh tomato when I can't be bothered to cook. There are no rules. And, for me, it's been this way for a while.

As a schoolboy I made mid-morning excursions to Chinatown in Melbourne with my friend Simon and his family, where we were greeted by yum cha trolleys laden with piles of steamed dumplings, white fluffy barbecued pork buns and spring rolls. Then, ten years or so on, backpacking across Thailand and India, I brunched on pretty much every type of street and beach food; from green chilli omelettes with cumin and fresh chutney in a soft bread roll to fried rice, with banana coconut pancakes drenched in palm syrup. These days, when I'm in Japan, I love onigiri with salted fish, or steaming bowls of udon with spring onions, egg and crunchy tempura batter. Anything goes.

And the same applies to whether you're having a lazy morning-into-afternoon at home or refuelling in a favourite local café or restaurant. Brunch should feel like a treat, never an effort or a rigid commitment.

America has always had a culture of diners, that wonderful idea that you can eat at any time of the day, not unlike the English caff. This has inspired me no end and, to this day, I love to be able to serve anyone whatever they want whenever they want it, not constrained by societal ideas of when we should be eating. I like the rebelliousness of brunch and I wholeheartedly encourage anyone who is eating in one of my dining rooms to be as rebellious as they like.

There is no other meal but brunch that can be stretched from 9am until 5pm, depending on who you are, your stage in life and what your mood dictates. It's the most flexible meal and the most intimate, best served with close friends and family.

It helps if the sun is shining, of course, and that sense of light, bright, laid-back dining is something I've always tried to instil in my restaurants, but even the gloomiest of days and spirits is lifted by that most indulgent of gastronomic pursuits.

One of the other reasons I'm obsessed with brunch dates back to my early starts cooking in the café in Sydney. I'd have to be at the fruit and vegetable and flower markets at around 4am to clinch the best produce and get the best buys. And once I'd finished my shopping and I could go and have my toasted egg, spinach and provolone focaccia and stiff espresso with the Italian market traders. Having this early snack meant I was ready for brunch by late morning, usually something Asian which Sydney does so well. I'm still an early riser, an enthusiasm for seizing the day that my wife doesn't share, but luckily she *does* share my passion for eating at around 11am most days.

In a time when we're all increasingly busy brunch seems to have a new importance. Sure, in some ways it's a luxury, like afternoon tea, but we need these feel-good rituals that give us the chance to reconnect with friends, families, food and ourselves, all the more. The fact that brunch is not on the everyday 'schedule' in the same way that breakfast, lunch and dinner are gives it an air of spontaneous, devil-may-care, unstructured abandon that we all deserve to indulge in from time to time.

Dishes

Legend

E **Easy** - A very basic recipe, eg, putting together a sandwich or tossing salad ingredients.

M **Medium** - Suitable for the average home cook.

C **Complex** - Several parts to make, or lots of ingredients to prepare, or a specific technique involved that may take some practice.

 Vegetarian

Knife and fork

Spoon

Chopsticks

Hands

Healthy

Indulgent

* Açai Bowl *

BRAZIL

It looks like ice cream, and tastes like ice cream, but this tropical Brazilian superfood snack couldn't be healthier. Refreshingly cool and satisfyingly filling (it's low GI), it's heaven in a bowl.

What is it?

An açai (ah-sah-ee) bowl (*açai na tigela*) is a mixture of slightly thawed, super-healthy Amazonian açai berries blended with liquid (such as guarana, almond milk, coconut water or apple juice) and served in a bowl topped with fresh fruit, granola and/or nuts, providing a crunchy counterpoint to the softness of the açai mixture.

Origin

Packed with antioxidants, amino acids, omega-3 fatty acid, fibre and protein, the berries of the Amazonian açai palm were barely known outside the Amazon until the 1970s. Legendary Brazilian Jujitsu founder Carlos Gracie popularised açai bowl in Rio de Janeiro in the 1980s, and it wasn't long before local surfers adopted the snack as the perfect post-session pick-me-up. In the early noughties, the first batch of açai pulp winged its way to the USA, and Hawaii and Southern California became the first places where açai bowl found a foreign home. Fast forward a decade and various incarnations can be found from Sydney to London.

Tasting

Waking up on a hot, sticky morning by the Brazilian seaside (especially when nursing a Caipirinha-induced hangover) the cool combination of berries and nuts in an açai bowl provide the ultimate wake-up call, with a health kick to boot.

With a similar consistency to lightly-defrosted gelato, the rich, deep-purple acai pulp or powder mixture forms the basis of this attractive tropical dish. Traditional Brazilian toppings include sliced banana and a sprinkling of granola, but Western cafes usually also offer an additional range of healthy toppings such as blueberries, shaved coconut, seeds and nuts.

While the açai mixture, which tastes a little bit like blackberries mixed with dark chocolate, is deliciously moreish by itself, the crunch of granola and nuts provides delightful texture. The fruity toppings add a healthy dimension, and help to tone down the chill of the açai mixture. But you'll have to scoff it all down before the mixture melts.

Finding it

Açai bowls are usually sold in beachside kiosks and juice bars for around BRL9 (US$3.69) (with banana and granola).

* TIP * While you'll gain more health benefits eating fresh açai in Brazil (outside the country, it can usually only be purchased in pulp or powder form), keep in mind that açai is traditionally blended with the juice from another Amazonian berry, guarana. Super-high in caffeine, it provides a great energy boost in the morning, but doesn't make the most ideal pre-bedtime snack.

By Sarah Reid

Recipe Açai Bowl

Choose the liquid to blend with the açai powder/pulp to suit your personal taste; the milkier the liquid, the creamier the mixture will be.

INGREDIENTS

1 heaped tbs freeze-dried açai powder or about 110g (4oz) slightly thawed açai pulp

1 heaped tbs milled seeds (chia, flax, sunflower etc)

⅓ cup almond milk, coconut milk, coconut water, or apple juice

¾ cup frozen blueberries and/or sliced banana

For the toppings

⅓ cup fresh seasonal berries and/or figs

½ ripe banana, sliced

2 tbs granola, muesli or oats

1 tbs seeds or other toppings (try flaxseed, chia seeds, shredded coconut, jungle peanuts and/or bee pollen)

METHOD

1. Blend the açai powder/pulp with the milled seeds, liquid and frozen fruit.

2. Add more liquid until it reaches the desired consistency, according to your personal taste.

3. Transfer the mixture to a breakfast bowl and serve immediately.

4. Top the mixture with fresh berries, sliced banana, granola and seeds, in whichever combination you prefer.

SERVES 1

* Ackee and Saltfish *

JAMAICA

Hungry Jamaicans have been known to sprint like Usain Bolt in order to procure their morning fix of ackee and saltfish, the much-loved breakfast of champions that's revered nationwide.

What is it?

The dish has two key ingredients and a number of interchangeable accompaniments. Ackee, a tropical fruit with a buttery, egg-like consistency, is pan-fried with dried, preserved saltfish (usually cod) along with onion, tomatoes and spices. The sautéed stew is heaped alongside optional sides of fried breadfruit, dumplings, boiled plantain or bammy (cassava pancake) to create a rich, starch-heavy breakfast.

Origin

Ackee and saltfish has its roots in the slave era when it was served as a cheap breakfast for indentured workers. The ackee fruit is native to West Africa, but was transported to Jamaica on slave ships sometime in the 1770s. Saltfish is a cheap and nutritious food source that was easy to import and, due to its non-perishable nature, could be stored for long periods without spoiling. Ackee's scientific name, *Blighia Sapida,* honours William Bligh of HMS *Bounty* fame, who first shipped the fruit to London in 1793.

Tasting

Unusually for a fruit, ackee is highly toxic if consumed before it's ripe, hence there are strict rules surrounding its export. The ackee you find outside Jamaica is nearly always the canned variety. The best fresh Jamaican ackee has a mild, creamy flavour and a texture not unlike scrambled eggs. Its faint sweetness counterbalances the saltiness of the fish to create a marriage made in Caribbean heaven. The sides – boiled plantain, breadfruit, bammy and, occasionally, rice and peas – are assembled to provide bulk, starch and mellowness, supporting the main act in the same way that the Wailers once supported Bob Marley.

Served all over Jamaica, ackee and saltfish is best enjoyed in some quintessentially ramshackle food shack within sight of the beach with a reggae beat thumping in the distance. Wash it down with a mug of super-smooth Blue Mountain coffee – possibly the best java you'll ever drink.

Finding it

For taste, authenticity and atmosphere, look no further than Smurf's Café in Jamaica's Treasure Beach where the dish costs US$8.

* TIP * Ackee's toxicity means that only skilled cooks should attempt to prepare the raw fruit. The uninitiated are better off using canned ackee. Although the fruit is cultivated in a variety of countries, Jamaica is the only place where it is consumed with gusto.

* By Brendan Sainsbury *

Recipe Ackee and Saltfish

INGREDIENTS

230g (8oz) saltfish

1 onion, finely chopped

3 garlic cloves, finely chopped

1 green bell pepper, finely chopped

3 spring onions, finely chopped

1 Scotch bonnet chilli, seeded if liked and finely chopped (wear gloves to do this and take care not to get any on your skin or near your eyes)

1 tbs olive oil or vegetable oil

1 tomato, chopped

1 thyme sprig

ground black pepper

540g (19oz) can of ackee

bammy and/or dumplings and/or boiled plantain and/or or rice and peas, to serve (optional)

METHOD

1. Soak the saltfish in a bowl of cold water overnight.

2. Drain the saltfish.

3. Put the fish in a pan, cover with cold water. Bring to the boil and cook the fish for 20 minutes.

4. Remove the fish from the water and leave until cool enough to handle, then break the fish into small flakes.

5. Place the prepared onion, garlic, pepper, spring onions and chilli in a large frying pan with the oil. Fry over a medium heat for about 5 minutes, until the ingredients soften.

6. Add the chopped tomato, flaked fish, thyme and black pepper to the frying pan. Stir and cook for another 10 minutes, until the vegetables are cooked and tender.

7. Carefully stir in the ackee (it's delicate). Cook for 2–3 minutes, until the ackee is heated through.

8. Serve with optional sides of bammy, dumplings, boiled plantain, or rice and peas.

SERVES 4–5

* Aussie Steak Sandwich *

AUSTRALIA

The Aussies love a good barbecue and what better dish to have for brunch than a steak sandwich? It's simple to make but stuffed full of great ingredients.

What is it?

Sandwiches come and sandwiches go, but the steak sandwich remains a firm Aussie favourite thanks to its hearty nature. Yes, it's sloppy (in the best possible way) but who can resist a juicy slab of steak sandwiched in a fresh flatbread with caramelised onions, tomatoes, rocket, beetroot and a fried egg?

Tasting

The Aussie sandwich sounds like it has a lot going on. This recipe contains no fewer than six ingredients – juicy minute steak, caramelised onions, a fried egg, sliced tomatoes, rocket and the kicker, beetroot – yet each item plays a role and it all comes together well. Eating a steak sandwich means encountering a range of different textures and flavours – from the tender to the crunchy, sweet to the savoury. If you ever find yourself in a patch of good weather in Australia, you'll find barbecues going on in parks and backyards. Try to get yourself invited to one! Yes, biting into a steak sandwich could get messy, but don't worry, you won't be the only one making a mess... and everyone else at the barbecue will be too busy stuffing their faces to care.

Origin

Some histories say that the sandwich was named after John Montagu, the 4th Earl of Sandwich (and also patron to Captain James Cook, who explored Australia, among other places). The legend goes that the Earl, an inveterate gambler, asked for meat to be put between two bread slices so that he could keep gambling instead of having to stop to eat a meal on a plate. Today, sandwiches are ubiquitous the world round. In Australia, where cattle farming is worth $12.3 billion, it's no surprise that the steak sandwich is the bread-and-filling combo of choice at barbecues.

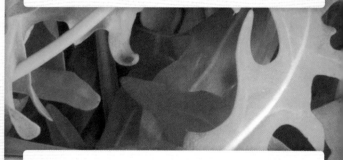

Finding it

Get yourself invited to an Aussie barbecue (free!) or sample a steak sandwich for $25.25 (US$22) at the Perth Merrywell, Burswood.

* VARIATIONS * In the USA, ferret out the cheese steak and the reuben sandwich. The cheese steak has roots in Philadelphia and is made by stuffing thinly sliced steak and melted provolone cheese into a long bread roll. The reuben is made with hot corned beef, Swiss cheese, sauerkraut and Russian dressing in between rye bread. The Aussies will, of course, claim that their version is better.

* By Shawn Low *

Recipe Aussie Steak Sandwich

INGREDIENTS

salt and ground black pepper

2 minute steaks

4 tbs olive oil

1 onion, sliced

1 tsp balsamic vinegar

1 tsp brown sugar

2 eggs

2 Turkish pide, split, toasted and buttered

1 tbs mayonnaise

4 cooked beetroot slices, drained

1 tomato, sliced

40g (1½oz) rocket, shredded

cold beer, to serve

METHOD

1. If you are using a charcoal barbecue, get it going first.

2. Season the steaks with salt and pepper and rub them with 1 tbs of the olive oil.

3. Set aside the steaks to rest at room temperature while you prepare the onion.

4. Heat 2 tbs olive oil in a frying pan over a low heat.

5. Once the oil is hot, add the onion.

6. Cook the onion for 15 minutes, until soft and golden.

7. Add the balsamic vinegar and sugar to the onion.

8. Cook for 20–25 minutes, stirring occasionally, until the onion is caramelised.

9. Set aside the onion.

10. The charcoal should now be a dull, uniform grey and ready to cook on. If you are using a gas barbecue or a griddle pan on the stove, set them to a medium-high heat.

11. Once the barbecue or griddle is searing hot, add the steaks.

12. Cook the steaks to your preference; they only take about 2 minutes to cook for rare steaks, or a little longer for medium or well-done ones. Flip them once during the cooking time.

13. Remove the steaks to a warm plate to rest.

14. Place a frying pan on the barbecue or stove and add the remaining 1 tbs olive oil.

15. Once the oil is hot, crack in the eggs.

16. Fry the eggs sunny-side up.

17. Assemble the sandwiches: spread the mayonnaise over the base of pides, then top each with a steak, some onions, beetroot, tomato, rocket and a fried egg.

18. Enjoy immediately with cold beer. And some napkins.

SERVES 2

* Beer Damper *

AUSTRALIA

A painless bread to make (if you don't mind donating a beer to the cause), damper is also one of the most delicious – particularly eaten alfresco while camping.

What is it?

Damper is a traditional soda bread, long favoured by Australian bushmen for its simplicity. The ingenious use of beer instead of water makes it even tastier (and more Australian). It can be baked on a campfire in the outback, or in a kitchen oven deep in suburbia – either way it's best served warm with butter and lashings of wild fruit jam.

Origin

Indigenous Australians have been making damper for millennia, using ground-up grains and nuts mixed with other bushtucker and baked on the hot ashes of firepits. When Europeans arrived, those who took to the outback – stockmen, drovers, bushrangers and swagmen – adopted this cooking style, but introduced wheat flour, bicarb soda (baking soda) and sometimes milk or beer into the mix. Now damper is typically cooked in camp ovens (heavy metal pans that can be covered in hot coals) by recreational travellers, or at home. It also appears on menus in trendy coffee shops and restaurants, accompanied by native fruit jams.

Tasting

Baking your own bread on a campfire in the midst of the outback, under a ceiling of a stars, is a quintessentially Australian experience. As any seasoned old swagman will tell you, it's best to allow the damper to cool slightly once you've taken it out of the camp oven, but get stuck in while it's still warm. Tear it open, smudge a bit of butter on it and a slathering of jam, and then serve with a cup of billy tea. It doesn't really matter if you're nowhere near Australia, just shut your eyes and the smell and taste of the bread will do the rest. This is a recipe for impressing your camping mates – it really is a deceptively simple dish to smash out, and the result is a brilliant brunch.

Finding it

Experience sunrise over Uluru and Kata Tjuta while eating damper on the Desert Awakenings Tour (Ayers Rock Resort) for $168 (US$146).

* TIP * Try experimenting with different kinds of beer and compare flavours. Unfiltered beers (seek out some Coopers if you want the genuine Aussie article) make a really tasty damper. For darker bread, use stout.

* By Patrick Kinsella *

Recipe Beer Damper

INGREDIENTS

4 cups self-raising flour

1 tsp bicarb soda (baking soda)

1 tsp salt

2 tbs butter

350–375mL (12–13fl oz) beer

METHOD

1. Prepare your camp oven by heating it over moderate coals. If you are cooking the damper at home, preheat the oven to 180°C (350°F).

2. Place a baking tray or pizza stone in the oven, if you are making the damper at home.

3. Sift together the flour, bicarb soda (baking soda) and salt into a large bowl. If you are cooking in the bush and don't have a sieve, simply mix together the dry ingredients in a bowl (or bucket!).

4. Add the butter.

5. Rub the butter into the flour mixture using your fingertips, until no lumps remain.

6. Gradually add just enough beer for you to be able to form a dough that you can knead. The dough shouldn't be too sloppy.

7. Knead the dough for a couple of minutes, to bring it together and ensure it is smooth.

8. Shape the dough into a round.

9. Place the dough on the preheated baking tray or pizza stone in the oven, or directly into the camp oven. If you are using a camp oven, make sure there are plenty of hot coals on the lid.

10. Bake the damper for 30–35 minutes. When it is done, the crust should be golden and the base should sound hollow when tapped.

11. Remove the damper from the oven and leave it to cool slightly on a wire rack, or on whatever camping gear seems an appropriate alternative!

MAKES 1 MEDIUM-SIZED LOAF

* Bill's Ricotta Hotcakes *

AUSTRALIA

These lighter-than-light pancakes, speckled with clumps of soft ricotta, deliver up a dash of Australian sunshine on a plate.

What is it?

Bill Granger's signature dish packs quite the punch, as pancakes go. Disarmingly fluffy, they're also surprisingly substantial, thanks to the nuggets of protein-rich ricotta cheese crumbled into the batter. Served up warm in a higgledy-piggledy pile, they're rounded off with fresh banana, butter studded with crisp honeycomb and a dusting of icing sugar. One thing's certain: you won't be leaving hungry.

Origin

Every restaurant's brunch menu needs a good pancake – it's practically breakfast law. On a quest to create the perfect specimen, Bill took inspiration from Eastern Europe, with its traditional Jewish holiday fare of blintzes – pancakes stuffed with cheese and fried in oil. And when he discovered in Sydney a supplier of the freshest, creamiest ricotta, he knew he'd struck culinary gold. The ricotta's creamy texture and mildly sour tang offset the lashings of sweet goo drizzled on top.

Tasting

On a weekday morning in Bill's restaurants, suits rub shoulders with media folk and parents with pushchairs. Brunch here isn't just a meal, it's a way of life. You'll see neighbours running into one another and strangers striking up conversation across huge, communal tables strewn with newspapers. And then there's the hotcakes. Fluffy fried batter: so far, so delicious. But it's the surprise pockets of ricotta that provide the *pièce de résistance* of these fabulous little soufflés. Their crisped edges give way to a spongy centre flecked with the creamy curd, adding smooth texture and a fresh, savoury kick. Sweet, sliced banana is served alongside them and over the whole lot oozes honeycomb butter, drenching pancakes and bananas alike with crunchy, toothsome sweetness.

Finding it

Bill's restaurants can be found in London, Tokyo, Seoul and even Honolulu, but there's nowhere better to experience ricotta hotcakes than in bills in Darlinghurst, Sydney, where it all began. Expect to pay A$20 (US$17.80).

* TIP * Hosting a brunch party? Save time by preparing the batter the night before. Combine the wet ingredients and the dry ingredients in separate bowls, and whisk the egg whites: all you'll need to do come morning is throw them all together. If you're preparing lots of hotcakes you can avoid having to cook them in batches by slightly undercooking them in the pan, then finishing them off together on a baking tray in the oven.

* By Jessica Cole *

Recipe Ricotta Hotcakes with Banana and Honeycomb Butter

Hotcake batter can be stored for up to 24 hours, covered with plastic wrap in the refrigerator. Store leftover honeycomb butter in the freezer – it's great on toast.

INGREDIENTS

for the honeycomb butter

250g (8oz) unsalted butter, softened

100g (3 ⅓oz) sugar honeycomb, crushed with a rolling pin

2 tbs honey

for the hotcakes

1 ⅓ cups ricotta

¾ cup (6fl oz) milk

4 eggs, separated

1 cup plain (all-purpose) flour

1 tsp baking powder

a pinch of salt

50g (1 ½oz) butter

to serve

banana

icing sugar for dusting

METHOD

1. First, make the honeycomb butter. Place all ingredients in a food processor and blend until smooth. Shape into a log on plastic wrap, roll, seal and chill in a refrigerator for 2 hours.

2. Place ricotta, milk and egg yolks in a mixing bowl and mix to combine.

3. Sift the flour, baking powder and salt into a bowl. Add to the ricotta mixture and mix until just combined.

4. Place egg whites in a clean dry bowl and beat until stiff peaks form.

5. Fold egg whites through batter in two batches, with a large metal spoon.

6. Lightly grease a large non-stick frying pan with a small portion of the butter and drop 2 tbs of batter per hotcake into the pan (don't cook more than 3 per batch). Cook over low to medium heat for 2 minutes, or until hotcakes have golden undersides.

7. Turn hotcakes and cook on the other side until golden and cooked through. Transfer to a plate and quickly assemble with the other ingredients.

8. Slice one banana lengthways on to a plate, stack 3 hotcakes on top with a slice of honeycomb butter. Dust with icing sugar.

SERVES 6–8

* Biscuits with Gravy *

USA

**Like the culinary version of your favourite teddy bear
and blankie, a big ol' helpin' of flaky biscuits and decadently
rich gravy is America's breakfast comfort food.**

What is it?

Flour, leavening, fats and a little milk or buttermilk
is all that's needed for biscuits. Kneaded lightly and
folded a few times to aerate, these cakey quick-
breads have a sturdy crust and delicate layers. The
milk-based gravy usually contains added sausage,
but, these days, it could be bacon, oysters or
vegetarian crumbles. Biscuits are eaten mostly at
breakfast, but can appear with stews, at picnics, or
on Thanksgiving.

Origin

In the post-Revolutionary agrarian United States,
breakfast had to be three things: cheap, filling,
and not British. While Scottish, Irish and English
immigrants brought the scone to the USA, the
recipe morphed to leave out the sugar and the name
changed to the French-inspired biscuit (*biscuit*:
literally, 'twice cooked'). Yeast-less biscuits were
made inexpensively from on-hand farmhouse
staples: flour, milk and fat.

Tasting

Although physicists and philosophers have tested
the many earthly substances, none have proved
as fluffily delicious as the perfectly baked biscuit.
First-timers: try splitting one in half slowly, watching
the layers of flaky strata burst with hug-flavoured
steam, and slather some freshly churned sweet
cream butter or homemade preserves on top.

 Some families in the American South have
their own closely guarded recipe that goes back
generations. Unless you need the calories for a full
day's work on the farm, a full plate of biscuits with
gravy is usually reserved for weekend brunches.
If you can't join a cattle drive, just find an old-time
diner – preferably one with decor from the 1960s
and a beehive hairdo-sporting waitress who calls
you 'hon' – or, even better, make the dish at home.

Finding it

Pine State Biscuits in Portland, Oregon, combines
North Carolinian recipes with local ingredients to
achieve superlative biscuitry. Dishes cost US$2–9.

*** TIP * You want real biscuits and gravy? Skip the fancy-schmancy restaurants
offering souped-up versions of the classic and instead look for truck stops, diners and
neighbourhood breakfast joints. While the Deep South's buttermilk biscuits are the most
famous, classic biscuits and gravy can be found all over the USA, especially in rural areas.**

* By Alex Leviton *

Recipe Biscuits with Sausage Gravy

If your country doesn't sell buttermilk, you can make your own version. Just add 1 tbs lemon juice or white vinegar to 1 cup regular milk and wait until it curdles (about 15 minutes).

INGREDIENTS

For the biscuits

1 cup unbleached all-purpose (plain) flour (or 2 cups all-purpose flour if cake flour is not available)

1 cup cake flour, if available (see above)

¾ tsp salt

3 tsp baking powder

2 tbs unsalted butter, cut into tiny pieces and, if possible, chilled in the freezer

2 tbs shortening (lard or white vegetable shortening)

¾ cup buttermilk

about 2 tbs melted butter, for brushing

For the sausage gravy

450g (1lb) country or breakfast sausages

⅓ cup unbleached all-purpose (plain) flour

3 cups milk

2 tsp black pepper

salt, to taste

METHOD

1. Preheat the oven to 230°C (450°F).

2. Combine the flours, salt and baking powder in a large bowl.

3. Quickly cut or rub in the chilled butter and shortening, using a pastry blender or your fingers. Blend until the mixture resembles coarse sand, then make a well in the centre.

4. Pour in the buttermilk and mix lightly with a spoon and then with your hands to create a sticky dough. Try not to handle the dough too much.

5. Transfer the dough to a well-floured surface. Gently pat the dough flat, using your hands. Fold the dough in half and pat it flat again, repeating a few times, to add in air.

6. Use a floured round or square biscuit cutter (the edge of a juice glass works in a pinch) to cut out biscuits that are 5cm (2in) in diameter.

7. Place the biscuits on an ungreased baking sheet lined with baking paper. For moister biscuits, space them close together during baking. For harder exteriors, space them well apart.

8. Brush the tops of the biscuits with a little melted butter.

9. Bake the biscuits for 12–15 minutes, until well risen and light golden brown.

10. Meanwhile, make the gravy. Remove the casings from the sausages, discarding the casings. Fry the sausage meat in a large pan without oil over a medium-high heat until it is browned, breaking up the meat into small pieces as it cooks.

11. Stir in the flour until it dissolves in the fat from the sausages. Slowly add the milk, incorporating it gradually and stirring all the time to form a smooth gravy containing lumps of sausage.

12. Reduce the heat to low and simmer the gravy, stirring constantly, for about 12 minutes, until it is thickened.

13. Season to taste with salt and pepper. Spoon the warm gravy mixture over the biscuits and serve fresh from the oven.

MAKES 8–12 BISCUITS; SERVES 4

* Blueberry muffins *

CANADA; USA

The wafting aroma of freshly baked blueberry muffins – could your brunch table be complete without them? No. No it couldn't.

What is it?

With the addition of fruit, what might be dismissed as a rustic cupcake becomes a pivotal member of a healthy diet. Almost. Maybe not exactly. Purists might argue the point in grand cake/muffin debates, but it would be a fine distinction and, ultimately, who cares? This moist, fragrant bakery item is the go-to choice for the sweet-toothed bruncher.

Origin

Muffins can be sweet or savoury, and are known as a quick bread – that is, a bread made to rise by methods other than yeast. In the case of muffins, the raising agent is bicarb soda (baking soda). This form of muffin is an American invention, likely starting life in savoury form before the genius addition of fruit and sugar struck. There's almost no limit to what ends up in a muffin, but it's safe to say that adding chocolate pushes it into cake territory.

Tasting

Blue is not a colour you long for in your food. But in a muffin, a blueberry is exactly what you want. It begins though, at the top. The muffin top. If you're lucky, there'll be a rock or two of large sugar crystals on the golden surface. And underneath there'll be that craggy, un-cake-like crumb which a muffin really should have. It's not a cake! The crumb is fine and it melts in your mouth. And then the majesty of the blueberry hits home, its fragrant, floral sweetness; its slight tang; its gift of moisture to the mouth to counterbalance the soft, sweet crumb. Despite its special blueness, it's the everyman ability of the blueberries to blend into the whole that lets you know that this is the king of muffins.

Finding it

Go for gold at Thomas Keller's Bouchon Bakery in New York (and elsewhere) and experience the perfect muffin for US$3.

* VARIATIONS * Cake/muffin debates aside, chocolate might be worth considering along your blueberry muffin adventure. Not for the purist obviously, but chocolate adds a little decadence and texture; life's too short for arguments, try it and make up your own mind.

Recipe Blueberry Muffins

INGREDIENTS

2½ cups all-purpose (plain) flour

2 tsp baking powder

½ tsp baking soda (bicarb soda)

1 cup caster sugar

½ tsp salt

2 eggs

½ cup melted butter

1½ cups buttermilk

1 tsp vanilla essence

1½ cups frozen or fresh blueberries

Demerara sugar, to glaze

METHOD

1. Preheat the oven to 190°C (375°F).

2. Grease a standard 12-cup muffin pan and line it with cupcake wrappers, or use a lightly oiled silicone muffin pan.

3. Sift the flour, baking powder, baking soda, sugar and salt into a bowl.

4. Whisk the egg in a separate bowl.

5. Add the melted butter, buttermilk and vanilla essence to the egg.

6. Pour the liquid mixture into the dry ingredients, stirring gently to just combine. Don't over-mix it.

7. Fold the blueberries through the batter.

8. Fill the 12 cupcake wrappers with the batter and sprinkle a little Demerara sugar on top.

9. Bake the muffins for about 25 minutes, until golden and firm to the touch.

10. Allow the muffins to cool in the pan for 5 minutes, then transfer them to a wire rack to cool further.

11. Eat the muffins while they are warm; the fresher they are, the better they'll be.

MAKES 12

* Breakfast Burrito *

NEW MEXICO, USA

Eggs: check. Potatoes: check. Spicy heat: check. A bit of grease: check. Energy-giving protein: check and check. The breakfast burrito is tailor-made for a restorative morning-after brunch.

What is it?

Breakfast burritos are available in handheld form, but for a proper sit-down brunch you want the version that takes up a whole plate, with a flour tortilla filled to bursting with eggs, potatoes and some kind of breakfast meat. That's all doused in spicy red or green chile sauce, the signature component of New Mexican cuisine.

Tasting

'Careful,' says the waitress, 'this plate is very hot'. These words are followed by the clink of a heavy porcelain dish being set on a glass-topped diner table. And there sits your burrito in all its glory, bathed in chile and draped with a thin layer of bubbling cheese. Dig into the tender flour tortilla – the ideal forkful is a mix of textures: softy, fluffy scrambled egg, a bit of chewy bacon or crumbly sausage, and the crunchy edge of a hash brown or pan-fried potato. The chile – either a smooth, brick-red sauce or a chunky, vegetal green one – should have real heat, but not overwhelm the other ingredients. And there should be enough of it to moisten every bite of the burrito, no matter how big.

Origin

The handheld breakfast burrito is thought to have originated at the Albuquerque Balloon Fiesta in the early 1970s – perfect food for chilly pre-dawn launches. A few years later, in 1976, Tia Sophia's opened a few blocks off the plaza in downtown Santa Fe, and its menu featured what is generally considered the first plated version. Unlike all the imitators that followed, though, Tia Sophia's default burrito is filled with only breakfast meat and potatoes – you have to request scrambled egg, and pay an extra dollar. Bologna is a meat option, served with additional bacon, sausage or ham on the side.

Finding it

A breakfast burrito at Tia Sophia's, 210 W San Francisco St, Santa Fe, costs US$8.75 (US$9.75 with an egg).

* **VARIATIONS** * You have two decisions to make. What kind of meat? None at all is fine, but bacon, sausage and ham are the standards, and some restaurants offer *chicharrón* (crispy pork skin), chorizo and even Spam. Then, red or green chile? Can't decide? Say 'Christmas' and you'll get half-and-half.

* By Zora O'Neill *

Recipe Breakfast Burritos with Red Chile

INGREDIENTS

For the New Mexican red chile sauce

½ cup New Mexico red chile powder*

½ tsp ground cumin (optional)

2 tbs all-purpose (plain) flour

2 tbs lard or vegetable oil

2–3 garlic cloves, crushed or minced (optional)

2–3 cups chicken stock or water

1 tsp dried oregano (optional)

For the burritos

2–3 tbs vegetable oil

12 bacon strips

3 potatoes

salt and ground black pepper

2 cups (or more) New Mexican red chile sauce

2 tbs butter

10 eggs

4 large flour tortillas

2 cups grated Cheddar or Monterey Jack cheese

Because it is sold dried, New Mexico red chile powder is easier to find than green chile. Don't use the chilli powder found in the spice section of grocery stores, as this uses a different chilli as the base and contains additional spices.

METHOD

1. To make the New Mexico red chile sauce put the chile powder, ground cumin (if using) and flour in a heavy pan. Place over a medium-high heat and stir continuously until the spices are fragrant and the flour has darkened slightly. Remove the pan from the heat and transfer the mixture to a small bowl.

2. Heat the lard or oil in the pan over a medium heat, add the garlic and stir-fry for about 2 minutes, until golden.

3. Stir the chile-flour mixture into the oil-garlic mixture to form a thick paste. Stirring constantly, slowly add half of the stock or water until the mixture becomes velvety in texture. Add the remaining stock or water and the oregano and mix well. Lower the heat and simmer the sauce for about 20 minutes.

4. To make the burritos, heat a little oil in a skillet and fry the bacon. Leave to cool, then cut into 2.5cm (1in) pieces. Pour off the excess grease so that 2 tsp of fat remains in the skillet.

5. To make the hash browns, coarsely grate the potatoes, wrap them in kitchen paper and squeeze out as much excess moisture as possible. Heat the oil in the skillet over a medium heat. Arrange the potatoes in the skillet in an even layer and fry for 3–4 minutes, until browned on the bottom. Flip over the hash brown using a spatula and cook until it is crispy. Remove the hash brown to a piece of kitchen paper to absorb excess oil, then cut or tear into 5cm (2in) pieces.

6. Preheat the oven to 200°C (400°F). Gently warm through the New Mexican red chile sauce in a small pan.

7. Melt the butter on a medium-low heat until bubbling. Lightly beat the eggs and a pinch of salt with a fork in a large bowl. Pour the eggs into the skillet and slowly stir until cooked.

8. To assemble the burritos, place a dry skillet over a medium-high heat and warm each tortilla. It should puff up slightly.

9. In each tortilla, lay out a quarter of the bacon, potatoes and egg, along with ¼ cup of grated cheese. Roll up the burrito and place it on an ovenproof plate. Ladle a quarter of the red chile sauce over each, then top with the remaining cheese.

10. Place the burritos in the preheated oven, uncovered, until the cheese has melted and is bubbling.

MAKES 4 BURRITOS

* Bún Riêu Cua *

VIETNAM

**Sometimes a big bowl of *phở* is just too much –
for a lighter brunch, the Vietnamese fall back on *bún riêu
cua*, vermicelli in a rich and nourishing crab broth.**

What is it?

Bún riêu cua consists of thread-thin rice noodles, served in a fragrant broth flavoured with tomato and crab paste. As with most Vietnamese dishes, these core ingredients are just the starting point for a build-your-own one-pot meal. Common extras include congealed pigs' blood (even stranger than it sounds), fried tofu, water spinach, bean sprouts, banana flowers and Vietnamese mint.

Origin

Bún riêu cua is a northern Vietnamese dish born of the paddy fields that are such a feature of the country's rural landscape. The flooded rice terraces provide the perfect environment for freshwater crabs, which are harvested as a bonus crop when the fields are drained. To create the distinctive crab flavour, whole crabs are ground down in a pestle and mortar, creating a fine paste containing all the goodness of the crab, including the calcium-rich shell.

Tasting

If your seafood limit is fish and chips, *bún riêu cua* might not be the dish for you. With 100 per cent whole crab in the mix, the crab flavour is rich and intense – hell, you almost feel like you are in there swimming around with the things. The congealed pigs' blood is another acquired taste – a soft, slippery, iron-flavoured, chocolate-coloured jelly – but you can't deny that it's packed with vitamins. In fact, the whole dish functions as a kind of vitamin tonic; you can almost feel your body surging as it stores away all these useful nutrients for later use. One thing everyone loves is the ritual of assembling your own Zen garden of extra ingredients on top of the broth, and the texture of the rice noodles – lubricated by soup, they hardly touch the sides as they slip down.

Finding it

Seek out *bún riêu cua* at itinerant stalls around Hanoi's Cho Hom market. Expect to pay VDN 10,000–20,000 ($0.50–$1).

* VARIATIONS * *Bún riêu* comes with all sorts of extra ingredients as well as crab. Seek out *bún riêu ốc*, prepared with snails, and *bún riêu cá*, with pieces of river catfish. Many cooks also bulk up the crab meat with tasty ground pork.

* By Joe Bindloss *

Recipe Bún Riêu Cua

The trick to preparing *bún riêu cua* is to prepare the rice vermicelli separately.

INGREDIENTS

400g (14oz) dried rice vermicelli

For the soup

5 tomatoes

12½ cups chicken stock

3 tbs *gạch cua xào dầu ăn* (Vietnamese crab paste in soybean oil)

3 tbs *gạch tôm xao dau an* (shrimp paste)

170g (6oz) canned crab meat

5 eggs

salt, sugar and *nước mắm* (Vietnamese fish sauce), to taste

For the garnish

handful of water spinach

200g (7oz) firm tofu

pinch of salt

1 tbs vegetable oil

handful of beansprouts

handful of Vietnamese mint

METHOD

1. Soak the vermicelli in warm water until they are flexible but not too soft. Wash the vermicelli in cold water and drain.

2. Prepare the garnishes. Split the stems of the water spinach leaves and pull them into small clumps.

3. To prepare the tofu, sprinkle it with a little salt then leave it for 15 minutes to draw out excess moisture

4. Blot the tofu dry with kitchen paper. Cut the tofu into 5cm (2in) cubes.

5. Heat the oil in a frying pan. Add the cubed tofu to the pan and fry it on a low heat, turning it once when the bottom side is browned, until it is browned on two sides.

6. Remove the tofu to kitchen paper, reserving the oil in the pan for cooking the tomatoes for the soup.

7. Prepare the tomatoes by removing the skin. Cut the tomato into segments. Sauté the tomato segments in the oil remaining in the frying pan for 1–2 minutes, adding a little more oil if necessary, until slightly softened. Set aside.

8. To prepare the broth, bring the chicken stock to the boil in a large pan.

9. Beat together the *gạch cua xào dầu ăn* (crab paste), *gạch tôm xao dau an* (shrimp paste) and eggs in a bowl.

10. Stir the crab meat into the mixture. Then drop spoonfuls of the crab mixture into the boiling broth.

11. Add the tomato segments and continue to cook for a few minutes, until the crab balls are cooked.

12. Season the soup lightly with salt, sugar and *nước mắm* (fish sauce) to taste.

13. To serve, place a handful of rice vermicelli in each of four bowls. Ladle some soup over each portion of vermicelli. Top each portion with water spinach, fried tofu, beansprouts, and Vietnamese mint immediately before you serve the dish.

SERVES 4

* Buttermilk Pancakes *

NORTH AMERICA; EUROPE

Pancakes are a quintessential breakfast and brunch food. In the pantheon of pancakes, buttermilk pancakes are especially beloved for their light, spongy texture and rich flavour.

What is it?

A stack of pancakes made with buttermilk, eggs and flour, cooked on a griddle to a light-golden brown and served with butter, maple syrup or even (for the especially decadent) chocolate chips and whipped cream. Popular with adults and children alike, this dish is best avoided by those avoiding the 'three C's': carbohydrates, calories and cholesterol.

Origin

Pancakes have been around in various forms about as long as humans have been eating cereals made from grains. Basically, if it's made from a starch-based batter and cooked on a hot surface – be it griddle, frying pan or hot stone – you can call it a pancake. While the French national pancake is a thin crepe, which is wrapped around fillings, the North American pancake is more reflective of the continent's rugged nature, thick and bold enough to hold almost any filling dropped in the batter before it is cooked.

Tasting

While in America the crepe is considered haute cuisine, its humble cousin the buttermilk pancake is a distinctly blue-collar dish, served day and night in diners, greasy spoons and truck stops from Maine to California. Whether using a pre-made mix or whipping up the batter from scratch, any eatery with this dish on the menu should serve a few variations using fruits (banana, blueberry and strawberry, served on top or mixed into the batter) or chocolate chips (always added to the raw batter). At their most basic a stack of buttermilk pancakes presents a tasty, carb-loaded meal. But made well, the dish can be transcendent, satisfying the senses from the moment the pancakes reach your table piping hot (enough for pats of butter placed between the golden discs to melt in 30 seconds) until the last satisfying bite.

Finding it

Pancakes come no finer than those made using local flour at Portland's Bob's Red Mill. Expect to pay US$7.

* TIP * No buttermilk in the fridge? No problem! Make your own soured milk by adding 3 tbs lemon juice to 3 cups full-fat milk and leaving it to stand at room temperature for 5 minutes.

* By Joshua Samuel Brown *

Recipe Buttermilk Pancakes

INGREDIENTS

For the dry mix

3 cups all-purpose (plain) flour

2 tbs white or soft light brown sugar

3 tsp baking powder

1¼ tsp bicarb soda (baking soda)

¾ tsp salt

For the wet mix

3 cups buttermilk

3 eggs

⅓ cup melted butter

oil, for greasing

METHOD

1. Combine the dry ingredients in a large bowl.

2. In a separate bowl, mix together the wet ingredients using a whisk.

3. Heat a lightly oiled griddle or pan over a medium heat.

4. While the pan is heating up, add the wet mix to the dry one and combine with a wooden spoon, until they are just blended. Do not over-mix the batter.

5. When the pan is hot enough to cause a drop of water splashed on to its surface to sizzle, you're ready to cook. Pour or scoop about ½ cup of batter on to the griddle. (If you are adding fruit or chocolate chips, now is the time to do so.)

6. Cook for about 3–4 minutes, until the surface has dulled in colour slightly and tiny bubbles appear.

7. Flip over the pancake with a spatula.

8. Cook on the other side for 2–3 minutes, until browned all over. Voilà: Buttermilk pancakes!

MAKES ABOUT 12 PANCAKES

* Chawan-mushi *

JAPAN

Seemingly humble and delicate, yet at the same time intensely flavoured, Japan's ultimate egg dish is an intriguingly savoury and refreshing delight that will ease you into the day.

What is it?

Chawan-mushi is a pale and silky steamed egg custard traditionally filled with pieces of chicken, prawn, ginkgo nuts and lotus root and garnished with mitsuba leaf. The name *chawan-mushi* literally means 'steam in a cup' and refers to the lidded teacups especially used for this dish, which are found in virtually every Japanese home.

Origin

A classic of Japanese cuisine, *chawan-mushi* has been around for centuries, possibly dating as far back as the Heian period (794–1185) when court banquets were all the rage among the Japanese aristocracy. *Chawan-mushi* is likely to have started life as a soup, and is one of only a few Japanese dishes to be eaten with a spoon. These days, it is served as just one item in a multi-course Japanese breakfast, or as an appetiser – hot in winter or chilled in summer.

Tasting

This is about as light and delicate as egg dishes come. Creamy, slippery-smooth *chawan-mushi* is a delight to eat, with comforting mouthfuls of soft egg punctuated with bitesize morsels of meat and vegetables, as though you're on a treasure hunt. More than just an egg custard, the use of *dashi* or Japanese fish stock lends the dish its characteristic *umami* savouriness, while the various fillings make for a tasty surprise. The ultimate expression of *chawan-mushi* can be found in Japan's most prestigious restaurants, where revered chefs elevate the humble dish to tantalising heights with the expert preparation of quivering, perfectly cooked custard and the use of the finest, seasonal ingredients such as the slightly bitter and unique-tasting ginkgo nut or the matsutake mushroom, both only available for a brief spell during autumn.

Finding it

Experience sublime *chawan-mushi* as part of a *kaiseki* (tasting menu) at Kitcho Hirashiyama restaurant in Kyoto for ¥35,000 (US$300).

* DID YOU KNOW? * Increasingly in Western countries, *chawan-mushi* is gaining popularity as a special-occasion dish served on Mother's Day, the egg being a symbol of fertility.

* By Johanna Ashby *

Recipe Chawan-mushi

Use heatproof cups with 200ml (7fl oz) capacity. You can use fillings of your choice, such as crabmeat, white fish, mushrooms, bamboo shoots, peas or cashew nuts. Making your own *dashi* is easy and the ingredients can be found at many large supermarkets. However, powdered or instant *dashi* may be used as a substitute, and this can be purchased from Asian stores.

INGREDIENTS

For the *dashi*

5cm (2in) piece of *kombu* (dried seaweed)

1L (1.75 pints) water

1 cup *katsuobuoshi* (bonito flakes)

For the filling

80g (3oz) chicken breast, diced

1 tsp light soy sauce

1 tsp cooking sake

4 small raw prawns, peeled, deveined and blanched in hot water for about 30 seconds

4 water chestnuts or sliced bamboo shoots or sliced button mushrooms

For the custard

4 medium eggs

2½ cups chicken stock or *dashi*, at room temperature

1 tbs *mirin* (rice wine)

1 tbs light soy sauce

pinch of salt

small parsley or coriander leaves and/or finely grated lemon rind, for garnishing

METHOD

1. To make the *dashi*, soak the *kombu* in the water in a small pan for at least 30 minutes.

2. Bring the water to the boil, removing the *kombu* just before it boils.

3. As soon as the water has boiled, add the *katsuobuoshi*, then turn off the heat.

4. Let the *katsuobuoshi* infuse for 1–2 minutes.

5. Strain the *dashi* through muslin or kitchen paper into a bowl and set aside.

6. To prepare the filling, marinate the chicken breast in the light soy sauce and sake for about 15 minutes.

7. Discard the marinade and set the chicken aside.

8. To make the custard, beat the eggs in a bowl.

9. Add the *dashi*, *mirin* (rice wine), soy sauce and salt.

10. Place a bamboo steamer over a pan of simmering water.

11. Divide the fillings evenly between four heatproof cups.

12. Strain the egg mixture into the cups, filling them to 1.5cm (⅔in) from the top.

13. Cover each cup with cling film or foil.

14. Place the cups in the steamer and cover with the lid.

15. Steam the custards for about 15 minutes, until the custard is set, ie slightly jiggling but not cracked or too firm.

16. Garnish with a parsley or coriander leaf and serve immediately, or leave to cool down if serving chilled.

SERVES 4

* Chilaquiles *

MEXICO

What drives locals to wait in long lines to get their *chilaquiles* fix? Must be the spicy goodness of crispy tortillas bathed in salsa – Mexican comfort food at its best.

What is it?

Chilaquiles are fried corn tortilla wedges in a spicy red or green salsa with toppings such as shredded chicken, diced onion, crumbled cheese and sour cream. Make no mistake: *chilaquiles* are hardly the healthiest brunch option, but die-hards insist that the hot salsa works wonders for hangovers.

Origin

The word *chilaquiles* has its origins in Náhuatl terms: *chilli* (chilli), *atl* (water) and *quílitl* (green herb). Náhuatl, the language spoken by the Aztecs, hails from central Mexico, where corn tortillas have been a food staple since the pre-Hispanic era. *Chilaquiles* make use of leftover corn tortillas and the ingredients are ridiculously cheap, making them a working-class favourite in Mexico.

Tasting

Ideally, the tortillas in *chilaquiles* should be lightly fried and retain their crispy texture; unfortunately some become a mushy mess. For the salsa, spicy is good, but remember that a fiery four-alarm salsa can render this dish inedible. Anything goes when it comes to toppings: scrambled or fried eggs pair perfectly with the tortillas and salsa; beef or pork can replace chicken; and shredded lettuce, avocado slices and Mexican *cotija* cheese make excellent vegetarian fixings.

You'll find *chilaquiles* on breakfast menus at street stalls, diners and even in up-market restaurants. Another option is eating them in a *mercado* (market), where you can get homemade cooking just like *mamá* used to make. The *mercado* experience allows you to sit at a counter and chat it up with locals while the cook slings those *chilaquiles*.

Finding it

Chilakillers in Mexico City offers an alternative *chilaquiles* experience with bean and *mole* (chocolate and chilli) salsas for M$75 (US$5.50).

* VARIATIONS * A street stand in Mexico City's trendy Condesa quarter does a roaring trade in *tortas de chilaquiles*, a roll stuffed with *cochinita pibil* (pulled pork), shredded chicken, or *milanesa de pollo* (breaded chicken fillet) and topped with *chilaquiles*. Try *la bomba* (the bomb), which combines all ingredients. Known as 'La Equina del Chilaquil,' the stand is open daily from 8am–noon, at Avenida Tamaulipas and Alfonso Reyes.

* By John Hecht *

Recipe **Chilaquiles in Salsa Verde**

INGREDIENTS

8 corn tortillas, preferably day-old

⅓ cup vegetable oil

4 pinches sea salt

1 cup shredded chicken breast or 2 eggs

2 tbs diced onion

4 tbs crumbled *cotija*, parmesan or feta cheese

2 tbs sour cream

2 sprigs cilantro (coriander)

For the sauce

6 tomatillos, husks removed

2 serrano chilli peppers, stems removed

1 garlic clove, peeled

pinch sea salt

⅛ cup water

⅛ cup chicken stock

⅛ cup chopped fresh cilantro (coriander)

METHOD

1. Slice the corn tortillas into bitesize wedges.
2. Preheat the oil in a large pan to 180°C (350°F).
3. Fry the tortillas in the hot oil for about 3 minutes or until crispy.
4. Carefully lift out the fried tortilla wedges with a slotted spoon and transfer them to a plate lined with kitchen paper.
5. Sprinkle the fried tortilla wedges with 2 pinches sea salt.
6. For the sauce, place the tomatillos, serrano chilli pepper and garlic clove in a small pan with water to cover.
7. Bring to the boil and cook for about 5 minutes, until softened.
8. Transfer the tomatillos, serrano chilli pepper and garlic to a blender along with the remaining 2 pinches sea salt, water and chicken stock.
9. Blend until smooth.
10. Pour the mixture into a wide, lightly oiled pan and cook over a medium heat for 10 minutes, until thickened.
11. Once the sauce reaches the desired consistency, mix in the chopped cilantro (coriander).
12. Add the crispy tortilla wedges to the pan containing the sauce. Allow the tortilla chips to absorb the salsa, but avoid letting them become soggy.
13. To serve, divide the tortilla wedges between two plates.
14. Top with the shredded chicken breast or eggs any style, diced onion, crumbled cheese and sour cream.
15. Garnish with sprig of cilantro and serve immediately.

SERVES 2

* Churros y Chocolate *

SPAIN

Churros y chocolate are a traditional Spanish breakfast treat: an irresistible dunking duo of mouthwatering doughnuts, eaten piping hot and perfectly shaped to dip into the accompanying hot, thick chocolate.

What is it?

Spanish *churros* are light, crispy doughnuts made with a simple batter mix that are quickly deep-fried before being immediately dipped either in sugar or dunked satisfyingly in a cup of thick hot chocolate. They are standard fare at every Spanish fiesta as well as being an essential component of a traditional Spanish breakfast.

Origin

Churros have humble nomadic origins. They were the traditional morning food of goat- and sheep-herders in Spain who, lacking any corner-bakers, whipped up a basic concoction of flour, water and oil to cook over an open fire. The *churro* is so-named after the horns of the churro breed of sheep reared in the grasslands of Castile y León province. Chocolate (named after the Aztec word *xocolatl*) was brought from the New World back to Spain in the 16th century, where it was enjoyed as a drink long before it reached the rest of Europe.

Tasting

Although a European-style doughnut may be the closest thing to a *churro*, the comparison really does this Spanish tastebud-treat no favours. One of the delights of the *churro* is that it is neither too sweet nor too doughy. Best enjoyed straight from the cauldron of bubbling oil, bite into a reputable *churro* and you will be struck by just how crisp and light it is. Light, that is, until that fateful moment of dunking. Forget any preconceived notion of milky cocoa at bedtime, the hot chocolate here is so thick you can stand a *churro* up in it and so rich you will be spooning up the very last drop. For the most authentic *churros* in Spain just look for the *churreria* sign posted above a cafe or simple counter. Alternatively, consider making your own...

Finding it

Founded in 1894, Chocolatería San Ginés is a Madrid institution where *churros y chocolate* for one costs about €3.80 (US$4.75).

* VARIATIONS * A common variation of the churro, particularly in Madrid, is the porra. This is longer, softer and thicker than the traditional churro, as well as being more expensive as one porra roughly equals three churros size-wise. The difference in texture is caused by the use of lukewarm, rather than boiling, water in the preparation.

* By Josephine Quintero *

Recipe Churros y Chocolate

INGREDIENTS

For the churros:

2 cups plain flour

1 tsp baking powder

2 cups water

1 tbs vegetable oil

¼ tsp salt

olive or vegetable oil, for frying

For the chocolate:

4 tsp cornflour

4¼ cups milk

2 cups grated dark chocolate

METHOD

1. To make the *churros*, sift the flour and baking powder together into a bowl.

2. Place the water, oil and salt in a large pan and bring to the boil.

3. Add the flour and baking powder gradually, stirring constantly with a wooden spoon, and reduce the heat. Continue stirring until a ball forms.

4. Remove the pan from the heat and leave the dough to cool.

5. Using a pastry bag or cake decorator with a 10cm (4in) fluted nozzle, pipe the dough into strips around 10cm (4in) long on to a sheet of greaseproof paper.

6. Line a baking tray with sheets of kitchen paper.

7. Two-thirds fill a deep pan with oil and heat until a cube of bread browns in 45–60 seconds.

8. Fry a few *churros* at a time, turning once, until they are crisp and an even golden brown in colour.

9. Carefully lift out the *churros* with a slotted spoon and transfer to the kitchen paper to drain.

10. Repeat the process until all the *churros* are cooked.

11. Serve immediately or keep the *churros* warm by covering them with a clean dish towel while you make the chocolate.

12. To make the chocolate, combine the cornflour with a little of the milk in a small bowl.

13. Heat the remaining milk in a pan until it is hot but not boiling, then remove from the heat.

14. Whisk the cornflour paste and grated chocolate into the hot milk, until the chocolate is melted and the mixture is smooth.

15. Return the pan to the heat and gently heat the chocolate until the mixture has thickened slightly.

16. Pour into cups and serve immediately with the *churros*.

MAKES 20 *CHURROS*; SERVES 3–5

* Çılbır *

TURKEY

Poached eggs for brunch? Why yes, that sounds perfect. Give me mine on a swirl of garlic-and-dill-infused yoghurt, warm pita bread on the side. That would be lovely, thank you.

What is it?

Çılbır is a dish comprising yoghurt flavoured with garlic and dill, a couple of poached eggs and a drizzle of pepper-infused butter, all served with Turkish pide to scoop up the rich yolk and tangy sauce. Familiar ingredients combine to take you to another place, and it's so easy to make you'll be taking yourself there regularly.

Origin

This Turkish dish has quite a heritage, with records dating it to as far back as the 1400s. It seems that the culinary mastermind behind the dish has disappeared from view, but it's not a stretch to imagine it was borne out of a 'what-have-we-got-on-hand' dining imperative. Whatever its genesis, today the dish is much enjoyed at breakfasts and brunches all over Turkey, providing a nutritious and soothing start to the day with just enough oomph to wake up the tastebuds.

Tasting

You choose an outdoor cafe to absorb the sights and sounds of Istanbul as it wakes up. The morning rush is on show, a blur of modern life set against an ancient backdrop. You start with a treacle-black (and thick) coffee, but it's the *çılbır* you're waiting for. When it's placed in front of you, the aroma of melted butter and paprika hits you first, then the faint tang of the yoghurt. The balance is perfect; the creamy richness of egg yolk swirling through the soft sourness and bite of the yoghurt. Warm pide completes the picture, the chewy flatbread adding texture to the dish as well as providing lasting sustenance and a ready means of transporting the scrumptious mixture from the plate to your mouth. As fast as you can manage, without appearing to be gobbling…

Finding it

Kahve 6 in Istanbul is set in a beautiful garden and serves generous portions of *çılbır* for TL 16 (US$7).

* TIP * You're in Turkey: coffee is the breakfast tipple of choice. Strong, rich and dark, the brew is made from fine-ground coffee boiled with sugar in a pot. The grounds are part of the experience, so let your cup rest and sip gently to avoid a dusty mouthful.

* By Ben Handicott *

Recipe Çılbır

The easiest exotic breakfast you'll ever make!

INGREDIENTS

1 garlic clove

1 cup full-fat unsweetened yoghurt

½ cup fresh dill, finely chopped

salt, to taste

4 eggs

2 tbs butter

½ tsp ground black pepper

1 tsp smoked paprika

METHOD

1. Finely mince the garlic.

2. Stir the garlic into the yoghurt.

3. Add the chopped dill to the yoghurt.

4. Season the yoghurt mixture to taste with salt, and stir to combine.

5. Bring a pan of water to the boil, then reduce it to a simmer.

6. Crack an egg into a dish or ramekin.

7. Swirl the simmering water and gently slide the egg into the whirlpool.

8. Repeat with the remaining eggs.

9. Reduce the heat to low.

10. Cook the eggs cook for about 3 minutes, until the white has set. The yolks should be runny.

11. Place the poached eggs on kitchen paper.

12. Place a separate pan over a medium heat.

13. When the pan is hot, add the butter and the pepper.

14. Heat the butter, stirring constantly, until it becomes a light tan colour.

15. Remove the pan from the heat; the butter will continue to brown in the residual heat but should not burn.

16. Divide the yoghurt between two bowls and rest two eggs on top of each.

17. Pour the melted butter over the two portions.

18. Sprinkle ½ tsp smoked paprika over each portion and serve.

SERVES 2

* Colcannon *

IRELAND

Deceptively creamy, this easy recipe turns simple ingredients into a hearty brunch that will take the sting out of a hangover or fuel you for the day ahead.

What is it?

Often offered as a side dish – but substantial enough to serve as a main – colcannon is simultaneously beautifully basic and wonderfully satisfying. There are three core ingredients – bacon, potatoes and cabbage – but the addition of butter and cream introduces a smooth texture and delightful dairy layer. Vegetarians can replace bacon with shredded carrot and chopped leek.

Origin

The name of this dish is an anglicisation of the Irish Gaelic *cál ceannann*, meaning 'white-headed cabbage'. Originally it would have been served as a staple in many Irish households, using two cheap/homegrown ingredients: spuds and cabbage. The introduction of bacon and cream elevates colcannon from a stodgy stomach-filler to a creamy treat, and it's now being rediscovered in Irish restaurants and kitchens. There are regional varieties and some Irish families serve colcannon on Hallowe'en (itself originally a Celtic tradition), with items such as coins, rings and thimbles hidden in the mash.

Tasting

The trick to creating a cracking colcannon is getting the potato mash as light and fluffy as possible, before adding a bit of sizzle in the form of good-quality bacon, and some dollops of dairy indulgence – ideally produced from milk made by herds grazing on the verdant fields of Kerry. It's the kind of dish that warms you from the inside out, perfect internal armour for surviving even the wooliest day, or for aiding recovery from a wild night. It's most often served in people's homes, but if you come across it on a pub or restaurant menu – probably as a side dish – don't go past it. Grab a black beer, settle into a comfortable seat, ignore the rain streaking the window outside and tuck into a hearty serving of real Irish fodder.

Finding it

Colcannon is best enjoyed in a place such as Johnny Foxes, Glencullen, County Dublin, where a side dish costs around €4 (US$5).

* VARIATIONS * There are regional versions of colcannon, and most Irish families will have a variation of the classic recipe that they favour. Some keep it simpler than the one described here, others add more vegetables such as leeks. Kale can be used instead of cabbage. Sausages are a good accompaniment to this dish.

* By Patrick Kinsella *

Recipe Colcannon

INGREDIENTS

1kg (2lb 2oz) potatoes, well scrubbed

1 tbs vegetable oil or butter, for frying

150g (5½oz) sliced back bacon, finely chopped

small bunch spring onions, finely chopped

½ small Savoy cabbage, shredded

110g (4oz) butter

150ml (5fl oz) double cream

cooked sausages and a pint of stout, to serve (optional)

METHOD

1. Boil the potatoes in their skins in a large pan of lightly salted water for around 25 minutes, until soft.

2. Meanwhile, heat the oil or butter in a large frying pan over a medium-high heat.

3. Add the bacon, spring onions and cabbage to the pan.

4. Fry for 6–7 minutes, until the bacon is golden and crispy and the vegetables are softened slightly.

5. Drain the cooked potatoes and allow them to steam-dry in the colander for 2 minutes.

6. Mash the potatoes with half the butter (with their skins on for more vitamins). If you prefer smooth mashed potatoes, peel off the skins from the potatoes just before mashing them.

7. Melt the remaining butter in a small pan over a low heat.

8. Add the cream to the pan and heat through, without letting the mixture boil.

9. Pour the butter and cream mixture over the mashed potato and fold it in.

10. Mix in the bacon, cabbage and spring onions.

11. Serve the colcannon on its own, or with sausages and a pint of stout.

SERVES 4

* Congee *

PAN-ASIAN

Nourishing and soothing, ubiquitous yet as multi-faceted as Asia itself, this delicious dish is a culinary canvas into which a nearly unlimited variety of tastes and textures can be added.

What is it?

Although there are as many variations on this quintessentially Asian dish as there are languages and dialects in the region, the generally accepted definition is this: if it's a thick porridge made from rice that's been slow-cooked, it's *congee*. This staple breakfast food is served from Beijing to Singapore and Manila to Goa (and pretty much everywhere in between).

Origin

People have eaten *congee* as long as they've cooked rice. The main differences between *congee* and regular cooked rice are the grain-to-water ratio and the cooking time. Because *congee* is so easy to digest, it is commonly considered the ideal food for the elderly and infirm (and also the hung-over). Nearly every culture in Asia has developed its own style of the dish, based on local tastes and produce.

Tasting

Though the Burmese child preparing for kindergarten and the Tokyo salary-man at the end of a drinking spree share little in the way of language or lifestyle, the chances are good that the next meal for both will be a bowl of *congee*. The child's *hsan byok* might be plain, or it might be flavoured with pork or chicken stock and served with fried onions and a bit of meat. The salary-man's *okayu* might be garnished with fish eggs, seaweed flakes or salted pickles. The Beijing real-estate mogul eating *zhou* topped with salted duck eggs and bamboo shoots may not see eye-to-eye on political issues with the Taipei taxi driver eating *xi fan* with sweet potato chunks, pickled vegetables and fried gluten, but they're all enjoying variations of this pan-Asian dish.

Finding it

Universally revered, Hsiao Lizi Restaurant on Fuxing Road in Taipei serves a full meal with *congee* for about NT180 (US$6).

* VARIATIONS * Traditional Chinese medicine considers *congee* to be an excellent base for healing tonics thanks to the ease with which it is digested. Healthy variations include brown rice *congee* (which retains more fibre and nutrients than its white-rice cousin), *congee* made with chicken or mutton broth (considered a panacea for cold and flu) and *congee* made with fresh ginger (considered a balm for digestive issues).

* By Joshua Samuel Brown *

Recipe Congee

Congee is so easy to prepare that even people who can't normally cook rice properly should have no problem making basic *congee*. In general, too much liquid is better than too little. A truly flexible dish, *congee* can be made on the stovetop, in a crock pot or using a rice cooker. From a traditional medicine viewpoint, the slower and longer it cooks, the more nutritious it becomes. The following is the stovetop method.

INGREDIENTS

1 cup long grain white rice

9 cups water (or mixed water and chicken stock)

salt, to taste

condiments of your choice, to serve (chunks of cooked sweet potato, pickled vegetables, fried gluten, salted duck eggs, bamboo shoots, seaweed flakes, fish eggs, shredded cooked meat or chicken, or even just a dollop of jam!)

METHOD

1. Place the rice, liquid and salt in a large pan.
2. Bring to the boil over a medium heat.
3. Reduce the heat to low and cover the pot with loose-fitting lid.
4. Simmer the mixture for about 1½ hours, stirring occasionally, until the *congee* has a rich, creamy texture.
5. Serve the *congee* plain or with condiments of your choice.

SERVES 6

* Cullen Skink *

SCOTLAND

**One of the world's finest seafood soups, Cullen skink
pulls the flavours of the earth and sea together in
a hearty chowder that packs a real punch.**

What is it?

A creamy smoked haddock soup made with potatoes and onions, Cullen skink rivals haggis as Scotland's signature dish, and served steaming-hot on a cold winter's day it's very hard to beat. Chefs disagree about how best to create its rich flavour and velvety texture, but at its heart it's a humble fisherman's supper that shouldn't be overworked.

Origin

Popular across Scotland, this traditional soup has its roots in the fishing village of Cullen on the Moray Firth. 'Skink' is an old word for 'shin of beef', which became synonymous with a cheap soup. However, in this part of Scotland – where fish was more plentiful – cooks decided to replace the meat with fish and thus this much-loved classic came into being.

Tasting

Smooth and comforting and infused with a deep smokiness, Cullen skink is one of those dishes that are easy to make but hard to perfect. Very fresh fish is essential, as are floury potatoes and the best stock. The finished result should have a rich taste of the sea layered with the sweetness of slow-cooked onions and the silkiness of starchy potatoes and cream. A wholesome yet indulgent dish, the smoothness can be counterbalanced by leaving some chunks of fish or potato intact if you prefer a meatier texture.

Cullen skink is best enjoyed by the seaside, ideally with a view over a harbour where brightly coloured fishing boats bob in the water against a backdrop of stone harbour walls, brooding clouds and craggy islands on the distant horizon.

Finding it

For the best, go to Cullen itself, where the Rockpool Cafe serves up a fine version for £3.95 (US$6.50).

* VARIATIONS * Cullen skink is traditionally made with undyed smoked haddock but this can be hard to find outside northern Europe. Any smoked fish could be substituted in the recipe and even in Scotland kippers (smoked herring) are often used. Some chefs use mashed potatoes to thicken the soup, others add fennel, bacon or mussels, and in one atypical variation Jerusalem artichokes are substituted for the potatoes.

* By Etain O'Carroll *

Recipe Cullen Skink

INGREDIENTS

knob of butter

1 medium onion, finely chopped

2 medium potatoes, skins on, cut into chunks

1 bay leaf

120mL (4fl oz) good chicken stock

500g (1lb 1 oz) undyed smoked haddock

1 leek, cut into chunks

568mL (1 pint) full-fat milk

120mL (4fl oz) single cream

salt and ground black pepper, to taste

chopped parsley, to garnish

crusty bread and butter, to serve

METHOD

1. Melt the butter in a large pan over a medium heat.

2. Add the chopped onion and cook for about 10 minutes, until transparent but not browned.

3. Add the potatoes, bay leaf and chicken stock to the pan and simmer for 10–15 minutes, until the potato is cooked.

4. Remove the bay leaf and lightly mash the potatoes against the side of the pan using a fork.

5. In a separate pan, poach the haddock and leek in the milk over a medium heat for about 5 minutes, until the fish is opaque and cooked and the leeks are just tender.

6. Remove the fish from the milk and gently flake it, removing any bones.

7. Add the milk, leeks and fish to the potato mixture, stir well to combine and cook for a further 5 minutes.

8. Add the cream and season to taste with salt and pepper.

9. Sprinkle with chopped parsley and serve with crusty bread and butter.

SERVES 4

* Devilled Kidneys *

UNITED KINGDOM

Hot pepper, Worcestershire sauce, verdant parsley and salty butter: the devil is in the details of this awfully good breakfast dish of sizzling kidneys served on hot buttered toast.

What is it?

Fresh lambs' kidneys combine a delicate flavour and a whole alphabet of nutrients into a compact package. This dish features kidneys that have been spiced with traditional British condiments – Colman's mustard from Norwich and Worcestershire sauce – and cooked in butter, served on warm buttered toast. Garnishes are simply a squeeze of lemon juice and some chopped parsley.

Tasting

The delight of devilled kidneys lies in the contrast between the soft, savoury kidneys and the crunchy toast. Your first bite tells you how the cook has seasoned the kidneys – is there a fiery blast or a gently warming piquancy? The next moment reveals whether the kidneys have been cooked with a careful hand or have been callously abandoned in an overheated pan. With any luck it's the former and the buttery, lemon-infused juices will soak into the toast, creating a delicious platform for the meaty mouthfuls. A speckling of herbaceous parsley brings everything together, providing a whiff of freshness to cut through the butter. Goodbye muesli, hello devilled kidneys, a thoroughly British breakfast that will set you up for a day of Empire-building.

Origins

In Edwardian-era Britain, breakfasts were decidedly robust. Nowhere else was the adage 'breakfast like a king, lunch like a prince' taken so seriously. British breakfast tables were laden with hams, pies, oysters and lobsters – and offal dishes such as this classic recipe. 'Devilling' is a way of seasoning fish and meats with hot-flavoured condiments found in most kitchen cupboards, typically mustard and various peppers. It was probably a way of disguising ingredients that were past their best, but it's a great way of adding a little (or a lot of) pep to your breakfast.

Finding it

Devilled kidneys cost £7.80 (US$12.85) on the bar menu of offal evangelist Fergus Henderson's St John restaurant in Farringdon, London.

* VARIATIONS * For a more luxurious experience, add a splash of dry sherry to the kidneys as they cook, along with 1 tsp redcurrant jelly and finally a little double cream. This elevates the dish to the truly divine.

Recipe Devilled Kidneys

If you have some chicken stock in the fridge, adding a couple of tablespoons will keep the kidneys moist as they cook and add extra goodness to the sauce.

INGREDIENTS

6 lambs' kidneys

2 tbs plain (all-purpose) flour

½ tsp dry mustard powder

½ tsp of cayenne pepper, to taste

salt and ground black pepper, to taste

2 tbs butter

couple of shakes of Worcestershire sauce

handful of parsley, chopped

hot buttered toast (preferably wholemeal or sourdough), to serve

½ lemon

METHOD

1. Gently rinse the kidneys in cold water.

2. Slice the kidneys lengthwise, so you have two B-shaped halves.

3. Use scissors to cut out the little white core from the kidneys.

4. Mix together the flour, mustard powder, cayenne pepper and salt and pepper to taste in a bowl.

5. Toss the kidneys in the flour mixture, until they're thoroughly coated.

6. Melt the butter over a medium heat in a heavy frying pan until it foams.

7. Add the kidneys and cook for a couple of minutes per side. Avoid over-cooking them or they will become chewy. They should be slightly pink in the centre and still soft.

8. As the kidneys are cooking, sprinkle a dash of Worcestershire sauce over them.

9. Once the kidneys are cooked, chuck in a handful of chopped parsley and take them off the heat.

10. Arrange the kidneys on the hot buttered toast.

11. Spoon over the juices from the pan.

12. Squeeze over the lemon and serve immediately.

SERVES 2

* Dim Sum *

HONG KONG; SOUTHERN CHINA; EVERY CHINATOWN

A dizzying variety of small, delectable delicacies including shrimp, meat and vegetable dumplings, steamed buns of many sorts and more exotic fare (stewed chicken claw, anyone?) served off food trolleys.

What is it?

As much a way of dining as any single dish itself, dim sum is a traditional brunch in Hong Kong and Southern China, where carts filled with plates and steaming baskets of delicious bitesize morsels are pushed through a noisy restaurant and consumed alongside endless cups of hot tea.

Tasting

That cacophony and variety are hallmarks of the dim sum experience should come as no surprise. Such elements are in no short supply in Hong Kong, the city most associated with the classic lengthy, leisurely and loud dim sum brunch. Dim sum restaurants tend to run big, holding dozens of large circular tables and plenty of room for numerous carts to be simultaneously wheeled through, each bearing a cornucopia of dishes from all corners of the middle kingdom. Dumplings are a dim sum staple, with fragrant steamed shrimp *hargow* vying for space with pan-fried pork and cabbage *jiaozi*. *Baozi* –baked or steamed buns with fillings ranging from meat to sweet bean – can be dipped in a variety of sauces, or eaten straight. If you're in the mood for something more exotic, try the tofu skin roll, or the moist and tasty chicken claws, braised and steamed in a fragrant sauce.

Origin

Dim sum traces its roots back to the teahouses located along the Silk Road in China, which began serving small morsels of food to accompany (but not overshadow) the tea. Over the centuries, this practice has been transformed into the venerated culinary tradition practised in Chinese communities around the world, a tradition that brings friends and families together to share a vast variety of little dishes in lively dining halls. Though the recipes have changed over the centuries, tea – dim sum's original *raison d'être* – is, of course, still ubiquitous.

Finding it

Maxim's Palace, City Hall, Hong Kong is a must-visit, where you are likely to spend at least HK$120 (US$15).

* VARIATIONS * Pan-fried *jiaozi* (also known as 'potstickers') are assembled the same way as the steamed variety, but the cooking process (fried in a pan of light cooking oil for about 4 minutes each side) produces a crispier counterpart to the steamed dumpling's more doughy texture. Serving the two together will double your culinary credibility.

* By Joshua Samuel Brown *

Recipe Dim Sum: Vegetarian Jiaozi

Most of the items found on a dim-sum trolley can be bought in the freezer section of any Asian market and either pan-fried or heated in a bamboo steamer, but it is worth having a go yourself, especially if you are vegetarian as this recipe is one of the few types of dim sum suitable for those who don't eat meat.

INGREDIENTS

About 30 dumpling wrappers

For the filling

2 tbs warm water

2 tsp cornflour

¾ tsp sugar

2 tbs soy sauce

2 tbs peanut oil

½ cup shredded carrots

½ cup finely chopped shiitake mushrooms

½ cup finely chopped spring onions

½ cup finely chopped celery or bok choy

2 tbs cooking oil

2 tbs finely shredded fresh ginger

METHOD

1. Mix together the warm water and cornflour in a small bowl to form a smooth paste. Add the sugar, soy sauce and peanut oil to the cornflour mixture and stir to combine.

2. Mix together the carrots, mushrooms, spring onions and bok choy in a large bowl.

3. Heat the cooking oil in a wok over a high heat. Add the fresh ginger and fry for 30 seconds or until fragrant. Then add the vegetables and stir-fry over a high heat for 1 minute.

4. Add the cornflour mixture to the wok. Cook, stirring constantly, for 2 minutes, until the sauce is thick and glossy.

5. Remove from the heat and transfer the dumpling filling to a bowl. You should have about 2 cups of filling. Leave the mixture to cool enough to be handled. (Refrigerate the mixture to speed the cooling process if you like.)

6. Line a bamboo steamer with baking parchment.

7. Lightly flour a work surface and your hands. Holding one dumpling wrapper in the palm of one hand, fill it with ½–1 tbs dumpling filling (depending on the size of the wrapper), placing the filling slightly off-centre and leaving a clear rim of wrapper about 1.25cm (½in) wide all around. Fold the dumpling to create a half-moon shape that encloses the filling, pleating the edges to seal them as you fold.

8. Place each finished dumpling in the steamer, taking care that they touch neither each other nor the sides of the steamer or they may stick. If you have a steamer with one tier, place the ones that won't fit on a piece of baking parchment and cover with a damp dish towel until you are ready to cook them.

9. Steam the dumplings over boiling water for 7 minutes. Finished dumplings should be slightly translucent. Repeat the process if necessary, until all the dumplings are cooked.

10. Serve immediately with dipping sauce.

MAKES 18–30 DUMPLINGS

* Donegal Oatcakes *

IRELAND

Coarse, dry oatcakes with their nutty flavour and crumbly texture are a cross between a cracker and a flatbread and taste delicious served with soft goat's cheese and smoked salmon.

What is it?

Oatcakes are a type of traditional cracker, popular across the north of Ireland and Scotland for generations and made using just four ingredients: oatmeal, butter, water and salt. These were combined and fried on a griddle or baked in an oven and then hardened in front of a roaring fire.

Origin

Oats were the most common grain grown in ancient Ireland and, combined with some butter, they could be baked into a simple cracker-type cake that made a good long-lasting alternative to bread. Oatcakes were taken into the fields by labourers, on long journeys by itinerant workers, and even on transatlantic voyages. The recipe has changed little in centuries and the original one remains the best.

Tasting

Crunchy, nutty and oaty, light yet somehow substantial, oatcakes carry far more clout than a humble cracker. Their dry, crumbly texture contrasts wonderfully with the moistness and softness of a topping of butter, jam or soft cheese and, washed down with strong tea, they are quintessential Northern Irish. Oatcakes aren't something you'll find on a restaurant menu though; they're associated with a much more personal feast, ideally one enjoyed outdoors on the slopes of Mount Errigal, in the dunes on Marble Hill Beach, or while sitting in a bed of heather listening to the mournful whistle of golden plovers flying overhead as you relax after a hard morning cutting turf on the bog. In such places there's something almost spiritual about eating oatcakes, knowing you are carrying on a tradition held dear to Donegal natives for centuries.

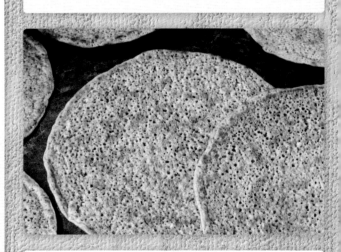

Finding it

Served with artisan cheeses and chutney, for €7.50 ($9.50), the oatcakes at the Drift Inn in Buncrana, County Donegal, shouldn't be missed.

* DID YOU KNOW? * **Oatcakes in Scotland are pretty much a national dish and are served instead of toast at breakfast or alongside soups and stews. There are even records of 14th-century Scottish soldiers carrying sacks of oats and a metal plate in their packs in order to cook their own as they marched.**

* By Etain O'Carroll *

Recipe Donegal Oatcakes

INGREDIENTS

2 cups stoneground oatmeal

½ tsp salt

¾ cup water

2 tbs butter

METHOD

1. Put the oatmeal and salt into a bowl, mix them together and make a well in the centre.

2. Heat the water and butter in a pan until it is almost boiling.

3. Add the hot liquid to the dry ingredients.

4. Mix everything together with a wooden spoon to form a stiff dough.

5. Sprinkle the dough with a fine coating of oatmeal.

6. Roll out the dough thinly, about 5mm (0.2in) thick, on a lightly floured surface.

7. Cut out circular shapes with a cookie cutter.

8. Place the rounds on a lightly greased baking sheet.

9. Cover the baking sheet with a clean dish towel and leave the rounds to dry out for about an hour.

10. Heat the oven to 200°C (400°F).

11. Bake the oatcakes for 20 minutes.

12. Turn over the oatcakes with a spatula – be careful as they can be quite fragile.

13. Cook the oatcakes for a further 10 minutes.

14. Remove the oatcakes from the oven.

15. Leave the oatcakes on the baking sheet for 2 minutes to firm up a little.

16. Transfer the oatcakes to a wire rack using a spatula and leave to cool. Oatcakes will keep in a sealed container for up to a week.

SERVES 8

* Eggs Benedict *

USA

That first forkful seals the deal: creamy eggs, Canadian bacon, a crispy muffin and rich sauce in one magnificent bite. Make no mistake: eggs Benedict is the king of brunch dishes.

What is it?

Not unlike many Americans, eggs Benedict is a curious hybrid of nationalities, consisting of poached eggs served atop Canadian bacon and an English muffin, with the undeniably French hollandaise sauce drizzled over the top. It's served and eaten year-round, typically in mid- to upmarket restaurants all across the USA (and in a handful of other countries).

Tasting

What makes eggs Benedict the brunch dish par excellence is its rich combination of textures and flavours. Knife and fork cuts into the combo, the creamy egg yolk and hollandaise sauce spilling over the juicy Canadian bacon and crisp English muffin. Then up and into the mouth for that first taste as the flavours meld into one decadent mouthful — equal parts luscious eggs and salty bacon, with the crunch of muffin underneath.

New York City remains one of the best places to eat this brunch classic. On a weekend morning, join hung-over New Yorkers at a buzzing spot in the East Village or in Brooklyn and recount the previous night's adventures over plates of eggy perfection.

Origin

While the exact origin of eggs Benedict is shrouded in mystery, this much is known: it was invented in New York City, most likely during the 19th century. One much-told story goes like this: Lemuel Benedict was a Wall Street banker by day, *bon vivant* by night, who partied hard in 1890s-era NYC. One morning he strolled into the Waldorf Hotel, where he created an open-faced sandwich out of toast, poached eggs and bacon and then poured hollandaise over the top. The astute maître d'hôtel Oscar Tschirky noticed this creation and refined it, naming the dish after Benedict.

Finding it

Cafe Mogador in NYC is an especially good spot for sampling this classic, where it will set you back $16.

* **VARIATIONS** * There are countless variations of this legendary dish. Along the east coast (especially in Maryland), you can find crab Benedict, which uses lumps of crabmeat in place of Canadian bacon. There's also smoked salmon Benedict (popular in the Pacific Northwest) and country Benedict — a southern speciality consisting of eggs over biscuits (similar to British scones) and smothered with gravy. Vegetarians need not be left in the lurch as eggs Florentine substitutes spinach for bacon.

* By Regis St Louis *

Recipe Eggs Benedict

INGREDIENTS

4 slices bacon (Canadian if available)

2 English muffins, halved

4 tbs white wine vinegar

4 eggs

For the hollandaise sauce

8 egg yolks

2 cups clarified butter, cut into pieces

4 tbs lemon juice

salt and ground black pepper, to taste

METHOD

1. First prepare the hollandaise sauce. Bring a large pan of water to the boil, then reduce it to a simmer.

2. In a heatproof non-metallic bowl, beat the egg yolks until the mixture begins to foam. Position the bowl over the pan of barely simmering water.

3. Whisk in the clarified butter, a little bit at a time, until the mixture begins to thicken and emulsify. Do not let the bowl get too hot or the sauce could split.

4. Whisk in the lemon juice and salt and pepper. If the sauce is too thick, you can add a little warm water from the pan (use just 1 tbs at a time) to thin it down to the desired consistency.

5. Cover the surface of the hollandaise with cling film to prevent a skin from forming and keep it warm while you prepare the rest of the dish.

6. In a large frying pan, cook the bacon for a few minutes, until it is lightly browned.

7. Toast the English muffin halves.

8. Bring a deep pan of water to the boil, then reduce the temperature until the surface of the water is just shimmering. If it is boiling too vigorously it will break up the eggs when you add them to the water.

9. Mix in the vinegar and give the liquid a swirl.

10. Break the eggs into small cups or ramekins and carefully lower them into the water. Cook the eggs for about 3 minutes, until the whites are set but the yolks remain runny.

11. Place a slice of bacon on top of each of the toasted English muffin halves.

12. Carefully remove the eggs from the water using a slotted spoon; try not to break the yolks. Place the eggs on top of the bacon.

13. Cover the eggs with warm hollandaise sauce and serve at once.

SERVES 2

* Eggs Baked in Avocado *

AMERICAN SOUTHWEST, USA

Creamy, zesty, and more buttery than a dish without butter should be, eggs baked in avocado are guaranteed to impress seekers of the culinary unique.

What is it?

This devilishly simple dish takes advantage of the fact that the hole left in a pitted avocado is the perfect shape to accommodate an egg. Though at first glance it seems an odd pairing, the avocado's creamy texture and mild, slightly sweet flavour pair brilliantly with the taste and versatility of the humble egg.

Origin

Baked egg dishes are a brunch classic, and omelettes – especially in the American Southwest, where this dish may have originated – have long been made using diced avocado as a filling or served with a side order of guacamole. At some point we can only assume a clever chef realised that removing the avocado's pit left a hole large enough to accommodate a small egg and decided that combining two of nature's more ovoid foods would result in a tasty (and rather photogenic) dish.

Tasting

The first thing you'll notice about this dish is its aesthetic prettiness. The sunshine-yellow yolk surrounded by a white ring floating inside the deep green oval of a halved avocado has a fun, almost Dr Seuss-like quality to it. The dish is equally pleasurable to eat, the avocado's creamy texture combining perfectly with the eggs to create something as easy to eat with a spoon as it is to spread over freshly toasted bread.

As with any egg dish, the final texture depends on the cooking time, so your yolk can be anything from lightly poached to solid, depending on your preference. Diners looking to add crunch can sprinkle crispy bacon bits, fried garlic or croutons on the top, while those seeking a more Southwestern flavour will want to add a dash of hot sauce and perhaps some piquant salsa.

Finding it

Specialising in unique culinary creations, Rumfish y vino in Placencia, Belize sometimes features this item on its lunch menu for US$8.

* VARIATIONS * Avocados come in all sizes, so why stop at chicken eggs when nature provides a veritable plethora of potential egg/avocado combos? Quail eggs baked in small avocados (or doubled up in medium-to-large ones) create a unique version of this dish. If you've got especially large avocados, try duck eggs.

* By Joshua Samuel Brown *

Recipe Eggs Baked in Avocado

There are two keys when it comes to making this simple dish. First, match the size of your eggs and avocados, using a spoon to make the hole left by the pit larger if necessary. Second, arrange the avocado halves snugly in a baking tray or ovenproof dish so that the uncooked egg doesn't spill out.

INGREDIENTS

2 large avocados, ripe but not overly so (a day or two away from being suitable for guacamole should do)

4 small or medium eggs

salt, pepper and paprika, to taste

crisp-fried bacon bits, crumbled croutons and/or crisp-fried garlic, to serve (optional)

METHOD

1. Preheat the oven to 220°C (425°F).

2. Cut the unpeeled avocados in half, then remove the pits with a small spoon and enlarge the hole if necessary (depending upon the relative size of the avocados and the eggs).

3. Crack the eggs into a bowl, taking care not to break the yolks.

4. Arrange the avocado halves in a baking tray or ovenproof dish so the cut sides are facing up and are as level as possible.

5. Carefully place one egg yolk into each avocado half, then add enough egg white to each to completely fill the cavities. The best way to scoop up an egg yolk is to use an empty egg shell as a receptacle.

6. Season with salt, pepper and paprika to taste.

7. Carefully place the baking tray or ovenproof dish in the oven and bake for 12–15 minutes, depending on the desired consistency of the cooked eggs.

8. Remove the tray or dish from the oven and transfer the avocados to serving plates, allowing two halves per person.

9. Add bacon bits, crumbled croutons or fried garlic if desired.

SERVES 2

* Eggs Sardou *

NEW ORLEANS, USA

Some people believe eggs Sardou is a lighter version of the classic eggs Benedict. Wrong! This dish was invented in New Orleans, a city that's proud of its rich gastronomy.

What is it?

We get why the cliché exists. Eggs Sardou consists of poached eggs served over artichoke bottoms and creamed spinach – a green Benedict, right? But even though the dish is also topped with hollandaise sauce, it has a totally different feel, especially once New Orleans chefs sex the whole thing up with anchovies, crumbled ham and, if they're feeling racy, black truffle slices.

Origin

Eggs Sardou was invented at Antoine's in New Orleans, in 1908, to celebrate the arrival of French dramatist Victorien Sardou. Antoine's, which can also claim credit for oysters Rockefeller, remains the oldest functioning restaurant in New Orleans, and continues to serve locals and tourists in the heart of the French Quarter. The history of New Orleans is written, in no small part, upon its menu pages, and while Antoine's may not be the gastronomic powerhouse it once was, it is the oldest, most iconic repository of New Orleans Creole cooking in the world.

Tasting

A good plate of eggs Sardou strikes a textural golden mean between the creaminess of the spinach, the smoothness of the egg yolk and hollandaise, and the light but noticeably firm yield of the artichokes, upon which the structural integrity (as it were) of the entire dish relies. The taste is uniformly rich – again, egg yolks, hollandaise – but done right, the artichoke and spinach provide a slight green counterpoint, a little bit delicate and just starchy enough to be comforting.

With all of this said, if you have the dish in New Orleans, chances are any subtle nuances are joyfully smothered with what locals call, in Louisiana French, *lagniappe* – 'something extra'. That extra may be truffles, anchovies, seared asparagus, pieces of ham or bacon, whatever. It will be there, and in force.

Finding it

Head straight to the source – Antoine's, 713 St Louis St, New Orleans – where the dish costs US$20.

* TIP * If you're going to have this New Orleans dish, wash it down like a New Orleanian: with a cocktail, or as locals call it when served before noon, an 'eye-opener'. Go the full measure and order the city's signature drink: a Sazerac. That's rye whisky in an absinthe-coated glass, with a dash of bitters and orange or lemon peel. Who needs to get anything done today anyways?

* By Adam Karlin *

Recipe Eggs Sardou

INGREDIENTS

8 artichoke bottoms

1 tbs olive oil

450g (1lb) spinach

2 garlic cloves

1 tsp salt

2 tsp white wine vinegar

8 eggs

8 anchovies

pieces of ham or cooked bacon
(optional)

For the hollandaise sauce

3 egg yolks

1 tsp red wine vinegar

⅓ tsp cayenne pepper salt and
ground black pepper, to taste

⅓ tsp salt

1½ cups melted butter

juice of ½ lemon

1 tsp water

salt and ground black pepper,
to taste

METHOD

1. Bring a pan of water to the boil. Add the artichoke bottoms and cook for 10 minutes, until tender.

2. Remove the artichoke bottoms from the pan using a slotted spoon and keep warm.

3. Put the egg yolks, vinegar and cayenne pepper in a large heatproof bowl. Place the bowl in the top of a double boiler or over a pan of simmering water.

4. Whisk the mixture until it is thick and smooth, removing the bowl from the heat as required to prevent the eggs from overcooking. Gradually stir in the salt, butter, lemon juice and water, until the sauce thickens. This is the hollandaise.

5. Season the hollandaise to taste, then keep it warm.

6. Heat the olive oil in a large pan over a medium heat. Add the spinach and garlic and saute for 2–3 minutes, until the spinach is wilted. Season to taste and keep warm while you poach the eggs.

7. Half-fill a pan with boiling water. Add the salt and white wine vinegar and bring to a simmer.

8. Crack an egg into a small bowl or (ideally) a ramekin. Stir the water vigorously, creating a small whirlpool in the pan. Slide the egg carefully into the centre of the whirlpool in the pan.

9. Turn off the heat, cover the pan and leave it to sit for 5 minutes. Then use a slotted spoon to lift the now-poached egg out of the water.

10. Plunge the egg into a bowl of iced water to arrest the cooking while you poach the remaining eggs. Poached eggs can be reheated with a dunk in warm water once you are ready.

11. To serve, place one anchovy on each piece of artichoke, then top with spinach and a poached egg. Pour hollandaise sauce over each egg. Add salt, pepper and pieces of ham or cooked bacon, if liked, to taste.

SERVES 4

* English Crumpets *

ENGLAND

Imagine: a white tablecloth. A china cup. A pot of tea. And a warm crumpet, a pat of butter disappearing into its honeycomb caverns... could anything be more English?

What is it?

Is it a bread? Is it a cake? No, it's a crumpet! This yeast and flour pastry is the love-child of a pancake and a slice of bread. Traditionally round, crumpets are about 2cm (1in) thick and 7.5cm (3in) across. They're characterised by a flat bottom and a holey top that looks something like a sponge. And, of course, they're delicious.

Origin

As you might guess, a food as mysterious-looking as a crumpet has no certain history, but its Anglo-Saxon roots are a given. It seems likely that, perhaps 1000 years ago, crumpets began as a pan-cooked flat bread or cake known as a *crompid*. But the soft, squidgy things we've come to know and love were an 18th-century invention, with the addition of yeast making all the difference. This version is unquestionably English, so with our pinkies pointed away from the tea cup, let's have a taste...

Tasting

Batter in the pan, cooked in rings until the perfectly round cake is shot through with holes, it's turned out and it's ready to... toast! You could flip it and give it a bit of colour on top, but toasting it under the grill or in a toaster (especially if it has cooled) is essential. But even more essential is the butter. No one said this was a health food!

We say unique far too often, but the texture of a crumpet is truly so. A weird sponginess, a distinct chewiness, it's bread, but it's not doughy. It's cake but it's not sweet. It's warm and its bottom is smooth despite the tunnelled top. There are no corners. There's no crust! The melted butter adds a hint of saltiness and a lot of richness. You will eat more than one.

Finding it

Try Caravan at Exmouth Market, London for a crumpet of distinction. Two crumpets, with lashings of butter, cost £2.50 (US$4).

* TIP * Butter. We mentioned butter, right? The best you can find. It's difficult to describe the bliss of a fresh crumpet, its holes laden with melted butter. While honey is a fine addition, and maybe even Marmite if you're wanting to take it up an English notch, the butter-adorned crumpet is it. Butter. Say it again.

* By Ben Handicott *

Recipe English Crumpets

Like most baking endeavours, crumpets are a labour of love – not arduous, but they can be a test of patience. If you are going to attempt them, it's best to invest in some crumpet rings.

INGREDIENTS

2 cups of milk

½ cup double cream

⅔ cup boiling water

2 tsp caster sugar

1 tbs dried yeast

4 cups strong white bread flour

1 tsp salt

1 tsp bicarb soda (baking soda)

2 tbs water

butter for greasing, cooking and eating

METHOD

1. Put the milk and cream in a heatproof jug and add the boiling water.

2. Stir the sugar and yeast into the liquid.

3. Leave the mixture to stand for 15 minutes – it will become active and foamy.

4. Combine the flour and salt in a large bowl.

5. Make a well in the centre of the dry ingredients.

6. Add the milk and yeast mixture, stirring constantly until a thick, slightly elastic batter forms.

7. Cover the bowl with oiled cling film or a clean dish towel and leave it to prove in a warm place for 1½–2 hours. It will grow and become foamy again.

8. Dissolve the bicarb soda (baking soda) in the water in a small bowl. Mix it into the batter.

9. Leave the dough to stand for 30 minutes more.

10. Heat a greased heavy frying pan over a low heat.

11. Place greased 7.5cm (3in) crumpet or metal rings in the pan and put a dab of butter into the bottom of each.

12. When the butter starts to sizzle, add 1–2 tbs of the batter to each ring so that it is two-thirds full.

13. After 4–5 minutes you'll see bubbles form and pop on the surface – the tunnels are forming! Cook for a further 3 minutes, until the top of the crumpet is firm to the touch (not at all sticky). This can take 10–15 minutes.

14. If you're eating the crumpets immediately, flip them over for 1 minute to toast the tops. If you're saving them for the next day, remove the crumpets from the pan, leave them to cool on a wire rack and then toast them just before eating them.

15. Repeat the cooking process until all the batter is cooked. Get stuck in with the butter and serve immediately.

MAKES ABOUT 12

* Ezogelin Çorbasi *

TURKEY

This slightly spicy and satisfyingly heart-warming orange-hued lentil soup is a popular and nutritious way to start the day in Turkey, served with hunks of warm *pide* (bread).

What is it?

This Turkish red lentil soup is a creamy and comforting yet intensely flavoured dish made from softened red lentils and cracked bulgur wheat, seasoned with the subtle flavour of dried mint and a uniquely sweet and slightly bitter red pepper paste. Turks usually squeeze some fresh lemon into it just before serving, for extra zing.

Tasting

As a breakfast item or afternoon snack in Turkey, *Ezogelin çorbasi* is light and delicately flavoured with just enough kick from the distinctive red pepper flakes, an indigenous condiment found all over Turkey that is used to season most foods in the same way as salt and pepper are employed elsewhere. The addition of lamb, chunks of tomato and other flavourful spices, a popular way of preparing the soup in Anatolia, makes for a hearty and satisfying meal in its own right. Hot from the soup pot, soft lentils and cracked bulgur wheat give an earthy, mealy texture while the quintessential Turkish triumvirate flavourings of dried mint, red pepper paste and red pepper flakes lend the soup a uniquely aromatic and exotic character, which is virtually impossible to replicate with substitute ingredients.

Origin

Legend has it that a beautiful but unhappy bride named Ezo attempted to impress her future mother-in-law by cooking this soup, hence the name Ezogelin ('Ezo, the bride'). References to red lentil soup and its soothing properties can be found in Turkish medicinal manuscripts, as far back as the 14th and 15th centuries. Prepared with unripe grape juice or vinegar or even chicken meat, the soup was deemed a cure for everything from headaches to the flu and smallpox.

Finding it

Ciya Sofrasi in Istanbul has a roof terrace and serves this wonderful soup daily for TL11.25 (US$5).

* TIP * Red pepper paste and red pepper flakes lend an authentic flavour to the soup but can be difficult to find unless you happen to be in the vicinity of a well-stocked Turkish grocer. Tomato paste and paprika are acceptable substitutes. Don't be tempted to use fresh mint, which will lend the soup an unwanted menthol flavour that is best reserved for Turkish mint tea.

* By Johanna Ashby *

Recipe Ezogelin Çorbasi

INGREDIENTS

1 tbs butter

1 tsp flour

1 tbs tomato paste

1 tbs red pepper paste (or an equal quantity of additional tomato paste)

1 tbs dried mint

1 tsp red pepper flakes (or an equal quantity of hot paprika), plus extra to serve

1 cup red lentils, washed but not soaked

⅓ cup bulgur wheat

5 cups vegetable stock

lemon wedges, to serve

METHOD

1. Melt the butter in a large pan over a medium heat.

2. Stir in the flour to make a paste.

3. Cook the flour paste, stirring, for 1 minute.

4. Stir in the tomato paste, red pepper paste, dried mint and red pepper flakes.

5. Cook, stirring, for 2 minutes.

6. Add the red lentils, bulgur wheat and stock and bring to the boil.

7. Reduce the heat to low and simmer for 20–30 minutes, stirring occasionally, until the lentils are soft.

8. Serve immediately with a squeeze of lemon and extra red pepper flakes to taste.

SERVES 4

* French Toast *

USA; FRANCE; GERMANY

A particularly indulgent and decadent way to start the day, the starch and sugar hit from French toast makes it one of the world's all-time great brunch dishes.

What is it?

French toast is sliced bread soaked in a gently spiced egg-and-milk batter, fried until crisp and golden in melted butter and served hot with a sprinkling of sugar or all manner of sweet accompaniments, such as maple syrup, honey or even chocolate sauce.

Origin

Known variously as eggy bread, Roman bread, German toast, Spanish toast, and every other iteration in between, French toast is unlikely to have originated in France given the ubiquitousness of some form of egg-soaked bread in most cuisines. That said, it is possible that a classic French dish called *pain perdu* or 'lost bread' could have been the precursor to today's modern version, involving as it does disguising stale pieces of bread with egg batter, fried butter and sweet toppings.

Tasting

First, there's the crunch from the crispy edges, followed by the soft but substantial heft of dense bread – rich, unctuous and golden from being fried in butter. The sweetness from the sugary topping makes a nice foil to the slight savouriness of the egg batter, which is also complemented by the aromatic and subtle spicing from cinnamon or nutmeg. Good French toast should be spongy and moreish but not soggy nor cloyingly sweet.

Perfect for indulgent weekend brunches, French toast is comfort food at its best, soothing with its eggy base yet undeniably decadent with toppings only limited only by the imagination. Experiment with all manner of tantalising combinations including sliced bananas with caramel sauce, stewed cherries and yoghurt, cream or custard fillings, or even savoury versions with cheese and herbs.

Finding it

Schmuck in Paris serves decadent French toast with homemade salted caramel and vanilla ice cream for €13 (US$16.60).

* VARIATIONS * America has well and truly made French toast its own with weird and wonderful variations and toppings ranging from mascarpone, cornflake crusts, cream stuffings and even sausage, eggs and bacon.

* By Johanna Ashby *

Recipe French Toast

Day-old or stale bread is best for this recipe, preferably one with a dense texture such as brioche, but white bread is a fine substitute.

INGREDIENTS

2 medium eggs

3 tbs milk

pinch of cinnamon or nutmeg

4 thick slices day-old brioche or white bread

4 tbs butter

icing sugar, maple syrup, honey, chocolate sauce or fresh fruit, to serve (optional)

METHOD

1. In a small bowl, beat the eggs with the milk and cinnamon.

2. Coat each slice of brioche or bread in the egg mixture and set aside.

3. Melt 1 tbs of the butter in a small frying pan over a medium heat.

4. Once the butter is sizzling, add one slice of brioche or bread.

5. Fry the slice of brioche or bread on both sides until golden brown.

6. Remove the brioche or bread from the frying pan and keep it warm while you cook the remaining slices in the same way, adding 1 tbs butter to the pan each time.

7. Dust with icing sugar and serve the French toast immediately, on its own or with a topping of your choice.

SERVES 2

* Fresh Fruit Platter *

CUBA

Tropical fruit rarely tastes better than it does in Cuba where ambrosial fruit platters are the breakfast offering de rigueur in private homestays known locally as *casas particulares*.

What is it?

The breakdown of a Cuban fruit platter can vary according to season and location. The classic selection consists of a juicy quintet of banana, papaya, mango, pineapple and guava. The fruits are first peeled and cut before being placed unadorned on a platter for serving. Some fruits such as mango are seasonal (May–July), but most are available year-round.

Origin

Of the classic five fruits found on Cuban breakfast platters, only two – guava and pineapple – pre-date the arrival of the Spanish on the isles. Bananas and mangoes both have Asian origins and were brought to Cuba during the colonial period, where they quickly thrived in the tropical climate. Papaya originated in South America. Homegrown fruit products became a vital part of Cuban cuisine during the 'Special Period' in the 1990s when imported goods were in short supply. With the USA trade embargo still in place, they continue to inject nutrition and sweetness into the local diet.

Tasting

Breakfast fruit is often enjoyed alfresco in a colonial courtyard, on a scenic roof terrace or, if you're lucky, within catching distance of the tree/plant from which it was plucked. Eat it with the dulcet sounds of daily Cuban life resonating around you: the clip-clop of horses' hooves on cobbled streets, the intermittent crowing of roosters, and the cries of the morning baker doing his rounds on a bicycle. Most homestays offer fruit as an overture to a wider breakfast of pastries, fresh bread (from that door-to-door baker!), eggs and strong coffee. The pineapples and mango ooze with juicy sweetness, the guava with its pear-like texture has a sharper tart flavour, orange-red papayas are a more acquired taste that's hard to pinpoint (some people squeeze lime juice on them), and bananas are – well – *bananas*, although Cuba produces countless different varieties including the sweet, creamy 'dwarf red'.

Finding it

At Casa Terraza Pavo Real run by Juan Martí in Santiago de Cuba, breakfast (including a fruit platter) is US$4.

* **VARIATIONS** * The Cubans love blending their fruit to make fruit shakes, known locally as *batidos*. These natural drinks, augmented with crushed ice and a splash of milk, are served at weekend street parties or in town markets. They are often drunk from recycled jam jars. Popular flavours include *fruta bomba* (papaya), or mamey, a native fruit with a sweet, creamy taste and hints of almond and sweet potato.

* By Brendan Sainsbury *

Recipe Fresh Fruit Platter

INGREDIENTS

1 papaya

1 mango

2–3 guavas

1 medium pineapple

1–2 bananas

lime juice (optional)

METHOD

1. Cut the papaya in half.
2. Peel off the skin and scoop out the seeds.
3. Cut each papaya in half lengthways into slices.
4. Peel the mango.
5. Cut the flesh into cubes; discard the stone.
6. Wash the guavas.
7. Cut the guavas into thin slices (the skin is edible).
8. Cut off the top and base of the pineapple.
9. Stand the pineapple on a board and saw off the skin using a serrated knife.
10. Cut out any remaining 'eyes' using the tip of a sharp knife.
11. Cut the pineapple into quarters.
12. Cut off the hard core.
13. Dice the pineapple flesh into chunks.
14. Peel the bananas.
15. Cut the bananas into chunks.
16. Arrange all of the cut fruit on a platter.
17. Squeeze lime juice over the fruit if desired.
18. Serve immediately.

MAKES 1 MEDIUM-SIZED FRUIT PLATTER

* Ful Medames *

EGYPT

From street corners to five-star restaurants, Egyptians breakfast on a dish that has barely changed since 2000BC: slow-cooked spiced broad beans loaded on to stone-baked flatbread.

What is it?

Egyptians everywhere greet the day with a plateful of smoky broad beans, slow-cooked with garlic and cumin, for a sustaining and nutritious breakfast. A squeeze of lemon gives the musky bean a flavour lift, and the best *ful medames* glistens with olive oil. The dish is best topped with a quartered boiled egg, and mopped up with hunks of warm flatbread.

Origin

Egyptians have enjoyed broad beans since the time of the Pharaohs. Wily chefs used heat from the fires at bathhouses, left smouldering at the end of each day, by placing tureens of beans on top of the embers to slowly cook overnight into a flavourful stew. Egyptians so revered these beans that they offered them to the gods, but mere mortals were also voracious consumers and the recipe was exported across the Middle East and Africa. Today, *ful medames* is considered a national dish of Egypt.

Tasting

Even in frenetic Cairo, not everything happens in a hurry. And there's certainly no rushing a good *ful medames*. Before the city's chorus of car horns reaches a climax, when the early-morning fog is still draped over skyscrapers and minarets, Cairenes drift towards street vendors for a plateful. So follow the crowds (and your nose) when you choose a spot for breakfast. Liberal drizzlings of olive oil add to the rich, smoky flavour of the *ful*, which is best eaten by hand. Scoop it up with rounds of freshly baked bread, and cleanse your palate with pickled vegetables. '*Laziza*' (delicious) might be difficult to say with a mouthful of bread and *ful*, but your appreciative murmurs are sure to breach the language barrier.

Finding it

Expertly simmered *ful* at Cairo's El Tabei for EGP3 (US$0.40) is perfect for powering you around the nearby Egyptian Museum.

* VARIATIONS * Even the smallest street food stall has an arsenal of condiments, allowing you to adapt your *ful medames* to your own tastes. Tomato sauce gives more piquancy, a swirl of tahini (sesame paste) adds a creamier note, yoghurt freshens the flavour, and extra garlic is very popular. Midnight-dark Egyptian coffee is the ideal accompaniment, though mint tea might be an idea after all that garlic...

* By Anita Isalska *

Recipe Ful Medames

Using a slow-cooker is the best way to replicate the ancient method of making *ful medames*, and it ensures thorough infusion of the spices. But if you're short on time, boil the soaked beans for 1 hour before draining and mashing in the spices.

INGREDIENTS

250g (9oz) dried broad beans

5 garlic cloves

½ cup olive oil

juice of 1 lemon

¼ tsp cumin

½ tsp coriander powder

1 cup water

4 eggs

4 pita breads

tahini and extra olive oil, to serve (optional)

4 parsley sprigs parsley, to garnish

METHOD

1. Soak the dried beans in a large bowl of cold water, ideally for about 12 hours.

2. Once the beans are plumped up with water, peel and crush the garlic cloves.

3. Heat the olive oil in a large frying pan.

4. Add the garlic, drained beans, lemon juice, cumin and coriander to the olive oil.

5. Stir the mixture over a low heat for 5 minutes, until the ingredients are well mixed and heated through.

6. Pour the contents of the pan into a slow-cooker.

7. Add the water and leave the cooker on a low heat for about 12 hours (ideally overnight, so you can enjoy your *ful* in the morning). Stir occasionally.

8. In the morning, hard-boil the eggs in a pan of boiling water for 4 minutes.

9. Remove the eggs from the pan with a slotted spoon and place them straight into a bowl of cool water.

10. Allow the eggs to cool slightly, then peel off the shells.

11. Slice the hard-boiled eggs into quarters.

12. Toast the pita under a grill for 2 minutes on each side.

13. Place one pita on each of four plates.

14. Place a ladleful of the slow-cooked beans next to each pita.

15. Drizzle the remaining olive oil on each serving of *ful*.

16. Top each portion with a small sprig of parsley and four egg quarters.

SERVES 4

Full English Breakfast *

ENGLAND

Internationally recognised for its restorative properties, this hearty combination of fried eggs, sausages, bacon, tomato, mushrooms, beans, black pudding, toast and tea is England's national treasure.

What is it?

Definitions of what comprises a 'proper' full English breakfast are hotly contested across England. But it's generally agreed there are seven core components: bacon, eggs, sausage, tomato, mushrooms, toast and a pool of baked beans. Black pudding is a popular addition, as are 'bubble and squeak', potato cakes and hash browns.

Origin

We can trace back the concept of 'the full English' to 1861 when Isabella Beeton's *Book of Household Management* extolled the virtues of a big cooked breakfast. While some of her recommendations (broiled sheep's kidneys, anyone?) have since fallen by the wayside and fewer people tackle the fry-up daily (from more than half the English population in the 1950s to fewer than 1 per cent today), it's a dish that still straddles class divisions and remains a mainstay on B&B menus and in cafes worldwide.

Tasting

While it can be elevated to a fine-dining menu item, there's something a little bit dirty about an authentic fry-up. It's the ramshackle way it's put together, the usually dishevelled nature of those seeking its greasy delights and the down-to-earth cafes in slightly shambolic areas where it's served best. Seek out a traditional English cafe where you're going to be called 'luv', 'sweet'eart', 'chum' or 'mate'. You want to see gingham plastic tablecloths and to hear and smell the sound of bacon sizzling and sausages spitting. You won't see your plate for food. The saltiness of the crispy bacon is countered by the sweetness of the tomato, the runny egg seeps into the toast, a bit of juicy mushroom adds earthiness to the meaty sausage. Dribble orange beans down your chin and sip your steaming cup of tea. Grin at your winking neighbour. That's the way.

Finding it

Terry's Café in Borough, London, offers the real deal. 'The Works' is £9 (US$14.60), with tea costing just 20p (US$0.32)!

* VARIATIONS * **You can find slight variations on the full cooked breakfast in Ireland (soda bread and potato cakes) and Scotland (black pudding, haggis and lorne sausage).**

* By Karyn Noble *

Recipe **Full English Breakfast**

You could be fooled into thinking this concoction involves merely throwing things into a pan and frying them; appearances can be deceptive! The key to getting this dish right is the timing. You want the egg runny, the bacon crispy, the toast hot, and no ingredient overcooked – everything needs to maintain a perfect texture for maximum effect. Feel free to vary the quantities for personal preference.

INGREDIENTS

1 tomato, cut in half

1 sausage (do not prick it with a fork)

1 tbs vegetable oil

1 slice black pudding

2 rashers back bacon

6 whole button mushrooms/1 field mushroom, sliced

150g (5½oz) baked beans

1 slice white bread

2 eggs, at room temperature

tomato ketchup and/or HP sauce and/or English mustard, to serve

a cup of hot tea, to serve

METHOD

1. Preheat the oven to its lowest temperature and pop in a plate to warm. Preheat the grill to high.

2. Cook the tomato and the sausage under the grill for 10 minutes, occasionally turning the sausage.

3. Heat the oil in a large frying pan over a medium heat. Add the black pudding to the frying pan and cook for 5 minutes on each side.

4. Just before you turn the black pudding, add the bacon rashers to the frying pan, cooking them for a couple of minutes on each side, until crisp and golden.

5. Transfer the cooked sausage, tomato, black pudding and bacon to the pre-heated plate and cover with foil.

6. There should still be plenty of bacon fat in the frying pan, to which you can now add the mushrooms, at a medium heat.

7. Meanwhile, in a small pan, cook the baked beans over a low heat, leaving them to simmer away gently until you are ready.

8. Slice the bread in half to form two triangles and add these to the frying pan containing the mushrooms. Fry the bread for a few minutes on each side, until golden.

9. Push the bread and mushrooms to one side in the pan to make room for the eggs. Add a dash of extra oil if necessary.

10. Crack the eggs into the frying pan, spooning a little of the oil over them as they cook – keep an eye on the whites of the eggs; when they firm up, they're ready.

11. Add the cooked egg, mushrooms and toast to the warmed plate of sausage, tomato, bacon and black pudding.

12. Drizzle the pool of beans in between the sausage and the black pudding; you don't want the beans too near the runny egg, but everything should otherwise sit wherever you'd like it.

13. Serve with traditional English condiments: tomato ketchup, HP sauce and English mustard, along with a cup of hot tea.

SERVES 1 VERY HUNGRY PERSON

* Goetta *

CINCINNATI, OHIO, USA

There's only one place on earth where you can fork into the herb-spiced, oat-stuffed sausage known as goetta: Cincinnati, where the precious patties with their creamy-meat centre fry alongside eggs.

What is it?

Pork, beef, onions, spices and steel-cut oats combine to make goetta (pronounced *get*-uh), a hefty breakfast sausage. It's shaped like a loaf or roll that the chef slices into patties, browns to a crisp, then flips on to a plate to go with eggs and toast. It's served year-round throughout the city.

Origin

Goetta morphed out of sausage recipes that Cincinnati's droves of German immigrants brought with them in the mid-1800s. It's a variant of *Grützwurst* (spiced with marjoram and pepper) from Northern Germany and *Knipp* (spiced with clove and allspice) from Bremen. Both use oats as a filler to stretch the more costly meat. Initially, pork scraps were goetta's main protein. These were cheap and abundant, as Cincinnati was the nation's pig-processing hub circa 1840. Thus pork plentitude plus German sausage-saving strategies gave rise to goetta.

Tasting

Goetta works its magic best inside a classic diner, where you can grab a stool at the counter and watch the cook at work. He slices the sausage loaf and lobs the patties into the pan. As they sizzle, the oats puffing and popping, the zesty pork-beef scent slaps the air. The cook plates the meat beside over-easy eggs and thick-cut toast, and slides it across the counter. Sweet-smelling steam rises from the little slabs. You fork into the crisped exterior to reach a, well, *creamy* centre. The nutty taste (from the steel-cut oats) spreads across your tongue, followed by a slight peppery kick. To do it right, let the goetta absorb your plate's runny egg yolks or a dash of maple syrup.

Finding it

Tucker's Restaurant (1637 Vine St) fries juicy goetta in vintage diner style. A side order costs around US$3.

* TIP * Eating goetta is fine and dandy, but eating goetta amid thousands of other pork-and-oat enthusiasts is even better. Two festivals make it happen: the MainStrasse Village Original Goetta Festival (in mid-June) and Glier's Goettafest (in mid-August), complete with goetta-eating contests and goetta ring-toss games.

* By Karla Zimmerman *

Recipe Goetta

INGREDIENTS

675g (1½lb) boneless beef chuck, cut into 2.5cm (1in) pieces

340g (12oz) boneless pork shoulder, cut into 2.5cm (1in) pieces

4 cups beef stock

7½ cups water

1 cup steel-cut oats

¼ cup dried onion flakes

1¼ tsp ground white pepper

kosher salt, to taste

¼ cup canola oil

over-easy eggs or maple syrup, to serve (optional)

METHOD

1. Take a 23cm x 13cm (9in x 5in) loaf pan (tin) and line it with cling film. Be sure 10cm (4in) or so drapes over the edges. Set the pan (tin) aside.

2. Put the meats, stock, salt and 4 cups of the water in a 5.7L (6qt) pan. Bring to the boil over a high heat.

3. Reduce the heat to medium-low and leave everything to simmer for 1½–2 hours, until the meat becomes tender.

4. Strain the meat over a large bowl, retaining ⅓ cup of the cooking liquid.

5. Put the meat into a food processor and pulse to grind it finely.

6. Take a 3.8L (4qt) pan, pour in the remaining 3⅓ cups water, and bring it to the boil over a high heat.

7. Mix in the oats and salt, then reduce the heat to medium. Cook for 15 minutes or so, stirring periodically, until the oats become soft.

8. Put the oats, ground meat, reserved cooking liquid, onion flakes, white pepper and salt into a food processor.

9. Purée the ingredients until they form a thick paste.

10. Scoop the paste into the prepared loaf pan.

11. Tuck the overhanging cling film over the top to cover the meat completely. Place the pan in the refrigerator overnight.

12. To serve, unwrap the goetta, place it on a cutting board and cut into 1¼cm- (½in-) thick slices.

13. Heat the canola oil in a cast-iron skillet (frying pan) over a medium-high heat.

14. Add the slices of goetta. Take care not to crowd the pan, or they'll stick together. Fry the patties for 4–5 minutes, flipping them once or twice, until the meat is browned and crisp all over.

15. Serve the goetta solo or with eggs or maple syrup.

SERVES 6–8

* Greenlandic Open Sandwich *

GREENLAND

In this Greenlandic twist on Denmark's *smørrebrød* (open sandwich), fragrant angelica and smoky halibut combine elements of the land and sea, typifying the clean flavours of this remote island.

What is it?

To create this dish, angelica leaves are blended with butter to create a fragrant paste. This is lavishly spread on to dark rye bread and topped with smoked halibut. In Greenland, the type of fish used in this sandwich varies according to what is most abundant. Do as Greenlanders do, and adapt the recipe to suit the season.

Origin

Danish influence popularised open sandwiches in Greenland, but local flavours reign supreme. In remote Greenland, food follows the cycle of the seasons. Summers are spent in a frenzy of food preparation: endless daylight facilitates long hunting expeditions for muskox and caribou, fishing trips for halibut and Arctic char, and foraging sprees for herbs and berries. This bounty is then salted or bottled to preserve it. This dish contains all the elements required to protect the body against the brutal Greenlandic winter, featuring vitamin C-packed angelica and protein-rich smoked fish.

Tasting

Angelica grown in Greenland's harsh climate develops a distinct flavour – sweet, musky, with a whisper of anise. The scent is so strongly evocative of Greenland that expats say it rouses pangs of nostalgia for home. The first bite of this dish is infused with angelica, which lends fragrance to the salty chewiness of the halibut. The nutty flavour of rye bread gives an earthy note to each mouthful. The size of your brunch will depend on the time of year, as extremes of light and dark force Greenlanders to follow seasonal rhythms. In summer's glare, when the sun barely dips below the horizon, Greenlanders eat light meals, work long hours and hike the wilderness (for fun or food). In winter, hearty meals sustain families through the permanent darkness – as does the notoriously potent Greenlandic coffee (with splashes of Kahlua and Grand Marnier).

Finding it

Ilulissat's Restaurant Ulo, with views of the icefjord, whips up wonderful sandwiches made with homemade bread for 85DKK (US$14).

* LOCAL KNOWLEDGE * Whatever your personal opinions, tread lightly on the topic of hunting and fishing when you speak to Greenlanders. Though some cultures find it jarring, many Greenlanders describe their first kills with pride and reverence. Traditional hunting styles cause minimal environmental damage and no part of the slaughtered animals is wasted.

* By Anita Isalska *

Recipe Greenlandic Open Sandwich

INGREDIENTS

1 tsp angelica leaves

pinch of salt

1 cup butter, softened to room temperature

150g (5½oz) smoked halibut (or trout, salmon or cod)

4 large slices dark rye bread

METHOD

1. Finely chop the angelica leaves.

2. Blend the chopped angelica, salt and butter in a small bowl with a wooden spoon until it is smooth.

3. Spread about 1 tsp of the angelica butter on to each slice of rye bread. (Store the remaining butter in your fridge, or wrap small portions and freeze them for later use with baked meat or fish.)

4. Top each slice of buttered rye bread with a generous helping of smoked fish.

SERVES 2–4

* Hopper *

SRI LANKA

One taste tells you why it's a Sri Lankan obsession:
whether plain or garnished, this tangy, bowl-shaped pancake
is consummate Ceylon – a morsel of the past in the present.

What is it?

Hoppers are thin, crisp crepes made from a batter of fermented rice flour and coconut milk. They are cooked in mini hemispherical 'woks' and have a zesty flavour from added yeast or palm toddy. An all-seasons treat that is also eaten for dinner and dessert, hoppers are most common at breakfast, accompanied by a chilli or onion sambol (sauce).

Origin

The word 'hopper' is an anglicised version of appa, a Sri Lankan variation of the appam (which may include any rice-flour cakes) known all over India. Hoppers' true origins are unknown, but probably date back millennia to the southern Indian Tamil communities who favour appam and have always offered it to their gods. Today, some South Indian appam are hardly distinguishable from Sri Lankan appa.

Tasting

Before trying your first hopper, watch a professional make one, something best done in any *kade* (shop). Even at unassuming roadside stalls there's much to be learned from the white-shirted hopper chefs' quiet and deftness, a counterpoint to the surrounding irrepressible cacophony and bustle. In teams of two, the chefs mix and pour batter and juggle multiple concave pans for an uninterrupted flow of perfect paper-thin crusts and just-right coconut-gooey bottoms, sometimes thickened with an egg or extra coconut milk. The smell alone imparts the hopper's yeasty edge. Use the crunchy rim for dipping in a piquant sauce and then munch directly on the middle. The panoply of tastes – salty, spicy, creamy, sweet – adds to the sensation. Thus the seeds of obsession are planted.

Finding it

Reliably tasty hoppers can be bought in the Dehiwala and Wellawatte districts of Colombo. Plain/egg hoppers cost about Rs15/35 (US$0.10/0.25) each.

* VARIATIONS * Plain hoppers are the base element, a savoury snack served with spicy condiments. As the batter solidifies, however, you can crack in an egg for an egg hopper or pour in extra coconut milk for a milk hopper (*miti kiri appa*). Much-loved string hoppers (*idiyappam*) consist of flat tangles of thin rice noodles.

* By Ethan Gelber *

Recipe Hopper

INGREDIENTS

1½ cups white rice

1 tbs *urad dal* (black gram)

½ cup warm water

pinch of fast-action dried yeast

3 tbs white sugar

¼ slice white bread

coconut water or water

coconut milk

1 egg

coconut or vegetable oil, for frying

1 cup thick coconut milk or coconut cream or 1 egg (optional)

chilli or onion *sambol*, to serve

METHOD

1. The night before or 5 hours in advance, place the rice and *urad dal* (black gram) in a bowl of water and leave to soak.

2. After the soaking time, put the warm water into a separate large bowl. Stir in the yeast and then the sugar. Set aside the mixture in a warm place for about 10 minutes, or until the mixture is frothing and active.

3. Drain the rice and *urad dal* (black gram) and place them in a blender. Puree with the piece of bread and sufficient coconut water or normal water to make a thick batter.

4. Add the batter to the yeast mixture in the large bowl, adding a little at a time. Make sure it is well mixed and that the batter is still thick, but also smooth.

5. Cover the bowl with cling film and set aside for 6–7 hours. This is when the fermentation takes place. The result should be a thick and frothy pancake-like batter.

6. When you are ready to begin cooking, mix sufficient coconut milk into the batter to thin it. The result should be easy to pour but not too liquid. Beat the egg into the batter to combine thoroughly.

7. Wipe the hopper pan with a little oil using a piece of kitchen paper. Heat the pan over a medium heat until it is very hot, but not smoking. Reduce the heat a bit and then pour in a large spoonful of batter – enough so that when you swirl the batter around it coats the inner surface of the hopper pan. It should cover all of a small or medium-size hopper pan, or reach two-thirds of the way up a large one. The coating will be thin around the edges and thick in the middle.

8. Cover the pan. Cook the hopper over a low heat for about 3 minutes. The edges should be crisp and the centre soft.

9. Optionally crack an egg or pour 1 tbs thick coconut milk or coconut cream into the middle if you want to make an egg hopper or a milk hopper. Cook for about 3 minutes more.

10. Carefully transfer the hopper to a plate with a spatula. Repeat the cooking process until all of the batter is cooked. Serve the hoppers warm with *sambol*.

MAKES 9–12

* Huevos a la Mexicana *

MEXICO

Mexico's take on scrambled eggs is spicy enough to give you an all-day natural high. Chilli and tomatoes were born in Mexico and feature proudly in this zesty, easy-to-make dish.

What is it?

Scrambled eggs are spiked with green jalapeño peppers, diced raw white onion and juicy tomatoes. The green, white and red make up the colours of Mexico's flag and lend themselves to the dish's name. The vibrant colours also look great on the plate. Refried beans and hot corn tortillas are served on the side.

Origin

On 16 September 1810 a Mexican priest and revolutionary named Hidalgo rang his church bells and called on his parishioners to break free from Spanish rule. Today, Mexicans continue to re-enact his *grito* (cry) for liberty on Independence Day every year, with noisy celebrations and September-long feasts showcasing traditional Mexican dishes. One patriotic favourite is *huevos a la mexicana* for its Mexican-flag colours and typical local ingredients. The dish may have started as humble scrambled eggs, but today it means so much more in the hearts and bellies of Mexicans.

Tasting

This is a dish that's eaten in noisy *fondas* (cheap family restaurants) so it has to compete with musicians, giggling children, brightly painted walls and the smell of tacos wafting in from street stalls. From the moment your *huevos a la mexicana* land on your table and you smell that herbaceous cilantro (coriander) pierce the air, you know it's time for battle. The velvety golden eggs start you off gently, but it's the jalapeño pepper that brings the noise with a rush of fresh green spice. Then follow the exclamation points of raw onion one moment and sweet tomato juices the next. It's a beautiful brunch ballad. If things gets too hot for you to handle, reach for the refried beans (or sometimes slices of avocado); they're served at room temperature and provide a soothing richness. Then back to the chorus of flavours.

Finding it

Café la Blanca (40 Cinco de Mayo, Centro, Mexico City) serves Mexican eggs with juice and coffee for 75 pesos (US$5).

* TIP * This unpretentious dish is even better when you get in with your hands and eat it as makeshift tacos. Roll up a corn tortilla, load it up with the eggs and refried beans and douse it with a squeeze of fresh lime, and more salsa if you dare. A breakfast of revolutionaries.

* By Phillip Tang *

Recipe Huevos a la Mexicana

INGREDIENTS

3 tbs canola oil

1 small white onion, finely chopped

1 green jalapeño pepper, stemmed, seeded and finely chopped

1 ripe tomato, finely chopped

salt and ground black pepper, to taste

8 eggs, lightly beaten

1 tbs finely chopped cilantro (coriander) (optional)

few slices of avocado (optional)

refried beans (optional)

tortillas (optional)

METHOD

1. Heat the oil in a large skillet (frying pan) over a medium heat.

2. Add the onion, jalapeño pepper and tomato.

3. Season to taste with salt and pepper.

4. Cook, stirring, for about 4 minutes or until the ingredients are semi-soft.

5. Add the eggs and cilantro (coriander), if using.

6. Fold the eggs over in large curds whenever the edges cook, until it is all just about cooked through. This will take about 4 minutes. Do not overcook the eggs or the dish will be dry.

7. Serve immediately, with a side of refried beans, avocado slices and tortillas, if liked.

SERVES 3–4

* Huevos Divorciados *

MEXICO

Mexicans eat the most eggs in the world so it is little surprise that they star in so many national dishes, along with equally adored beans, salsa and tortillas.

What is it?

Huevos divorciados ('divorced eggs') is a popular Mexican brunch dish comprising two fried eggs (usually sunny-side up, and runny), one covered in *salsa roja* (red chile sauce), the other in *salsa verde* (green chile sauce). The two eggs are 'separated' by a generous line of refried beans and served on two heated tortillas. The dish is sprinkled with *cotija*, a hard cow's milk cheese, and *totopos* (corn chips).

Origin

The origins of *huevos divorciados* remain mysterious, but any mischievous storyteller could come up with a folkloric explanation for the 'divorce' – signified by two coloured salsas dividing the eggs. Traditionally, tortillas and eggs were the principal mid-morning fare of farm workers to help get them through the labouring day. Visually, *huevos divorciados* is a 'patriotic' dish – green, red and white being the colours of the Mexican flag.

Tasting

Head to a local cafe (follow the locals), especially on a Sunday when families en masse sit elbow to elbow (among the steam and aroma of hot corn tortillas) and boisterously engage over their egg dishes. *Huevos divorciados* is not the neatest of foods to eat – like any egg dish you must just dig in, and arm yourself with napkins... The yolks are generally prepared runny and made to ooze over the beans, while the spicy salsas give you (and your tongue) a morning pick-me-up. You soak up the mushy mess with the tortillas and, if you're still hungry, don't stop at one tortilla – extras are usually served at the table, steaming hot in a basket and covered with cloth. Perfect for wiping your plate clean.

Finding it

Head to Casa Valadez in Guanajuato to enjoy tasty *huevos divorciados* for M$5 (US$0.37), while looking over Teatro Juárez.

* VARIATIONS * Mexican food is spicy, but you can of course modify this dish to suit your tastes by using less salsa, or by making the salsas themselves less spicy by reducing the number of chillies used in their preparation. You can also prepare the eggs to your personal preference, or try using poached or scrambled eggs in place of fried ones for a slightly healthier variation.

* By Kate Armstrong *

Recipe Huevos Divorciados

INGREDIENTS

For the *salsa verde*

4–6 small tomatoes, washed and quartered

3 serrano chilli peppers, washed and halved

1 slice white onion

sprig of parsley

salt and ground black pepper, to taste

For the *salsa roja*

1 jalapeño chilli

1 garlic clove

2 red tomatoes

salt and ground black pepper, to taste

For the refried beans

1 tbs olive oil

½ onion, finely chopped

2 garlic cloves, crushed

400g (14oz) canned or cooked red kidney beans (or canned or cooked pinto beans), drained and rinsed

1 tsp cumin (optional)

pinch of salt

2 tbs vegetable oil

4 tortillas

4 eggs

¾ cup refried beans

½ cup *salsa roja*

½ cup *salsa verde*

¼ cup *cotija* or parmesan cheese

salt and ground black pepper, to taste

5 corn chips

METHOD

1. First make the *salsa verde*. Combine the tomatoes, chilli pepper and onion in a pan with a little water to keep it moist. Bring to the boil and cook for around 15 minutes, until soft and mushy, stirring frequently. Add a little water if the mixture is too dry.

2. Transfer the cooked vegetables to a blender. Add the parsley and blend until smooth. Add a small amount of water only if the sauce is very dry. Season to taste and set aside.

3. Make the *salsa roja*. Preheat the oven to 180°C (350°F). Put the chilli, garlic clove and tomatoes on a baking tray and roast for 10–15 minutes, turning them over midway through the cooking time. They should be browned and softened.

4. If you don't want too spicy a sauce, carefully remove and discard the seeds from the roasted chilli. Process the tomatoes, chilli and garlic in a blender until as chunky or smooth as you prefer. Season to taste with salt and pepper and set aside.

5. For the refried beans, heat the oil in heavy frying pan. Add the onions and garlic and fry over a medium heat for 5 minutes, until softened. Add the beans, cumin and salt.

6. Stir to combine everything, then 'mash' the beans with a potato masher as they cook until the refried beans achieve the desired texture (runny or chunky is fine). Set aside the beans.

7. To make the *huevos divorciados*, heat 1 tsp vegetable oil in the frying pan. Add one tortilla at a time to the pan, frying it gently over a medium heat for 1–2 minutes, until heated through. Remove the tortilla to a plate and keep it warm while you heat the remaining ones.

8. Add the remaining oil to the frying pan. Crack in two eggs and cook them sunny-side up for 2–3 minutes, until the whites are set but the yolks remain runny.

9. Heat the refried beans in a pan over a medium heat.

10. Place two tortillas on a large plate, overlapping them slightly in the middle. Place a spoonful of refried beans in the middle of the tortillas. Place one egg either side of the refried beans. Cover one egg with *salsa roja* and the other with *salsa verde*. Sprinkle a little cheese on the refried beans and add corn chips on top. Repeat for the second plate.

SERVES 2

* Huevos Rancheros *

NEW MEXICO, USA

In the southwest of the USA, Mexican 'farmer's filler' has become a brunch favourite: the combination of spicy chile sauce and mystical blue corn tortillas keeps you going till the cows come home.

What is it?

Huevos rancheros is a brunchtime favourite across the Southwestern USA, and you'll find it on morning menus from Sedona to San Antonio. Two over-easy eggs are served on warmed blue corn tortillas and topped with copious amounts of New Mexican chile sauce (red, green or both), strong Cheddar and a generous spoonful of pinto beans on the side.

Origin

Originally, *huevos rancheros* ('ranch-style eggs') was a simple dish of eggs, tortillas and salsa eaten by Mexican farmers to refuel after the morning's chores. Like many of the region's classics, it was transported up the Rio Grande Valley when the Spanish settled in what is now Southwestern USA in the 16th and 17th centuries. Mexican and Spanish conventions (salsa, tortillas) mixed with indigenous ingredients (chile, blue corn) to form *huevos rancheros*.

Tasting

The perfect *huevos rancheros* fill a rectangular oven plate from end-to-end with oozing chile, cheese and beans. The ingredients don't stand on ceremony here – they're *supposed* to get all mixed up together in a delightful concoction so your mouth doesn't know where the runny egg yolk ends and the smoky chile-cheese love-child sauce begins. You have to gobble up most of this delicious mess first before you find the final prize at the bottom of the plate: a chile-cheese-egg-soaked blue corn tortilla. The joy of *huevos rancheros* is that it's a food for everyone: posh brunchers wash this down with freshly squeezed orange juice on sunny, wildflower-fringed patios while builders and truckers fill up on it over strong cups of joe in no-nonsense diners.

Finding it

The San Marcos Cafe on Hwy 14 south of Santa Fe doles out perfect homemade *huevos rancheros* for US$8.50.

* VARIATIONS * Chile is a key ingredient in huevos rancheros, but will you take yours with red, green or both? The green sauce – made from the unripened chilli peppers – tends to be spicier, especially during the autumn harvest period, while the red sauce – made from ripe red chilli pods – is often milder and smokier in flavour. Savvy New Mexicans always order this dish 'Christmas' for a hit of both beloved sauces.

Recipe Huevos Rancheros

New Mexico chiles can be difficult to source, as they are rarely grown or indeed sold outside the state. If you want to make the sauce from scratch, you need fresh roasted or dried chiles. Instead, we recommend using jars of locally made sauce, which can be ordered online.

INGREDIENTS

4 cups cooked pinto beans

pinch of garlic salt

450ml (15fl oz) New Mexico chile sauce (red, green or both)

2 tbs vegetable oil

1 tsp extra-virgin olive oil

8 eggs

salt and ground black pepper, to taste

8 corn tortillas, preferably blue corn

4 cups grated strong Cheddar cheese

2 cups shredded iceberg lettuce

4 cherry tomatoes, halved

METHOD

1. Place four plates in an oven set to 180°C (350°F) to warm.

2. Place the pinto beans and garlic salt in a pan and gently heat through.

3. Pour the chile sauce into a separate pan and warm until it is gently bubbling. If you're using both red and green sauces, heat them in separate pans.

4. While the beans are warming, heat the vegetable oil in a large frying pan.

5. Crack in the two of the eggs.

6. Fry the eggs sunny-side up until cooked, leaving the yolks runny.

7. Add a pinch of salt and pepper to season.

8. Transfer the eggs to the top plate in the oven.

9. Repeat steps 5 to 8 until all the eggs are cooked.

10. Meanwhile, warm each tortilla in a large skillet (frying pan) with a drop of olive oil, until soft. You'll need to flip each one several times to ensure that it doesn't go either soggy or crispy.

11. To assemble, place 2 tortillas on each plate and top with 2 fried eggs.

12. Spoon the beans on to the side of the plate and cover the eggs/tortilla and beans with plenty of chile sauce. If you're making 'Christmas' *huevos*, confine the red sauce to one side of the eggs/beans and the green sauce to the other, not mixing them.

13. Liberally spread grated Cheddar over the top of the dish.

14. If you like, return the plates to the hot oven until the cheese melts.

15. Garnish with lettuce and tomato.

SERVES 4

* Idli with Coconut Relish *

INDIA

Southern India's cuisine is as enticing as a tropical breeze. Begin the perfect day on India's sultry coast with the local speciality *idli*, lavished with piquant coconut dip.

What is it?

These springy rice doughnuts are served smothered in coconut relish on breakfast tables across southern India. Creating dough for *idli* requires some advance preparation – ground rice and black gram are left to ferment overnight – but come morning, the light batter is ready to be squished into banana leaves and steamed.

Tasting

Southern India's steamy climate is the perfect setting in which to eat these springy savoury cakes, although they are also served further north across the country, usually with *sambar*, a lentil and tamarind stew. There's a whisper of sourness to the taste, brought about by the fermentation of the batter, which is offset by decadently sweet side dishes such as honeyed tomato relish. The rainbow of accompanying chutneys is part of the fun, and they range from fresh coconut and coriander dip to tastebud-scorching gunpowder. Indians swear by *idli* as a healthy breakfast (the recipe contains no oil or ghee, and the fermentation process makes the pancakes easy to digest). So go ahead, pile the *idli* high, drown them in relish and munch until you've mopped up the last drop of *sambar*.

Origin

Used to mop up chutneys across the subcontinent, *idli* are claimed as a regional dish of Southern India. It's likely that the practice of steaming these savoury cakes was imported from Indonesia between 800 and 1200AD. The earliest versions of this dish, as described in the ancient Indian encyclopedia *Lokopakara*, used *dal* (black gram) soaked in buttermilk as the main ingredient, but recent centuries have finessed the batter as a blend of *dal* and rice.

Finding it

Why limit yourself? Grab a platter of four differently flavoured *idli* for INR190 (US$3) at Delhi favourite Sagar Ratna.

* TIP * It's almost unthinkable that you'll end up with a surplus of these doughy gems: they're dainty enough that a second (or third, or fourth…) doesn't feel like a sin. But if you have spare *idli* the next day, slice them into fingers and pan-fry them until crispy. Sprinkle with chilli powder and serve them as a snack with whichever chutneys you have to hand.

* By Anita Isalska *

Recipe Idli with Coconut Chutney

A dedicated *idli* steamer, with palm-sized indentations to hold the dough, produces the best results. But you can also wrap your *idli* in banana leaves before popping them into a pressure cooker, or even make them in a microwave.

INGREDIENTS

For the *idli*

3 cups rice

1 cup *dal* (black gram)

2½ cups water

½ tsp fenugreek seeds

1 tsp salt

pinch of sugar

For the coconut chutney

1 fresh coconut

¼ cup roasted chickpeas (if you can't find these already roasted, drain a can of chickpeas, toss them in olive oil and bake on a tray at 200°C (400°F) for 30 minutes, or until crispy)

2 green chillies, finely chopped

1 tbs finely chopped fresh ginger

1 fresh coriander sprig, finely chopped

juice of ½ lime

1 tbs coconut oil

METHOD

1. Rinse the rice thoroughly and leave it to soak in a bowl of water for a minimum of 2 hours. In a separate bowl of water, leave the *dal* and fenugreek seeds to soak for about 2 hours.

2. Drain the *dal* and transfer it to a blender. Grind it, gradually adding about ½–¾ cups of water until you have a smooth and foamy paste. Transfer to a large bowl and set aside.

3. Drain the rice and add it to the blender with the salt and sugar. Grind it, adding about 1–1½ cups water little by little, until you have a smooth, pourable liquid.

4. Add the rice paste to the *dal* paste in the bowl and combine. Cover with cling film and leave to stand for around 12 hours.

5. Meanwhile, make the chutney. Carefully skewer one of the 'eyes' of the coconut and drain the coconut water into a cup.

6. Open up the coconut husk. Use a blunt knife to separate the brown husk from the coconut flesh, then place the flesh in a spice grinder or food processor with the chickpeas, chillies, ginger, coriander, lime juice and coconut oil.

7. Grind or process the mixture, gradually adding just enough of the coconut water to achieve a smooth texture.

8. After 12 hours, you should have a fluffy rice-and-*dal* batter. Without mixing it, pour ladlefuls into an *idli* mould.

9. Add water to the pressure cooker to a depth of about 2.5cm (1in) and bring to the boil. Place the mould inside (ensuring your *idli* are above the waterline) and steam for about 10 minutes until the batter has fully solidified. Alternatively you can cook *idli* in your microwave: grease a few small bowls with vegetable oil and pour in the batter. Cover and cook on high for about 2 minutes. If the mixture is still runny, give the *idli* an extra 30 seconds of cooking time.

10. Transfer the cooked *idli* to a plate, and place a small bowl of coconut chutney in the centre. Eat immediately: *idli* are best enjoyed when piping hot.

SERVES 4

* Indian Masala Omelette *

INDIA

Indians would never settle for a plain old omelette, and neither should you – add chilli, coriander leaves and spices and make an omelette worthy of the subcontinent!

What is it?

India's take on an old-fashioned vegetable omelette, the masala omelette is upgraded to appeal to refined Indian palates. Eggs and milk are combined with finely chopped onions, bell peppers, chillies and coriander leaves, then spiced up with ground pepper, turmeric and garam masala and fried in oil or ghee (clarified butter).

Origin

The masala omelette dates back centuries in India, but locals had to wait until the arrival of European colonial powers for the word 'omelette', first coined in France in the 16th century. The dish's popularity as a snack food is almost certainly down to the British extension of the Indian rail network, promoting on-platform catering and creating a fusion of English and Indian cuisine.

Tasting

The best place to sample a masala omelette is still a train station platform. Even a short stop is time enough to leap from the carriage and order a quick masala omelette to go. The sounds and smells of preparation are gloriously evocative – a brief waft of stove fuel, a crackle of bubbling butter, the swoosh as the omelette hits the pan, then a rich aroma of spices, before the delightful end product is slapped between two slices of crust-less white bread and served. Pause to enjoy the texture of still-crisp onion, chilli and pepper and the jumble of spices, feel a pang of nostalgia for home upon tasting proper sliced white bread, then quickly leap back on board as the train starts to roll out of the platform.

Finding it

You'll find masala omelettes being sold on – or close to – every train platform in India for ₹40–100 (US$0.65–1.60).

* **VARIATIONS** * As the masala omelette made its way around India, it took on the colour of the regions it passed through. An omelette served in Bengaluru will be subtly different from an omelette served in Udaipur, thanks to the local spice preferences. In southern India, don't be surprised if ground coconut is added to the mix.

* By Helen Elfer *

Recipe Indian Masala Omelette

INGREDIENTS

4 eggs

2 tbs milk

2 large onions, peeled and finely chopped

2 green chillies, finely chopped (seeded if you prefer a less fiery omelette)

½ red bell pepper, seeded and finely chopped

1 tomato, finely chopped

handful fresh coriander leaves, finely chopped

¼ tsp ground black pepper

¼ tsp ground turmeric

½ tsp garam masala

ghee (clarified butter) or vegetable oil, for frying

salt, to taste

toasted white bread, crusts removed, to serve

Indian *chai* (tea), to serve

METHOD

1. Beat together the eggs and milk in a large bowl until the mixture is light and fluffy.

2. Add the chopped vegetables and spices to the bowl and stir gently to combine everything thoroughly.

3. Heat the ghee or oil over a medium-high heat in a frying pan or omelette pan.

4. As soon as the fat is hot, turn down the heat to medium.

5. Add half the omelette mixture to the pan, swirling it around so that it completely covers the surface of the pan.

6. Cook the omelette for 2–3 minutes, until the underside is lightly browned.

7. Flip the omelette over using a spatula.

8. Cook the other side for 2–3 minutes, until is browned.

9. Slip the omelette on to a plate and keep it warm while you make the second omelette in the same way.

10. Serve the omelettes with unbuttered white bread toast and cups of Indian chai (tea).

SERVES 2

* Israeli Breakfast *

ISRAEL

Chopped vegetable salads and creamy cheeses, eggs and freshly squeezed orange juice, green olives and *matias* herring, fruit salad and granola (muesli) – breakfast in Israel is a nutritious, meat-free smorgasbord.

What is it?

An Israeli breakfast is a lavish, all-you-can-eat, self-service buffet. A variety of spreadable cheeses are joined by slices of yellow cheeses, vegetable salads sprinkled with olive oil and lemon juice, hummus, green olives of various types, hard-boiled eggs, fruit salad, jams, butter, fresh rolls, granola (muesli), breakfast cereals, fresh juices and hot drinks. Because of kosher laws that prohibit the mixing of meat and milk, the only non-vegetarian components are *matias* herring and pickled herring in sour cream.

Origin

For over a century, Israeli kibbutzniks (members of kibbutzim, socialist collective farms) have started the work day early – shortly after dawn – to avoid doing field work in the midday heat. By breakfast time, they have already put in hours of hard work and are ravenous. Back in Ottoman times they started a tradition: heading to the communal dining hall for a hearty, nourishing buffet breakfast. Even in times of food rationing, kibbutzim could provide their members with products they grew themselves: vegetables from the fields, milk from the cow shed, cheese from the milk.

Tasting

You're about to climb Masada or hike through the Galilee, but before you head out you stop off at your hotel's dining room for breakfast, Israeli-style. Crunchy-fresh meets creamy-rich as chopped juicy tomatoes and fresh cucumbers mingle on your plate with extra-rich cottage cheese, tangy *labneh* (strained yoghurt cheese) and *gvina levana* (a creamy version of what the Germans call *Quark*). Lending a salty, savoury note to the affair is the tangy pickled herring, which melts into the bitter overtones of cracked suri (Tyre) olives. Keen for something sweet, you go back for seconds – this time beautifully presented seasonal fresh fruit salad; crunchy, nutty granola (muesli); aromatic warm rolls or slices of bread spread with butter and jam; and mugs of thick, sweet hot chocolate.

Finding it

The King David Hotel in Jerusalem is known for its Israel breakfasts, which cost 128NIS (US$34) if you're not staying there.

* **TIP** * **It's easy to create vegetarian, vegan, low-fat, organic, nut-free or gluten-free versions of the Israeli breakfast because the options are so varied. Simply substitute ingredients as you see fit to create the perfect breakfast buffet for you.**

* By Daniel Robinson *

Recipe Israeli Breakfast

INGREDIENTS

firm, flavourful tomatoes (eg Roma, Italian or plum tomatoes)

Mediterranean (Persian) cucumbers

extra-virgin olive oil

freshly squeezed lemon juice

salt

extra-rich cottage cheese

labneh (strained yoghurt cheese)

sliced hard cheeses

hummus

hard-boiled eggs

green, unpitted olives (if possible from Israel, Palestine, Lebanon or Jordan)

matias herring

pickled herring

jams

butter

fresh rolls

fresh sliced breads

granola (muesli)

breakfast cereals

milk

fruit salad (can be made with orange, grapefruit, apple, cantaloupe melon, watermelon etc)

fruit juices, including freshly squeezed orange and grapefruit if possible

hot drinks (coffee, tea, hot chocolate)

METHOD

1. Cut the cucumbers and tomatoes into pieces the size of unpopped popcorn.

2. Place the chopped cucumbers and tomatoes in a serving bowl.

3. Combine the olive oil, lemon juice and salt in a bowl.

4. Stir the dressing vigorously with a fork.

5. Pour the dressing over the chopped vegetables and stir to combine.

6. Put the tomato-and-cucumber salad and the rest of the brunch components into bowls or on to small plates.

7. Arrange the plates and bowls on a buffet table, roughly in the order listed above, along with serving plates, cutlery, napkins and glassware.

* Japanese Breakfast *

JAPAN

A tray full of treasures arrives. Freshly steamed rice, hot *miso* soup, pickled vegetables, a piece of grilled fish, an egg... it's disarmingly straightforward yet so clearly from another world.

What is it?

Prepare for a mini smorgasbord, Japanese-style. As is common with many Asian cuisines, rice is the must-have, but the beating heart of the spread is surely the thin but defiantly rich *miso* broth. Another dish beside it offers pickled daikon, carrot and cabbage. A whole egg in a tiny dish sits alongside a butterflied sardine. Where to begin?

Origin

For centuries Japanese meals have revolved around rice, fish and vegetables. A history of Buddhist restrictions on meat consumption and anti-Chinese sentiment has contributed to the somewhat austere philosophy. One characteristic of Japanese eating is the unique serving vessel used for each element of a meal, whereby each morsel is taken on its own, never mixed. And *miso*? Well, once again, a distant Chinese origin is likely.

Tasting

The taste of the food is unquestionably just a part of the experience when it comes to a Japanese set. You're immediately drawn into a miniature universe, a private world of dishes to lose yourself in as you prepare for the day. You take your rice bowl in your hand and with a deft scoop of your chopsticks take a mouthful of the short grain rice Japan is famous for. It's fragrant, nutty and comforting as well as being sustaining. Then a sip from the *miso* soup bowl and the warming completeness of it brings your senses to life. From there it's a journey through textures and flavours, crunchy raw vegetables, soft, salty fish and tangy pickles. A light, tasty, healthy breakfast to whet your appetite for the day.

Finding it

The traditional Japanese breakfast at Park Hyatt Tokyo is the real deal. Expect to pay ¥ 3900 (US$36.80).

* TIP * You might find your breakfast tray arrives with a raw egg. To bolster your meal, crack the egg into the bowl it came in, season it with a little soy sauce and beat it with your chopsticks. Then simply pour it over your rice!

* By Ben Handicott *

Recipe Japanese Breakfast

Preparing your own version of a Japanese breakfast is not difficult; you just need a good selection of little bowls and plates to get the traditional effect.

INGREDIENTS

For the beansprout pickles

1 spring onion, cut into finger lengths and finely sliced lengthways

1 cup bean sprouts

½ tsp salt

3 tbs rice vinegar

1 tbs *mirin*

For the rice

1 cup Japanese short grain rice

water

For the *miso*

2 cups *dashi* stock

¼ cup *miso* paste

2 tbs torn *nori* strips

½ cup diced soft tofu

For the grilled fish

2 sardines, butterflied and filleted (ask your fishmonger to do this if you prefer)

1 tsp vegetable oil

a small dish of soy sauce and a whole egg, to serve (optional)

INGREDIENTS

1. To make the beansprout pickles, combine the spring onions and sprouts in a bowl.

2. Mix together the salt, vinegar and *mirin* in a bowl, then drizzle it over the sprouts and spring onions. Leave to stand for at least 30 minutes.

3. To prepare the rice, place it in a small pan and add enough cold water to fill the pan to about a finger's width above the level of the rice.

4. Cover the pan and bring the water to the boil over a medium heat. Turn the heat to low and cook the rice, covered, for 20–25 minutes.

5. Turn off the heat. Fluff up the rice with a fork and leave it to stand with the lid on.

6. To make the *miso*, heat the *dashi* in a pan, but don't boil it. Add ½ cup of the heated *dashi* to the *miso* paste in a cup and combine.

7. Add the mixture to the *dashi* remaining in the pan and stir gently.

8. Add the *nori*, then the tofu to the pan. Keep the soup warm.

9. To cook the fish, place a heavy pan over a high heat.

10. Once the pan is very hot, add the oil and then the sardines, skin-side down. Cook the fish for 1 minute, then turn them over and cook them for 30 seconds.

11. Transfer the fish to kitchen paper to rest for a few minutes.

12. To serve, place each item in a separate dish on a tray.

13. Add a small dish of soy sauce and a whole egg in a separate dish, if you like. When you are ready to eat, crack the egg into its serving bowl, whisk in some soy sauce and pour the mixture over the rice.

SERVES 2

* Japchae *

SOUTH KOREA

Holiday feasts and social outings in South Korea simply aren't complete without *japchae*, a slippery tangle of veggies, beef and glass noodles that will test your chopstick mettle.

What is it?

Japchae is a side dish of noodles made from sweet potato starch, beef, shiitake mushrooms, carrots, spinach and bell pepper. It's served at room temperature and usually eaten in restaurants. Because of the prep time (50 minutes start to finish), homemade *japchae* is normally reserved for family events and holidays.

Tasting

Unlike Korea's famously fiery fare, *japchae* embraces subtlety. Vermicelli tossed in a sesame-oil sauce gives the chewy noodles an understated butter-sweet flavour and a slippery exterior. Handling *japchae* with chopsticks can be a daunting task. So grab a fork, avoid the embarrassment of dropping noodles on the floor and dig into a bounty of layered tastes and textures. *Japchae* is best enjoyed in a *hanjeongsik* restaurant, a delightfully chaotic banquet place offering the full panoply of Korean cuisine. Dishes shift back and forth while outstretched arms pluck food with aplomb. Hand gestures signifying the appropriate level of respect welcome every pour of beer or shot of *soju*. The din of shouts for refills is constant, as is the sound of slurped noodles, an unabashed signal of gastronomic delight.

Origin

Japchae first appeared in 1608 on a prince's dining table. It was, back then, a noodle-free vegetarian dish and remained that way for three centuries. The noodle version emerged in the 1920s when Korea was under the boot of Japanese rulers who, among other dastardly deeds, exported the country's rice. The ensuing grain shortage stimulated interest in alternate food sources, including *japchae* fused with sweet potato noodles. By the 1960s, cookbooks featured *japchae* with meat, fish and noodles.

Finding it

Sanchon, a restaurant in Insadong, Seoul, serves temple food so you'll get the vegan version. Lunch costs KRW 33,000 ($30).

* TIP * Making *japchae* is a labour of love, so don't skip the details and be sure to buy sesame seeds. Give them a quick roasting before using them to garnish the final noodle mixture. They add a crunchy layer of texture, a pleasant nutty aroma and a dash of sophistication to the presentation.

* By Rob Whyte *

Recipe Japchae

INGREDIENTS

170g (6oz) Korean sweet potato
starch noodles

110g (4oz) lean beef, such as sirloin

4–5 shiitake mushrooms

170g (6oz) fresh spinach

salt and ground black pepper, to taste

1 small carrot

1 small onion

1 small green bell pepper

2 eggs, beaten

vegetable oil, for stir-frying

2 tsp sesame seeds

For the sauce

3 tbs soy sauce

2½ tbs sugar

2 tbs sesame oil

2 tsp minced garlic

METHOD

1. Combine all the ingredients for the sauce in a bowl and stir until the sugar is dissolved.

2. Cook the noodles in boiling water according to the packet directions. Drain, rinse, and drain again. Cut them into 15cm (6in) lengths using scissors and place in a large bowl. Add 2 tbs of the sauce and combine.

3. Cut the beef into thin 5cm (2in) strips. Place into a bowl and stir in 1 tbs of the sauce.

4. Slice the mushrooms into 5mm-wide (¼in-wide) strips. Place the mushroom strips in a bowl and stir in 1 tbs of the sauce.

5. Wilt the spinach in boiling water, then drain and rinse in cold water. Squeeze out excess water, cut into 5cm (2in) lengths and season.

6. Cut the carrot, onion and green bell pepper into julienne strips and place each ingredient in a separate dish.

7. Pour the beaten eggs into a lightly oiled frying pan and cook over a medium heat until just set. Flip over and cook until just solid, then remove to a plate and leave to cool. Cut it into matchstick strips.

8. In a large non-stick frying pan, stir-fry the noodles over a medium heat for 3–4 minutes, until they are translucent and a bit sticky. Transfer back to the large bowl.

9. Stir-fry the prepared carrots with 1 tsp oil in the frying pan over a medium heat for 1–2 minutes, then season. Repeat with the onion and green bell pepper, cooking them separately. After cooking, transfer each to the large bowl of noodles.

10. Stir-fry the beef for 1–2 minutes until just cooked, and add to the noodles along with the spinach and the remaining sauce.

11. Toss the mixture by hand to combine everything thoroughly. Adjust the seasoning by adding soy sauce and/or sugar.

12. Dry-fry the sesame seeds over a medium heat until toasted.

13. Transfer the noodle mixture to a serving dish, top with the sesame seeds and egg strips and serve at room temperature.

SERVES 4

* Johnny Cakes *

ATLANTIC COAST, USA; CARIBBEAN ISLANDS

For almost half a millennium, the versatile Johnny cake – in various guises – has filled many a belly on the Atlantic Coast, from New England to the West Indies.

What is it?

From a griddle-fried Rhode Island cornmeal pancake to a deep-fried Caribbean flour dumpling, the basic form of the Johnny cake morphs depending on its host nation, state, region, or even county. It's often served for breakfast topped with honey, syrup or butter, or as a filling accompaniment to ribs, stews or roasts.

Tasting

While Johnny cakes are meant to be simple, filling grub, the flavours and fats they contain blend to create a delicate flatbread that is far more complex and densely rich than regular cornbread. Purists in Rhode Island use only white cornmeal made from flint corn, a sweet and buttery heirloom corn cob that nearly became obsolete in modern farming, as it yields less corn but requires more land and labour. In the Caribbean, the Johnny cake is leavened, made of more wheat flour than cornmeal, and deep-fried, giving it the consistency of a flattened cakey dumpling. Keep an eye out for roadside stands with long lines of islanders; this ultimate comfort food treat is often served at casual local establishments accompanied by salted fish, baked beans, ribs or a stew, or as a sandwich.

Origin

When settlers and African slaves first populated North America and the Caribbean in the 1600s, Native American tribes taught them to replace inefficient wheat flour with stone-ground cornmeal. The etymology of Johnny cakes is hotly debated: the savoury treat's name might have come from Native American tribes (the *Shawnee* cake or *jonekin* cake, meaning 'cornmeal' in local languages) or white settlers (a 'journey' cake). While the name remained, the Johnny cake itself evolved: the flour is often a mixture of corn and wheat and they're deep-fried rather than pan-fried.

Finding it

Jigger's Diner, Rhode Island for US$5, or Garvey's Sunshine Shack, Anguilla, US$15–25 for meals with a side of Johnny cakes.

* TIP * If you want to make authentic Rhode Island-style Johnny cakes with the traditional white flint cornmeal, prepare it in advance. By at least a week. Both Kenyon's Grist Mill in Rhode Island and Gray's Grist Mill in Massachusetts have been stone-grinding the corn for hundreds of years and now sell it online.

* By Alex Leviton *

Recipe Rhode Island-style Johnny Cakes

INGREDIENTS

1 cup ground white cornmeal

¾ tsp salt

1 tsp sugar (optional)

1¼–1½ cup boiling water

¼ cup butter or bacon grease, for frying

butter and honey, to serve

METHOD

1. Thoroughly combine the white cornmeal, salt and sugar in a large heatproof bowl.

2. Slowly pour in the boiling water, whisking constantly, to form a batter with a thick, soupy consistency.

3. Grease a griddle with a little butter or bacon grease and place it over a high heat.

4. Once the griddle is hot, slowly drop a spoonful of dough on to its surface.

5. Press down on the Johnny cake with a flat spatula while it is cooking.

6. Fry the Johnny cake for 2–4 minutes on each side or until the edges are just crispy.

7. Remove the cooked Johnny cake to a plate and keep it warm while you cook the remaining batter in the same way.

8. Top the hot Johnny cakes with butter and honey and serve immediately.

MAKES 10–12

* Kedgeree *

UNITED KINGDOM

Filling and flavoursome, this Anglo-Indian breakfast classic is long overdue a revival. Best made the night before, it is the perfect brunch dish for feeding a crowd of overnight guests.

What is it?

Flakes of smoky fish, fluffy white basmati rice, mild spicing, an egg or two and a generous handful of chopped parsley: mixed together and served hot or cold on a large plate it won't win any prizes for presentation but it is an eminently comforting and nutritious brunch that harks back to the days of the British Empire.

Origin

Of all the dishes conceived during the culture clash that was the 19th-century British colonisation of India, kedgeree is perhaps the most famous. A rice and lentil dish known as *khichri* had long been popular in India and kedgeree is thought to be a British adaptation. The fish component comes from the dilemma facing anybody in a hot country before adequate refrigeration was available: how to keep fish fresh? The solution was to catch fish early in the morning, as usual, but serve them for breakfast rather than letting them deteriorate all day.

Tasting

The perfect venue for your first taste of kedgeree should be a palace hotel in India, perhaps Jaipur. Surrounded by ornate architecture and impeccable service at the breakfast table (clad in its starched white tablecloth of course), the plate of kedgeree is perfectly at home. True, curry seasoning at breakfast might be an acquired taste, but the kedgeree's spicing should be mild, so the flavour of the fish isn't obliterated. It's the aroma that arrives first: earthy spices of coriander seed, turmeric and cumin, then the mouth-watering smokiness of the fish. The first mouthful combines the chewiness of the spiced rice with soft flakes of haddock. The hard-boiled egg adds a quaintly Victorian touch – practical and unfussy. This is more authentic than the oozy yolk of a poached egg but feel free to experiment.

Finding it

Look no further than The Wolseley, just off Piccadilly, London. The hotel's kedgeree costs £12 (US$19.31) and is beyond reproach.

---

* VARIATIONS * An authentic kedgeree recipe, like this one, is fairly basic. But as the dish has left its Empire roots in India more ingredients have been added: green peas or sultanas are a frequent addition. Many moisten the dish with cream. One thing we must insist on: parsley only, please, not coriander.

* By Robin Barton *

Recipe Kedgeree

INGREDIENTS

250g (9oz) smoked haddock

water, for poaching the haddock

¾ cup basmati rice

1½ cups water, for cooking the rice

1 tsp curry powder

large knob of butter

1 medium onion, finely chopped

2 hard-boiled eggs, halved

bunch of parsley, finely chopped

½ lemon

METHOD

1. If you are cooking the haddock in the oven, preheat the oven to 180°C (350°F).

2. Check the smoked haddock fillet for bones. The best smoked haddock is undyed and sourced from sustainable fisheries.

3. Place the haddock fillet in a baking tray, if cooking in the oven, or a pan, if cooking it on the stove. Cover the haddock with water.

4. Put the baking tray in the oven and cook the fish for 20 minutes, or cook the fish on the stove for 10 minutes, until the haddock can be flaked. Lift out the haddock from the water and set it aside.

5. Rinse the basmati rice thoroughly until the water runs clear. Place the rice in a pan with the water and bring the water to a simmer over a medium heat. Put a lid on the pan and simmer the rice for 10 minutes, without lifting the lid.

6. Turn off the heat and leave the rice to stand, undisturbed, for 10 minutes. Then fluff up the rice with a fork.

7. Melt the butter in a large pan over a medium-high heat, then add the chopped onion to the pan and cook until it is soft and golden (about 10 minutes).

8. Stir in the curry powder.

9. Add the cooked rice to the pan, mix thoroughly, then carefully stir in the flaked haddock, trying not break up the flakes of fish.

10. Serve the mixture on to two plates and garnish each with a halved boiled egg, a generous sprinkle of chopped parsley and a squeeze of lemon juice.

SERVES 2

* Khanom Krok *

THAILAND

This is sweet brunch on the go. Rice-flour puffs create a crispy pancake-like shell that gives way to a hot, sweet coconut cream that melts in the mouth.

What is it?

Each morning, all over Thailand, you'll find street stalls serving these grilled pancake balls. There are two layers to *khanom krok*. First a rice-flour batter is cooked in the ping-pong ball-sized dimples of a special iron pan. This is then filled with a mixture of coconut cream, onions and other savoury fillings before being sandwiched together with another half and scoffed.

Tasting

The first bite into the hot, crispy shell of *khanom krok* is exciting. The golden exterior is wafer-like rather than greasy, playing at being innocent. Yet bite down and the creamy contents burst into your mouth and are wonderfully wicked. At the same time, the onions and other additions provide a savoury counterpoint – think sweet Thai curry. There are no spices here though, just the smoothness of coconut and green onions, plus variations with dried shrimp or coriander. The play of crisp/soft and sweet/salty is addictive. They seem to have the perfect bitesize shape that leads you down a slippery slope to *khanom krok* addiction...

Origin

The dimpled pan used to cook *khanom krok* resembles the one the Danish use to make *aebelskiver* (round pancakes) and the square pan that the Japanese use to make *takoyaki* (octopus balls). Some believe that popular use of this pan began in Ayutthaya, the former capital of Siam (now Thailand), during the reign of King Narai (1657–1688), who had contact with both the Danish and the Japanese. Narai's royal kitchen was not shy about using new, foreign ingredients (such as egg, which the Portuguese brought) and it was perhaps then that the pan and the subsequent dish came into being.

Finding it

Stalls in Or Tor Kor Market (MRT station: Kamphaeng Phet) in Bangkok sell 10 *khanom krok* for 25 baht (US$0.80).

* VARIATIONS * **Fillings can include shrimp, chillies, peanuts, corn, taro, rice, coriander, pandan and sugar. Whatever you choose, having it to go means getting your *khanom krok* wrapped up in a banana leaf or just in paper with a skewer to eat them with. Similar snacks can be found in Myanmar and Laos. In Indonesia it's known as *serabi* and a savoury variation in Vietnam is the *bánh khọt*.**

Recipe Khanom Krok

Outside Thailand, you might find it hard to get your hands on a dimpled *khanom krok* pan or similar *aebelskiver* pan. This recipe has been adjusted to use a mini-muffin tin with any ovenproof pan lid. Results will be similar, just not as spherical. Alternatively you could use a cake pop mould that goes in the oven, and just reduce the cooking time by about 2 minutes.

INGREDIENTS

1 cup rice flour

2 cups water

⅓ cup steamed jasmine rice

½ cup desiccated coconut (optional)

2 tsp salt

vegetable oil, to grease the tin

1 cup coconut cream

½ cup sugar

1 green onion, chopped (optional)

other optional ingredients: shrimp, chillies, peanuts, corn kernels, diced cooked sweet potato, chopped coriander, all added to taste

METHOD

1. For the batter, mix the rice flour with half the water in a bowl until smooth. Leave to rest for at least 1 hour.

2. In a blender, process the jasmine rice, coconut (if using), ½ tsp of the salt and the remaining water, until almost smooth.

3. Add the mixture from the blender to the bowl containing the rice flour and water mixture. Mix everything together well to form a smooth batter, then set aside.

4. Preheat the oven to 180°C (350°F).

5. Lightly grease two 12-hole mini muffin tins or cake pop moulds with a little vegetable oil. If you only have one tin, cook the pancakes in two batches.

6. For the filling, mix the coconut cream, sugar and remaining salt in a bowl until the sugar and salt have dissolved. Mix in the green onion and other optional fillings.

7. Place the greased tins or cake pop moulds in the oven to heat up. When they are hot, remove them from the oven and spoon a layer of batter into each hole so that it is two-thirds full.

8. Return the tins or moulds to the oven and cook the bottom layer for 3 minutes (about 2 minutes for cake pop moulds). The pancake should be set.

9. Remove the tins or moulds from the oven once more. Spoon in enough of the filling mixture to fill the holes to the top. Cover with an ovenproof lid to prevent the tops from drying.

10. Return the tins or moulds to the oven and cook for about 8 minutes (6 minutes if using cake pop moulds), until the bottom layer is cooked. Test the edge with a teaspoon – you should be able to push the base layer loose from the tin or mould and see that it is golden and crisp.

11. Carefully spoon out each hemisphere and immediately join pairs together to form rough spheres. Eat while hot and gooey inside.

MAKES 12 BALLS

* Kimberley Barra Burger *

AUSTRALIA

Simple, yet satisfying, nothing cries out 'summer picnic' more than grilled fresh fish slapped between two bread rolls and enjoyed outdoors under a shady tree with a couple of beers.

What is it?

Barramundi is Australia's most popular fish and the thick white fillet can either be grilled (preferably with the skin on for added crunch) or, more commonly, battered and deep-fried. The fillet is sandwiched in a bun or slices of bread with a salad comprising at least tomato, beetroot and leaves, moistened with a dab of aioli, mayo or tartare sauce.

Origin

While pairing fried fish with bread dates back to biblical times, and is still common in many countries, the Australian version originates from the tropical north where anglers have long prized the barramundi's succulent flesh. Originally a pub staple across the Top End, the barra burger has migrated south into more upmarket city restaurants, and comes in countless variations and complexities, not to mention price brackets. Some less reputable establishments will substitute imported fish for Australian barramundi, considered by many as sacrilege.

Tasting

A barra burger is an outdoor dish, so forget about expensive restaurants and put away your cutlery. Find yourself a nice shady mango tree where the languid air is slightly cooler and your taste buds have just been caressed by an ice-cold lager. Your first bite should send you to fish nirvana – a salty, lemony crunchy goodness. With the second bite, you should notice the tang of the aioli, and by the third the beetroot is probably already trying to escape. Anything else in the bun is there purely either to hold it together (iceberg lettuce) or to jack up the price. The fish shouldn't be tough or dry on the inside; if it is, then it's overcooked. And if there's no beetroot then, alas, you don't have a barra burger, you have a sandwich.

Finding it

Five Rivers Café, Wyndham, East Kimberley, comes complete with mango tree and good, honest burgers for A$10 (US$8.76).

* VARIATIONS * Sourdough, Turkish pide or mountain bread might substitute for buns, while cos, rocket, baby spinach or even watercress impersonate foliage. Exotic-sounding aioli (wasabi, mustard, lime, red curry) are all the rage. Adding any other protein (eg cheese or egg) or wacky fruits (mango or pineapple) is simply wrong.

* By Steve Waters *

Recipe Kimberley Barra Burger

This recipe is equally easy to make at home or with one pan on the back of a ute up the Gibb River Road. If you can't get hold of barramundi, you can use other fleshy white fish – kingfish, cod, haddock, etc.

INGREDIENTS

2 ice-cold beers

1 fresh barramundi fillet, skin on

salt and ground black pepper, to taste

1 black tomato (Black Russian, Krim, Kumato etc) or any red tomato

1 tsp seeded mustard

¼ cup mayonnaise or aioli (add ½ garlic clove, minced, to the mayonnaise if you want aioli)

1 tbs oil or butter, for shallow-frying

¼ lemon or lime

Turkish pide, or any other type of roll or sliced bread

handful baby spinach leaves or any leafy green

few slices beetroot (roasted if you like, or the precooked type, drained)

METHOD

1. Crack open the first beer and take a long pull.
2. Season the fish by rubbing salt and pepper into both sides, then cover to keep off the flies.
3. Slice the tomato.
4. Mix together the mustard and mayonnaise or aioli in a bowl, cup, jar or sawn-off plastic bottle.
5. Heat the oil or butter in a heavy frying pan over a fire, or a medium-high heat if you are cooking the barra on a stove.
6. Once the fat is hot, add the fish, placing it skin-side down.
7. Cook the fish for 5 minutes or until it is three-quarters cooked through.
8. Finish the first beer while waiting for the fish to cook.
9. Flip the fish with a spatula.
10. Fry the other side of the fish for 1–2 minutes (depending on its thickness), until it is cooked and opaque all the way through.
11. Squeeze over the lemon or lime, then set the fish aside.
12. Split the Turkish pide in half.
13. Lightly toast the pide or fry one side briefly in the pan you've just cooked the fish in.
14. To assemble the sandwich, spread the pide with half the mustard mayo or mustard aioli.
15. Place the fish on top.
16. Dab a little more mustard mayo or mustard aioli on the fillet.
17. Top with spinach leaves, 2 tomato slices, at least 2 beetroot slices and finally the other half of the pide.
18. Sit down under a shady tree, crack open the second beer and hook in.

SERVES 1

* Kippers *

UNITED KINGDOM

Infused with a delicate smoky flavour, plump, succulent kippers are a quintessentially British morning dish that is not only delicious but impressively nutritious too.

What is it?

In a process known as 'kippering', a whole herring (aka 'silver darling') is split in half butterfly-style from head to tail along the dorsal ridge, then gutted, salted and smoked. It can be prepared in countless ways, but a kipper topped by a poached egg and served on wilted spinach with brown bread is an abiding classic.

Tasting

Fish have been smoked for centuries but kippers' popularity in Britain is commonly traced back to the village of Seahouses on northern England's windswept Northumberland coast. Here, in 1843, fish-preserver John Woodger accidentally left a fire burning overnight in the room in which he had left the day's catch. Unwittingly, Woodger had created a delicacy that quickly became fashionable in Victorian and Edwardian societies. Today, several places in the British Isles are famed for kippers, notably Peel, on the Isle of Man; Mallaig, Stornoway and Loch Fyne in Scotland; Northumberland's Seahouses and, just a little further south, the seaside village of Craster.

Origin

A kipper's complex, woody, caramelised flavour comes from the smoking process, which sees the fish strung up and smoked over smouldering oak sawdust and whitewood shavings for up to 16 hours. While a steaming hot, juicy, tender kipper warms the cockles on a chilly morning, its benefits go beyond the comfort-food factor. It's rich in DHA, an essential fatty acid that is key for brain growth and development, and which is most readily absorbed in the morning. Other essential fatty acids include omega-3 and omega-6. A kipper is also packed with antioxidants, vitamins and minerals such as vitamin D, B12 and B3, and calcium, and is low in saturated fat and calories. If that wasn't enough, it's good for your conscience, too, as an environmentally sustainable fish.

Finding it

Craster's fourth-generation fish smokers Robson & Sons sell premium kippers smoked on site for £9 (US$14.75) per 500g (1lb 1oz).

* VARIATIONS * The smoky flavours work fabulously in fish cakes, fisherman's pies and chowders, or you could whip up a kipper pâté. Cover a kipper in boiling water for 8 minutes, then drain, leave to cool and pick out the bones. Whizz half a spring onion, the juice of half a lemon, 2 tbs cream cheese and some pepper in a blender, add the kipper flesh, then whizz again. Chill for 30 minutes before serving.

* By Catherine Le Nevez *

Recipe Kippers

INGREDIENTS

3 drops white wine vinegar

1 egg

1 kipper

110g (4oz) baby spinach

1 slice brown bread, to serve

lemon wedge, to serve

METHOD

1. Fill a deep-frying pan with boiling water.

2. Add the white wine vinegar and bring to a simmer.

3. Swirl the water rapidly as you crack and release the egg into the water (this helps the egg white wrap around the yolk).

4. Poach the egg for 2–3 minutes, until the egg white is set but the yolk remains runny.

5. Carefully remove the egg from the water with a slotted spoon and drain it on kitchen paper.

6. Add the kipper to the simmering water and heat through for 2 minutes.

7. Remove the kipper with a slotted spoon and drain on kitchen paper.

8. Empty the water from the pan and add the baby spinach.

9. Return the pan to a medium heat and stir for 1–2 minutes, until the spinach is wilted.

10. Spoon the wilted spinach on to a serving plate.

11. Place the kipper on top of the spinach, then place the poached egg on top of the kipper.

12. Serve with brown bread (ideally just baked) and a squeeze of lemon.

SERVES 1

* Lowcountry Shrimp & Grits *

COASTAL REGIONS OF SOUTH CAROLINA AND GEORGIA, USA

Don't let the word 'grit' get to you – this iconic Southern dish is creamy, rich and packed with fresh coastal flavour, as well as being endlessly versatile.

What is it?

Shrimp & grits is a traditional coastal Southern breakfast dish with a stick-to-your-ribs heartiness that fuels you all day. The foundation upon which any savoury flavour profile imaginable can be built is grits – a porridge of boiled-down stone-milled corn – topped with shrimp that have been stewed with bacon or ham and a vegetable or two.

Tasting

Fewer dishes are as integral to the Southern brunch experience as the humble shrimp & grits. Life down south moves at a decidedly leisurely pace, and you'll want a hearty dish to hold you over as you take time to catch up with friends. Local shrimp and creamy grits are merely the foundation of the eating experience – smoky bacon, tart tomato or zingy, sharp Cheddar cheese are all flavours likely to appear. Perhaps the most authentic way to experience the dish is in the home of a local, where your host serves it up with their own twist, but if you're lacking that connection, the atmosphere at any Lowcountry eatery where it's on the menu may be just as charming. Fresh is best, so stay close to the coast.

Origin

Grits (from the Old English *grytte*, meaning 'coarse meal') were developed by the Native American Muscogee tribe, who prepared corn by grinding it in a stone mill. The Gullah peoples, descendants of West African slaves in the Lowcountry, combined grits with fish and shrimp captured in nets in tidal creeks. The dish was also a seasonal staple for coastal fishermen, who would top grits with shrimp (often sautéed with bacon) for a tasty breakfast.

Finding it

Great shrimp & grits are to be found at Hominy Grill, Charleston, SC for US$18 and Tubby's Tank House, Savannah, GA for US$14.

* VARIATIONS * Adaptations include: gravies made with ham or sausage; different cheeses added to the grits (commonly Cheddar, mascarpone, goat, Gouda or parmesan); and combinations of different vegetables, such as sweet onion, bell peppers, collard greens, mushrooms, or tomatoes. Some styles even feature a fried egg and it's not uncommon to find the grits themselves fried into a cake.

Recipe Shrimp & Grits

INGREDIENTS

For the grits

1 cup stone-ground grits

4 cups milk

1 tbs butter

salt and cracked black pepper, to taste

cheese (Gouda, Cheddar, mascarpone or goat), to taste (optional)

For the shrimp

675g (1½lb) jumbo shrimp, peeled and deveined (leave the tails on if you like)

1 tsp Old Bay seasoning (or mix your own with mustard powder, paprika, celery salt, a bay leaf, black pepper, crushed red pepper flakes, mace, cloves, allspice, nutmeg, cardamom, and ginger)

juice of ½ lemon

6 slices Applewood smoked or other quality bacon, diced

4 garlic cloves, minced

1 cup in total of a combination of: diced bell pepper, diced onion and diced mushrooms (optional)

For the garnishes (optional)

green onion, chopped

flat-leaf parsley, chopped

tomato, diced

smoked paprika

METHOD

1. To cook the grits, bring the milk to a gentle boil in a heavy pan.Slowly add the grits and reduce the heat to medium-low.

2. Boil the grits long and slow – 30 minutes or more – whisking occasionally at first to avoid lumps, then frequently as they thicken. Take care that the grits don't catch on the bottom of the pan and burn!

3. Remove the grits from the heat once they are thick and creamy. Add butter, salt, pepper and optional cheese to finish. Set aside.

4. To cook the shrimp, season them with Old Bay seasoning and lemon juice and set aside.

5. Heat a skillet (frying pan) over a medium-high heat. Add the bacon and sauté for 10–12 minutes, until the fat is rendered.

6. Remove the bacon from the skillet (frying pan) and set it aside. Drain all but 2 tbs of the fat from the skillet (frying pan).

7. Reduce the heat to medium and add the garlic. Cook for 3–4 minutes, until it browns slightly.

8. Add vegetables of your choice and cook until just tender.

9. Add the shrimp and sauté for 3–4 minutes, until they are pink.

10. Return the bacon to the skillet (frying pan) and remove the pan from the heat.

11. To serve, scoop 1 cup of grits into each of four shallow bowls.

12. Divide the shrimp mixture among the bowls.

13. Garnish with whichever combination of green onion, tomato, parsley, or smoked paprika you favour that day.

SERVES 4

* Lox and Bagels *

NORTH AMERICAN JEWISH DELIS

A fresh bagel, shmeared with cream cheese, piled high with tomato, salmon and red onion and topped with green capers makes a nutritious and outright delicious way to start the day.

What is it?

A deli classic, this dish consists of a bagel topped with full-fat cream cheese, slices of tomato and red onion and finally, the guest of honour, the lox. Technically, lox is the belly of a salmon brined in a salt solution, but these days the term is also used to refer to cold-smoked salmon as well as Norwegian-style cold-cured gravadlax (or gravlax).

Tasting

A genuine bagel is hand-rolled, but before it's baked it's briefly boiled, creating a glossy crust that locks in the dense, chewy interior. Paired with lox, the combination of bread and fish can turn any Sunday brunch table into a do-it-yourself delicatessen; but, for the ultimate lox-and-bagels experience, the place to go is an authentic, old-time Jewish deli. There, the baked-that-morning bagels will be the right combination of yeasty, crunchy and chewy; the lox will be hand-sliced and succulent; the red onion slices will be so thin they're translucent; and the cream cheese – the 'shmear' – will be rich and creamy enough to meld with and mellow the saltiness of the lox. Salty green capers provide the finishing touch. Devoured in the doorway of the premises or on the nearest park bench, the dish is the ultimate portable brunch.

Origin

Jews didn't eat much salmon in the impoverished shtetls of Eastern Europe because it was too expensive, but in America the railroads made brine-preserved salmon from the Pacific and the Atlantic affordable. Bagels had long been an Ashkenazi Jewish favourite; the idea of slathering on cream cheese – touted by Philadelphia Cream Cheese radio ads in the 1930s – transformed a simple bread ring into an indulgent treat. Adding a layer of lox (from the Yiddish word for salmon, *laks*, similar to the German *Lachs*) was the logical next step.

Finding it

An eat-in bagel with lox at Zabar's deli in Manhattan costs US$7.50, or take out a bagel (US$0.95) and lox (from US$26/lb (450g)).

* TIP * **If you plant a Cheerio, it will not grow into a bagel. And if it somehow did grow into a bagel with poppy seeds on top, you wouldn't be able to bring it into Singapore – the seeds are classified as 'prohibited goods' by the city-state's Central Narcotics Bureau.**

* By Daniel Robinson *

Recipe Gravlax

Once cured, the gravlax can be used to top fresh bagels together with a generous layer of cream cheese and thinly sliced red onion, or simply served on its own with fresh lemon squeezed over.

INGREDIENTS

1kg (2lb 2oz) extremely fresh, never-frozen salmon fillets with the skin on

30g (1oz) fresh dill

4 tbs white sugar

4 tsp sea salt

2 lemons

fresh dill and thin lemon slices, to garnish

METHOD

1. Rinse the salmon, handling it with the same hygienic precautions you would take when preparing sushi (ie keep all surfaces and your hands absolutely clean).

2. Dry the salmon with kitchen paper and remove any residual pin bones with tweezers. Trim off the thin edge of the salmon so the fillet is roughly symmetrical, then cut it in half.

3. Place the two pieces of salmon, skin-side down, on top of a layer of cling film.

4. Finely chop the dill, stems and all. Mix with the sugar and salt.

5. Sprinkle the dill, sugar and salt mixture on the fillets, with slightly more on the thicker parts (you can vary the relative quantities of salt and sugar depending on how salty or sweet you like your gravlax).

6. Carefully place one of the fillets on top of the other to create a salmon 'sandwich' with salt, sugar and dill in the middle.

7. Wrap the 'sandwich' as tightly as possible using the cling film it is positioned on.

8. Tightly wrap the fish in two or three more layers of cling film and place the fish on a plate. If you like, put a weight of some sort (eg a can) on top of the fish.

9. Put the fish in the fridge for about 2 days, turning it over twice a day.

10. Open up the package, discarding the cling film and spread out the fish on a chopping board.

11. Remove the dill (the salt and sugar will have been absorbed).

12. Slice the fish on a slant as thinly as you can (a very sharp knife is a must) and squeeze over a few drops of lemon juice.

13. Garnish with fresh dill and thin lemon slices.

MAKES ABOUT 1KG (2LB 2OZ)

* Mas Huni *

MALDIVES

A spicy Maldivian seafood salad with all the goodness of the Indian Ocean distilled into a brunch – perfect when you've just come back from a day of strenuous island-hopping.

What is it?

Perhaps the best description is 'shredded tuna salad'. Pieces of cured tuna are crushed together with chopped onion and chilli and shredded coconut flesh, and the crumbly mixture is served with freshly cooked *roshi* (Maldivian flatbread) to create a spicy, salty all-day breakfast that tastes just like food in the Indian Ocean ought to.

Tasting

The setting is everything when sampling *mas huni*. Eschew the five-star hotel breakfast buffets for the modest setting of a ramshackle Maldivian teahouse in Male, the Maldives' miniature capital. Here you'll find all of the varied and wonderful morsels that are collectively known as *hedhika*, or 'short eats'. Alongside assorted sauces and fritters, you are guaranteed to find *mas huni*, served with a pile of freshly roasted *roshi* and a cup of sweet tea – the perfect pick-me-up after a hard night of hauling fishing nets and landing your catch on the beach at sunrise (it's also not bad after a leisurely morning of sunbathing). As for the flavour, it's exactly what you would expect – salty, tangy, fishy, spicy – the kind of dish that Robinson Crusoe would have invented, only to discover that Man Friday's people had been making it for centuries.

Origin

When you live in a country of 1200 desert islands, fish is bound to be the key feature on the menus, and people are bound to find new and inventive ways of serving it. The traditional basis of *mas huni* was the enigmatically named 'Maldive fish' – hunks of tuna, boiled, smoked and dried to the texture and colour of aged driftwood. Once cured, Maldive fish lasts almost indefinitely, making it the perfect food for long sea voyages.

Finding it

Follow the locals to the tiny teahouse Irudhashu Hotaa, Male. A plate of *mas huni* and *roshi* will cost less than Rf15 ($1).

* TIP * Canned tuna is increasingly replacing Maldive fish as the cornerstone of *mas huni*, but seek out the traditional version, prepared with dry, fluffy, pounded flakes of Maldive fish (this is to canned tuna what Serrano ham is to Spam).

* By Joe Bindloss *

Recipe Mas Huni with Roshi

Mas huni is easy to make, but Maldive fish is hard to get hold of outside the Maldives and Sri Lanka; canned tuna is a good substitute.

INGREDIENTS

For the *mas huni*

2 fresh green chillies, finely chopped

1 large white onion, finely chopped

juice and zest of 2 limes

salt, to taste

300g (11oz) Maldive fish or canned tuna in brine, drained

1 cup grated fresh coconut

extra lime wedges and a handful coriander leaves, to garnish

For the *roshi*

1½ cups plain (all-purpose) flour

salt, to taste

2 tbs vegetable oil

½ cup boiling water

METHOD

1. To prepare the *mas huni*, crush the chillies, onion, lime juice and zest and salt together in a mixing bowl.

2. Flake in the Maldive fish or drained tuna.

3. Stir in the grated coconut – use fresh meat, not desiccated coconut.

4. Leave the mixture to steep for a few minutes.

5. Meanwhile, make the *roshi*. Sift the flour and salt into a bowl.

6. Add the oil, then pour on the boiling water little by little, stirring as you go, to form a soft dough.

7. Leave the dough until it is cool enough to touch, then turn it out on to a lightly floured surface.

8. Knead the mixture for 10–15 minutes, until it is soft and elastic.

9. Divide the dough into six balls.

10. Roll each ball flat with a rolling pin.

11. Heat a heavy frying pan over a medium heat.

12. Cook a dough circle in the dry frying pan, flipping it once the *roshi* starts to rise up and cooking it on the other side until lightly browned.

13. Remove the dough circle to a plate once it is cooked and cover it with a dish towel to keep it warm while you repeat the cooking process with all the dough.

14. To serve the *mas huni*, pack some into a small bowl.

15. Invert the bowl on to a serving plate to form a mound of *mas huni* in the centre.

16. Repeat with the remaining mixture.

17. Serve the *mas huni* with a wedge of lime and a few coriander leaves to garnish.

18. Eat the *mas huni* under a palm tree (if you have one close by), with the warm *roshi*.

SERVES 2

* Masala Dosa *

SOUTHERN INDIA

Spiked with a whiff of the subcontinent, yet reassuringly nutritious, these giant stuffed crepes from Southern India are vegetarian, sugar-free, low in fat, flavourful and fun to eat.

What is it?

A *dosa* is a wafer-thin crepe made with batter concocted from rice and lentils that's been fermented overnight. Once cooked, it's rolled with a filling of *masala* made from mashed potatoes, fried onions and a potpourri of spices. *Sambar* (spicy lentil stew) and coconut chutney are offered on the side.

Origin

The *masala dosa* has its genesis in southern India though its exact origins are foggy. *Dosas* were mentioned in Tamil literature as early as the 6th century AD, but the modern dish has stronger ties to the city of Udupi in Karnataka state. Legend has it that the original *masala* filling contained only potatoes; the onions were added during a potato shortage. They were supposedly placed inside the *dosa* to hide them from vegetarian Brahmins whose Satvik traditions prohibit their consumption. *Dosa* is enjoyed as a hearty but nutritious breakfast food in India.

Tasting

The key when eating *masala dosa* is to dig in straight away while the crepe is still fresh and hot, before it loses its crispiness. The *dosa* is usually rolled up like a huge cigar with the *masala* nestled invitingly in the middle, making it easy to eat with the hands. Some restaurants serve it on a plate shaped like a banana leaf with the *sambar* and chutney in small condiment dishes on the side. Though infused with chillies and spices, the *masala* is pleasantly mild, which counteracts the inherent sourness of the *dosa*. The *sambar* has a spicier kick, while the chutney captures the unmistakable coconut tang of southern India. Both can be used as dips, with the *sambar* being finished off like a soup at the end.

Finding it

Vinayaka Mylari is a haven of *dosas* in the city of Mysore in Karnataka. *Masala dosa* cost from ₹30 (US$0.50).

* **VARIATIONS** * The *dosa* has many derivatives: a paper *dosa* comes without the *masala* filling and is ideal for fussy kids, while a *Mysore masala dosa* is lined inside with red chutney to give extra oomph. Cooks also use different sorts of batter: a *pessaretu dosa* from Andhra Pradesh is made with a mung bean batter, while a *rava dosa* uses a batter made from semolina and rice flour.

By Brendan Sainsbury

Recipe Masala Dosa

INGREDIENTS

For the *dosa*

1 cup white rice

1½ cups parboiled rice

½ cup *urad dal* (black lentils)

½ tsp fenugreek seeds

salt, to taste

For the *masala*

3 tbs vegetable oil

½ tsp mustard seeds

1 tsp cumin seeds

1 tsp *urad dal* (black lentils)

10–12 curry leaves

2 onions, finely chopped

2 green chillies, finely chopped

1 red chilli, finely chopped

1 tsp grated ginger

½ tsp turmeric

5–6 boiled potatoes, lightly mashed and cooking water retained

2 tbs chopped fresh coriander

salt, to taste

sambar and chutney, to serve

METHOD

1. For the *dosa*, combine the uncooked white rice and 1 cup of the parboiled rice and soak the mixture in a bowl of cold water for 6 hours. Wash the *urad dal* and fenugreek and soak them in a separate bowl of cold water, also for 6 hours.

2. Drain the *dal*. Blend it with about 1 cup of the soaking water to form a thick batter. Transfer to a large bowl.

3. Drain the rice and blend it with the remaining ½ cup parboiled rice and about 1½ cups of the *dal* water to form a batter that is runnier than the *dal* one.

4. Add the rice batter to the bowl containing the *dal* batter. Stir in the salt and combine well to form a thick batter. Cover with a loose lid and leave overnight in a warm room to ferment.

5. Meanwhile, make the *masala* filling. Heat the oil in a large frying pan over a medium heat and add the mustard seeds, cumin seeds, *urad dal* (black lentils) and curry leaves.

6. Add the onions, chillies and ginger and sauté for approximately 7–8 minutes over a medium heat, until the onions are soft and translucent.

7. Add the turmeric and lightly mashed boiled potatoes. Stir in the salt, a little of the potato cooking water and the chopped coriander. The mixture should be loose. Simmer, stirring, for 2–3 minutes, until the ingredients combine and the mixture is a little less soggy. Set aside.

8. When you are ready to cook, put a large non-stick frying pan over a high heat. When hot, reduce the heat and splash in a little water followed immediately by a ladleful of batter. Do not stir the batter beforehand or you'll knock out the air bubbles.

9. Swirl the batter into a large, thin circle that covers most of the surface of the frying pan. Lower the heat and add a little oil at the edges to makes the *dosa* crispy.

10. After 5–7 minutes, when the bottom is brown, put the *masala* filling in the middle of the *dosa*. Fold over the edges and serve immediately with *sambar* and chutney.

11. Repeat the cooking process with the remaining batter.

MAKES ABOUT 10

* Matias Herring *

JEWISH DELIS; BELARUS; RUSSIA

A silky-soft piece of *matias* herring, flecked with finely diced onion, glides between your lips. As it melts in your mouth like butter, a delicate, salty-sweet flavour spreads across your tongue.

What is it?

Russian-style *matias* (pronounced 'ma-chess') herring, cured in brine, is lightly salted and spiced. The fish are caught in the North and Baltic Seas, where they live in huge schools often numbering hundreds of thousands. Some of the finest fresh herring comes from Norway and Iceland, but production of the Russian-style product often takes place in countries such as Belarus and Poland. *Matias* herring is an excellent source of vitamins A and D and is rich in omega-3 fatty acids.

Origin

In the shtetls of Czarist Russia, affordable sources of protein were hard to find – or, as Tevye summed up the situation in *Fiddler on the Roof*, 'when a poor man eats a chicken, one of them is sick'. Herring, caught in the Baltic Sea and preserved in brine, was rich in protein yet reasonably priced so that even households of modest means could afford it. As often happens, a dish considered 'poor man's food' in the Old Country became in the USA and other lands of immigration a beloved part of Ashkenazi-Jewish cuisine – even as it continued to be hugely popular in the USSR and its successor states such as Belarus and Russia.

Tasting

The bar or bat mitzvah service is over and amid a flurry of Yiddish greetings – *'gut Shabbos'* and *'mazel toff*!' – guests line up eagerly for a traditional Ashkenazi-style brunch. The tables are piled high and groaning under the weight of blintzes and bagels, whitefish and lox, egg salad and tuna salad, but the belle of the ball sits quietly in a small glass bowl: *matias* herring. A group of old-timers, friends from Manhattan's Lower East Side, ignore the flashier dishes and head straight for the *matias*, sprinkling the creamy-soft fish with finely chopped white onion before eating it with several slices of heavy black bread – and washing it all down with chilled beer and shot after shot of ice-cold vodka.

Finding it

Try the finest Santa Bremor *matias* herring at Brooklyn's Little Odessa, 281 Brighton Beach Ave, where 250g costs US$2.99.

* TIP * **Matias herring from the Baltic region should not be confused with pink-toned matjes (maatjes) herring, often from the Netherlands, made with herrings that are too young to have spawned.**

* By Daniel Robinson *

Recipe Matias Herring and Black Bread

Brining Russian-style *matias* herring from scratch is fiendishly difficult, in part because the right kind of fresh herring is hard to source outside of Norway and Iceland. But, once you've tracked some down, here's the way many connoisseurs like to serve it.

INGREDIENTS

4 *matias* herring fillets

1 white onion

fresh heavy black bread, such as Russian bread, dark rye bread or pumpernickel

METHOD

1. Lay out the *matias* fillets on a serving plate.

2. Finely dice the onion.

3. Sprinkle the diced onion on the *matias* fillets.

4. Cut the black bread into thick slices.

5. Serve the prepared fish and bread.

SERVES 2

* Muesli *

EUROPE, ESPECIALLY SWITZERLAND
AND GERMANY; USA; AUSTRALIA; UK

**Toasted or raw; three ingredients or 20; mushy or dry –
infinitely adaptable, muesli is simply one of the trendiest brunch
choices around and is packed with nutrition to boot.**

What is it?

Muesli is a tasty combination of oats, nuts, seeds, grains, dried fruits and spices. It's served with milk (cow, nut or soy) or yoghurt, or even fruit juice, and it can be topped with honey, fresh fruits, toasted nuts or dried fruit compote, or even with chocolate chips if you're feeling frisky.

Origin

A type of muesli was first devised in the 1900s for its health benefits by Swiss doctor Maximilian Bircher-Benner, after which the Bircher muesli dish is named. Bircher muesli is a 'wet' combination of oats and water, with chopped apples, nuts, lemon juice and cream (or sometimes condensed milk), topped with honey. Modern recipes sometimes call for healthier yoghurt in place of the cream. In later years, muesli took on various drier guises. Once considered a 'hippy' nibble, today this nutritious cereal is a permanent fixture at many breakfast and brunch tables.

Tasting

Tighten your dentures: it takes time and concentration to chomp through this nutty textured combination; muesli belongs to the 'slow food' movement of another kind. But it's worth being unhurried, as muesli is full of surprises: just as you're chomping into an almond, there's a soft, juicy sultana or, a coconut piece on the next chew. Don't skimp on quality yoghurts and accompaniments – this can make or break the eating experience. Fresh, tangy berries such as blueberries, raspberries and sliced strawberries add moisture and acidity that counterbalance the dryness and sweetness of the cereal, while banana provides a creamy, soft foil to the crunchy nuts. This is the type of dish you want to enjoy over a glass of freshly squeezed orange juice and a thick newspaper.

Finding it

The best place to try the definitive Bircher muesli is in Confiserie Café Sprüngli, Zurich, Switzerland, where a small bowl costs CHF6.50 (US$6.80).

* VARIATIONS * While oats are the principal ingredient in most muesli recipes, along with nuts and grains, the blend can be consumed either raw or oven-roasted ('toasted'). This latter type tends to have had oil and a sweetener, such as apple puree or honey, added and takes on a golden, crunchy texture. In the USA, this is often called granola and is sprinkled over fruits or yoghurt.

* By Kate Armstrong *

Recipe Muesli

The best thing about muesli? As well as being tantalising, nutritious, and easy to make and serve, all experimentation is good experimentation. Bircher muesli aside, there's no 'correct' muesli recipe. This means you can try any combination of seeds and nuts – and perfect it to meet your own needs. This recipe is just one of many blends.

INGREDIENTS

3 cups rolled oats

1 cup quinoa flakes

½ cup almonds, chopped

½ cup pumpkin seeds or hemp seeds

½ cup walnuts, chopped

1 cup sultanas

½ cup dried apricots, roughly chopped

½ cup dried coconut flakes (unsweetened)

½ cup sunflower seeds

½ cup goji berries or dried cranberries

1 tbs ground cinnamon

dash of nutmeg

milk or yoghurt, to serve

fresh or stewed fruits, to serve

METHOD

1. Place the oats in a large bowl.

2. Add the remaining ingredients.

3. Mix everything thoroughly using your hands or a large spoon.

4. Store the mixture in an airtight container in a cupboard (not in the refrigerator).

5. Serve with milk or yoghurt and top with fresh or stewed fruits.

MAKES 8½ CUPS

* Nasi Goreng *

INDONESIA; MALAYSIA; SINGAPORE

Nasi goreng, aka fried rice, is the ubiquitous one-dish wonder that's served in Indonesia, Malaysia and Singapore. While there are other staples, nothing fills you up like this speciality.

What is it?

Nasi (rice) *goreng* (fried) is a melange of ingredients wok-fried together with a base of plain white rice. The beauty of the dish is that no place cooks it quite the same. Pre-cooked white rice is tossed in a wok at high heat and fried with some, or all, of: eggs, shallots, garlic, sauce and strips of meat.

Origin

The dish's origins aren't documented, but many believe that its genesis lies with Southern Chinese traders who came to Southeast Asia as far back as the 10th century. Ostensibly cooked in the mornings with leftover rice and scraps from the previous day's meals, *nasi goreng* is fried in a Chinese-style wok. In 2011, CNNGo polled 35,000 people on Facebook to compile a list of the top 50 best foods in the world. *Nasi goreng* came in at number 2, behind *rendang* (Indonesian meat stew).

Tasting

When you're travelling in Southeast Asia, some of your best culinary experiences will undoubtedly be at local hawkers or *warung* (mom-and-pop eatery) where you get to rub shoulders with locals. There's just something authentic about rocking up to a hawker stall in the morning and tucking into a plate of steaming, freshly wok-fried *nasi goreng*. The dish is a perfect balance of rice that is coated with spices and savoury sauce and studded with bits of egg, meat and vegetables. It's truly the complete all-in-one meal. Those who can handle spice can request the chilli quotient to be upped. In Indonesia, moreish *krupuk* (prawn crackers) accompany the dish and add a crunchy, savoury bite. Don't be surprised if you end up ordering seconds!

Finding it

Try the nasi goreng sold at W.I.P Cafe, Bangsar Shopping Centre, Kuala Lumpur for US$5, or any local *warung*.

* VARIATIONS * In Indonesia, the use of *kecap manis* (sweet soy sauce) browns and sweetens the dish. In Singapore, try the Pattaya version: the rice is fried, wrapped in a thin omelette and flavoured with ketchup. You might find some fried with *sambal belachan* (chilli shrimp paste) and restaurants might posh up the dish with prawns.

Recipe Nasi Goreng

You can make a vegetarian *nasi goreng* by substituting the meat with vegetables such as carrots, cauliflower, peas, and corn. Remove the *sambal belachan.* All these ingredients should be available at a good Asian grocer.

INGREDIENTS

3 tbs vegetable oil

1–2 garlic cloves, chopped

1 onion, chopped

150g (5½oz) chicken, beef or pork, cut into small strips or cubes

2 cups long grain rice, cooked and left overnight

1 red chilli, finely chopped

1 tsp *sambal belachan*

3 tbs *kecap manis*

2 eggs

METHOD

1. Heat a wok over a medium heat and add 2 tbs of the oil.

2. When the oil is shimmering, add the chopped garlic and onions.

3. Stir-fry the onions for 5 minutes, until they are starting to soften.

4. Add the garlic and fry for 3 minutes, until the garlic and onion are softened.

5. Add the chicken, beef or pork and fry until the meat is just sealed on all sides.

6. Increase the heat to high and add the rice.

7. Stir the ingredients together, breaking down the clumps of rice.

8. Stir in the chilli, *sambal belachan* and *kecap manis*.

9. Stir-fry everything for a further 3 minutes, ensuring everything is thoroughly combined.

10. Set aside the rice and keep it warm.

11. Put the remaining 1 tbs oil in the still-hot wok.

12. Once the oil is hot, crack in the eggs and fry them sunny-side up.

13. Divide the rice mixture between two bowls or plates.

14. Top each portion of rice with a fried egg and serve.

SERVES 2

* Oat Porridge *

SCOTLAND

Whether you associate it with fairy tales, the lumpy gruel of boarding school, or comfort food, porridge has never gone out of fashion. And the bonus is that it's very healthy.

What is it?

In its most traditional, pure form, oat porridge comprises oats, water (or milk) and salt, slowly boiled together on the stove. To this nutritious base can be added a little milk or cream and sometimes a generous helping of poached fruits, a sprinkle of sugar or a dribble of honey. Hardy traditionalists might even add a dash of whiskey (shhh).

Origin

Traditionally (so it's believed) a Scottish recipe, porridge was a means of preserving oats by transforming them into a thick paste. In later years, especially in Britain where cooler climes prevail, hot porridge was useful given the ready availability of oats, its price (cheap) and its filling nature. Today, porridge purists argue about which type of oat is best to use – rolled or pinhead – and about whether it should be made with milk or water, salt or sugar. These porridge pros meet at the Annual World Porridge Making Championship in Carrbridge, Scotland, to show off their porridge-making skills.

Tasting

Frosty winter mornings and porridge are synonymous. So picture yourself in your flannelette pyjamas and fluffy slippers sitting at the kitchen table with a bowl of steaming porridge in front of you. The secret of eating porridge is not to rush. Porridge is hot. This means you must count to 20 so you don't burn your tongue (hint: blow on your spoon). Now, take a decent spoonful and enjoy its texture – admittedly, it's slightly mushy at first, but it has a pleasant 'after-chew'. Now, if *that* doesn't tantalise your tastebuds and give your teeth a workout... Go slowly now: because of its nature – high in fibre and low in fat – porridge is filling. This means it will set you up for your fully clothed day.

Finding it

Enjoy a bowl of oats with fruit or syrup for £3 (US$4.83) at Cafe Gandolfi, Glasgow, which champions local produce.

* VARIATIONS * Porridge has many relatives across the world, from the drier oat-and-water mixture Americans call oatmeal, to the ubiquitous buckwheat *kasha* found in Central and Eastern Europe. Elsewhere, other cereals such as maize, wheat, rice, quinoa, millet, sorghum and flax are used, depending on the availability of ingredients.

* By Kate Armstrong *

Recipe Oat Porridge

As the traditionalists would tell you: to 'keep the devil at bay', you must stir with a wooden implement, a spurtle, with your right hand and in a clockwise direction only. A wooden spoon will do if you don't happen to own a spurtle. Soak the oats overnight for a quicker cooking time.

INGREDIENTS

1½ cups rolled oats

3⅓ cups water or milk

pinch of salt

Serve with one (or more) of: milk; yoghurt; dried, fresh or stewed fruits; honey or brown sugar; a dash of whisky (for the traditionalists)

METHOD

1. Place the oats and milk or water in a large pan over a medium heat.

2. Bring the mixture to the boil, stirring constantly.

3. Continue stirring and cooking the porridge for about 5 minutes, until the mixture is thick and creamy.

4. Add a pinch of salt and stir.

5. Ladle into bowls and add your favourite topping.

SERVES 4

* Oeufs en Cocotte au Saumon Fumé *

FRANCE

Oeufs en cocotte au saumon fumé is an unashamedly decadent brunch. French flair and unctuous crème fraîche transform this simple breakfast of baked eggs and salmon into something truly magnifique.

What is it?

Leave it to the mellifluous French language to transform 'eggs in pots' into the altogether more alluring 'oeufs en cocotte'. But there's more to this dish than Gallic pout. An egg is cracked into a ramekin over a dollop of crème fraîche. Fine slivers of smoked salmon are scattered on top and it's cooked until the flavours infuse.

Origin

Recipes for oeufs en cocotte date as far back as 18th-century France. Since then, the dish has enjoyed plenty of gastronomic experimentation, crowned with delicacies ranging from foie gras to meaty cep mushrooms to asparagus. The usual breakfast in modern France, a snatched coffee and croissant, is a brief affair – perhaps surprising, in a culture famous for savouring a fine meal. Luckily brunch in France is a precious exception, with oeufs en cocotte rapidly becoming a fashionable favourite.

Tasting

This small baked dish cries out for crusty baguette. While other brunches around the world sprawl and spread across their plates, oeufs en cocotte typify French elegance and minimalism, an explosion of flavours in one tiny ramekin. And what better setting to watch steam curl upwards from your oven-fresh oeufs than sitting at a latticed wooden table in Paris' Montmartre district? When this brunch is cooked to perfection, the egg white becomes infused with the salty flavour of the fish. The yolk pops at the gentlest nudging of a fork, mingling with the crème fraîche and herbs. And it might be brunch, but a glass of pinot gris is the perfect accompaniment – this is France, after all.

Finding it

Le Jardin d'en Face in Paris' Montmartre is an atmospheric spot where creamy oeufs en cocotte costs €7 (US$9).

* **VARIATIONS** * **Finely tuned palates will detect the greatest regional imprint in the garnishes. In the south of France, oeufs en cocotte are finished with a sprinkling of marjoram, rosemary, oregano and thyme (the famous herbes de Provence). In the Auvergne, a sliver of its famous blue cheese adds tang. And closer to the Swiss border, Emmental cheese gives it a nutty flavour and a chewy texture.**

* By Anita Isalska *

Recipe Oeufs en Cocotte au Saumon Fumé

While some swear by inundating their *oeufs en cocotte* in a bubbling bain-marie, modern French chefs oven-bake these compact brunch pots.

INGREDIENTS

1 garlic clove

4 tbs crème fraîche

4 eggs

50g (2oz) smoked salmon

sprig of rosemary (optional)

French baguette (or other crusty bread), to serve

METHOD

1. Preheat the oven to 180°C (350°F).

2. Crush the garlic clove with the flat of a knife.

3. Rub the garlic on the bottom of each of four ovenproof ramekins.

4. Place 1 tbs crème fraîche in each ramekin.

5. Crack an egg into each ramekin, taking care not to break the yolk.

6. Slice the smoked salmon into slivers about 1cm (⅓in) in length.

7. Arrange the sliced salmon around the yolk, submerging it gently in the egg whites.

8. Place the ramekins on a tray.

9. Cook the eggs in the centre of the oven for 12 minutes, or until the egg whites look firm and cooked through.

10. Remove the ramekins from the oven and sprinkle with rosemary.

11. Carefully place the ramekins on to plates.

12. Serve with baguette or crusty bread.

SERVES 4

* Pain au Chocolat *

FRANCE

A buttery croissant is decadent by itself. But with a sinfully rich chocolate centre adding an irresistible layer of sweetness, a *pain au chocolat* is the ultimate French pastry indulgence.

What is it?

Found in virtually every French *boulangerie* (bakery) and *pâtisserie* (pastry shop), a *pain au chocolat* is essentially a chocolate-filled croissant, made from the same yeast-leavened dough. Yet unlike a croissant's crab-claw shape, a *pain au chocolat* is rectangular. Both are among the morning-time treats collectively known as '*viennoiseries*' (Viennese pastries).

Tasting

A lustrous, golden *pain au chocolat* has airy, feathery pastry and the mellowest chocolaty centre when it's eaten still warm from the oven. The tantalising yeasty aromas wafting out on to the streets across France from the early morning onwards are enough to entice you to pick one up, and it is best enjoyed immediately on a park bench (a shower of flaking pastry crumbs as you eat it is inevitable, but the local birdlife won't mind). If you're buying *pains au chocolat* in, make sure they're your last purchase so you can eat them at their best. When making them yourself, only bake the amount needed – it's easy to freeze the rest of the dough and bake a fresh batch another day. Hot, strong coffee makes the ideal accompaniment.

Origin

Although as emblematic of France as berets and baguettes, croissants actually originated in Vienna, Austria. To celebrate a failed Turkish attack during the Siege of Vienna in 1683, Viennese bakers shaped pastries in the form of the crescent found on the Ottoman Turks' flags. When Austrian Princess Marie Antoinette arrived in France to marry King Louis XVI in 1770, Parisian bakers recreated the pastry in her honour, renaming it a 'croissant' for its crescent shape. It's not definitively known when chocolate was added to create a *pain au chocolat*, but some believe it was as late as the early 20th century.

Finding it

Parisian patisserie Laurent Duchêne makes prize-winning *viennoiseries* using premium *beurre Charentes-Poitou* AOC (*appellation d'origine contrôlée*) butter. Expect to pay €1.60 (US$2).

* VARIATIONS * To make croissants using the same dough, follow the recipe to the end of step 5. Cut out triangles, each with a 10cm (4in) base, then roll each triangle snugly from the base, tucking the apex underneath. Pull the ends in slightly to form a crescent. Then continue from step 7, placing the croissants right side up on the baking tray.

* By Catherine Le Nevez *

Recipe Pains au Chocolat

INGREDIENTS

350g (12½oz) good-quality* unsalted butter

300g (10½oz) very strong white bread flour

200g (7oz) plain flour

2½ tsp fast-action dried yeast

50g (2oz) caster sugar

2 tsp fine sea salt

1¼–1½ cups semi-skimmed milk

1 egg yolk, beaten

175g (6oz) high-grade dark chocolate batons (sticks/elongated bars; these can be chopped from a larger block of chocolate)

Quality butter is integral to the pastries' success; cheaper butter often has a high water content, which can ooze during baking.

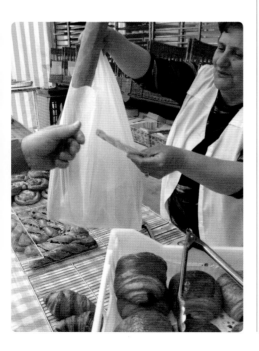

METHOD

1. Melt 50g (2oz) of the butter in a pan and allow it to cool.

2. Combine the dry ingredients (flours, yeast, sugar, salt) in a large bowl and mix well to combine thoroughly.

3. Add the cooled melted butter to the milk and stir to combine. Add the milk mixture to the dry ingredients. Gently work the ingredients together with your hands, adding a little more milk if necessary. Knead the dough just until it can be formed into a ball. Cover in cling film and refrigerate for 1 hour.

4. On a floured surface, roll out the dough to 50cm x 20cm (20in x 8in). Spread the remaining butter thickly over the centre of the dough in a square, leaving about 15cm (6in) of butter-free dough at each end. Fold the butter-free edges into the centre, taking care not to form air bubbles. Pinch the sides to seal them. Wrap in cling film and cool for 1 hour.

5. Remove the dough from the refrigerator. Fold in half on a floured surface. Turn through 90 degrees and re-roll it to 50cm x 20cm (20in x 8in). Bring the top third and bottom third of the dough into the centre. Cover in cling film and refrigerate for 1 hour. Repeat this step twice more, then refrigerate overnight.

6. Roll the dough to 100cm x 20cm (39½in x 8in). Cut out twenty 20cm x 5cm (8in x 2in) rectangles. Place one chocolate baton widthways 3cm (1¼in) from the top and another 3cm (1¼in) from the bottom of each rectangle. Roll the top and bottom strips over the batons into the centre and pat down.

7. Line two baking trays with greaseproof paper and place the filled pastries upside down on top of them. Lightly brush the beaten egg over the pastries. Cover with clean dish towels.

8. Leave the *pains au chocolat* to prove (rise) in a warm place for up to 2 hours, until they're puffy and almost doubled in size.

9. Preheat the oven to 190°C (375°F).

10. Brush the *pains au chocolat* again with beaten egg. Bake for 15–20 minutes, until risen and golden brown. Transfer the *pains au chocolat* to a wire rack to cool slightly.

MAKES 20–22

* Pan con Tomate *

SPAIN

This dish may sound drab – it really is just bread smeared with the insides of a tomato – but, prepared with care, it's a magical synthesis of Spanish ingredients.

What is it?

Pan con tomate (bread with tomato) hails from Catalonia, where it's called *pa amb tomàquet* and served all day. In the most traditional preparation, the bread is sliced and barely pink from being rubbed with tomato; in most of Spain, it's a heftier hunk of bread topped with a thick layer of tomato pulp.

Origin

Tomatoes were introduced to Catalonia in the 16th century, but at first they were not accepted as food. At this time, Catalonians ate dreary *pa amb oli* (bread with oil). Eventually, though, the tomato caught on, and *pa amb tomàquet* was documented in the 18th century as a peasant trick for salvaging stale bread. The preparation was so good it spread in the 19th century to restaurant kitchens in Catalonia, and eventually to the rest of Spain – where some still refer to it as *pan a la catalana*.

Tasting

A good *pan con tomate* is a staple of unfussy Spanish cafes, the sort where people gather to read the paper and sip *cafe con leche*. The least fussy cafes – usually only in Catalonia – will serve you just bread slices and a whole tomato, leaving you to halve the tomato and smear it over both sides of the bread. Most places, though, will have already toasted a slab of chewy bread and topped it with a layer of tomato pulp; it's up to you to dress it up with salt and olive oil. If the tomato is served on the side, resist the urge to ladle on too much – the trick is to get the right balance of the sweet-sour pulp and the chewy rustic bread.

Finding it

Try Barcelona's classic 24-hour bar El Velódromo (Carrer Muntaner 213, L'Eixample), where *pa amb tomàquet* costs €3.40 (US$4.25).

* VARIATIONS * Garlic is usually reserved for *pan con tomate* eaten in the afternoon or evening. The dish can also be dressed up to make a more substantial meal, with toppings such as *boquerones* (pickled white anchovies), crumbled hard-boiled egg and pieces of the ubiquitous Spanish *jamón* (ham). In Catalonia, it is also sometimes topped with slices of creamy cheese from the Pyrenees, or even smeared with fresh figs.

* By Zora O'Neill *

Recipe Pan con Tomate

For a group, you can prepare the tomato in advance, as most cafes in Spain do. For each serving, grate one tomato on a large box grater, being sure to catch all the juices. Optionally add 1–2 finely chopped garlic cloves to the grated tomato. Split a wide loaf, such as a ciabatta, in half lengthways and lightly toast each half. Top with the tomato mixture, then coarse salt and a generous quantity of olive oil.

INGREDIENTS

1 slice chewy rustic bread

1 garlic clove, cut in half (optional)

1 ripe tomato

coarse salt, to taste

good-quality olive oil, to taste

white anchovies, Spanish ham, hard-boiled egg or capers, to serve (optional)

METHOD

1. Lightly toast the slice of chewy, rustic bread.

2. If using the garlic, rub the cut sides across the warm bread.

3. Slice the tomato in half.

4. Rub the cut sides of the tomato over the bread, working from the edges of the bread towards the centre and pressing down slightly; discard the skin and dry flesh.

5. Sprinkle the tomato with coarse salt.

6. Drizzle the surface liberally with good-quality olive oil.

7. If you have the heel of the loaf of bread, use it to press the tomato-salt-oil mixture into the bread's surface; if not, use the back of a spoon.

8. If liked, serve with white anchovies, Spanish ham, hard-boiled egg or capers.

SERVES 1

* Pão de Queijo *

BRAZIL

Pão de queijo (cheese bread) is one of Brazil's darling domestic treats; a marriage of cheese and tapioca starch served fresh from the oven – the Brazilian breakfast of champions!

What is it?

Despite its name, *pão de queijo* is not actually bread; it's an unleavened breakfast snack made from tapioca (manioc) starch, cheese, eggs, salt and vegetable oil, all rolled together into balls and baked. Minas Gerais, famous for its hearty regional cuisine, is widely regarded as the best region in Brazil for bigger, tastier and cheesier *pão de queijo,* often made with regional *canastra* cheese.

Tasting

Pão de queijo is a simple dish eaten in a simple way. There are few variables: it must arrive warm and fresh from the oven. In fact, Brazilians won't serve *pão de queijo* that has been sitting around too long and to reheat it would be unthinkable. It's always nice to pull your first mouthful away from the rest with your fingers rather than biting directly into it; a hot, cheesy waft spills into the air, the chewy and moist inner core is revealed (a cheap industrial version is immediately exposed as not being a homemade artisan one by its cheese-to-manioc ratio). Chased with strong espresso, one of life's small pleasures comes to light as the clink and clank of Brazilian breakfast fills the air, the hustle and bustle of commuters merging with sustenance: let the day begin!

Origin

Like so many of Brazil's culinary staples, *pão de queijo*'s speculated history harkens back to the slave trade. As far back as the 1600s, slaves were producing manioc starch for farmers in the Brazilian state of Minas Gerais. In order to remove toxic residual cyanide from the root, manioc must be processed (peeled, grated, soaked in water and dried). Resourceful by necessity, slaves scraped away the leftover manioc starch, rolled it into balls and baked it. Eventually, the addition of milk and cheese turned it into gooey Brazilian goodness.

Finding it

Pão de Queijo Haddock Lobo in São Paulo specialises in *pão de queijo*, and one will cost R$5 (US$2.10).

* VARIATIONS * There are several variations, including *pão de queijo* filled with Brazilian cream cheese, called *catupiry*, as well as ones sweetened by guava or milk caramel. However, the classic recipe is far and away the most common.

* By Kevin Raub *

Recipe Pão de Queijo

INGREDIENTS

1 cup water

1 cup milk

1 cup canola or vegetable oil

salt (to taste)

500g (1lb 1oz) tapioca starch

110g (4oz) cheese (a combination of freshly grated parmesan or Asiago cheese along with small chunks of fresh white *queso fresco* from a Latin market work best outside of Brazil)

2 eggs

METHOD

1. Preheat the oven to 200°C (400°F).

2. Put the water, milk, oil and salt in a medium pan and bring to the boil.

3. Remove the pan from the heat and allow the liquid to cool sufficiently for you to be able to touch it.

4. Put the tapioca starch in a large bowl and make a well in the centre.

5. Add the warm liquid to the starch little by little, kneading constantly, until a pliant dough is formed.

6. When the dough is warm and elastic, add the cheese and eggs and knead briefly to incorporate into the dough.

7. Form the dough into balls the size of ping-pong balls and place on a lightly greased baking sheet, allowing space between them.

8. Bake for 15–20 minutes, until golden brown.

9. Remove from the oven and leave to cool for no longer than a few minutes – these are best served warm.

MAKES 6–12, DEPENDING ON SIZE

* Pastel de Nata *

PORTUGAL

Originating from a monastery just outside Portugal's sun-baked capital, the *pastel de nata* (Portuguese custard tart) is a heavenly mouthful of crispy pastry encasing a dense custard centre.

What is it?

Portugal's most famous sweet treat is a diminutive puff-pastry cup filled with wickedly thick, eggy custard. It's baked until it's a gleaming golden-brown and served hot from the oven, liberally sprinkled with cinnamon and icing sugar. A *pastel de nata* delivers an instant morning sugar hit and is the perfect accompaniment for a shot of strong black coffee.

Origin

Monasteries historically used egg whites to starch clothes and clarify wines, and monks of the Hieronymite Order at the Mosteiro dos Jerónimos at Santa Maria de Belém, to Lisbon's south-west, salvaged the yolks to create these now-famous tarts. After the 1820 Liberal Revolution, the monks raised money by selling the tarts at a nearby sugar refinery. When the monastery was shut in 1834, they sold their secret recipe to the refinery's owners, who opened the Antiga Confeitaria de Belém in 1837. It remains the only place in the world where the tarts can be called *pastéis de Belém* (singular: *pastel de Belém*); elsewhere they are known as *pastéis de nata* (singular: *pastel de nata*).

Tasting

Unlike light, fluffy pastry used in many other cuisines, little palm-sized *pastéis de nata* have papery shards of pastry that provide a sharp contrast to the smooth, soft custard centre. Shimmering on top of the pastries, the burnt-brown blistered skin has a subtle caramelised flavour and adds another layer of texture, while a dusting of cinnamon and icing sugar balances the rich intensity of the egg custard.

All over Lisbon and beyond you'll see locals starting their day perched at the counter of *pastelarias* (pastry shops) and *padarias* (bakeries), knocking back *uma bica* (an espresso-style coffee) and tucking in to a *pastel de nata*, with tray after tray of the pastries being pulled from the ovens to keep up with demand. Look for the words '*fabrico próprio*' (made on the premises) to ensure you get the real deal.

Finding it

Eat in or take away an authentic *pastel de Belém* at Antiga Confeitaria de Belém. Expect to pay €1.05 (US$1.30).

* TIP * Professional ovens are capable of reaching much higher temperatures than household ones, so you may find the tarts don't develop the classic burnt-brown blistered effect on the skins when you make them yourself. If that's the case, 2 minutes before the end of the cooking time, place the baking tray under a hot grill and keep a close watch while the caramelisation takes place.

* By Catherine Le Nevez *

Recipe Pastel de Nata

INGREDIENTS

For the puff pastry

125g (4½oz) unsalted butter, cold

1 cup plain flour

1 tsp salt

½ cup ice-cold water

For the custard filling

¼ cup cornflour

1 cup full-fat milk

¾ cup water

2 cups caster sugar

1 cinnamon stick

strip of peel from ¼ small lemon

⅓ cup double cream

1 tsp vanilla bean (or ½ tsp vanilla extract)

6 large egg yolks

1 tbs icing sugar, for dusting

1 tbs ground cinnamon, for dusting

METHOD

1. Cut the butter into small cubes and pulse it in a food processor 10–15 times with the flour and salt until it forms clumps. Continuing to pulse, slowly add enough iced water to form a smooth dough. Place on a floured surface and shape into a 10cm x 15cm (4in x 6in) rectangle that is about 2.5cm (1in) thick. Wrap in cling film and refrigerate for 1 hour.

2. Roll out the dough on a floured surface in one direction until it's three times its original length. Fold both ends into the centre, then fold it in half again. Rotate the dough 90 degrees and repeat. Wrap it in cling film and cool for 30 minutes.

3. Roll out the dough until it's 1.25cm (½in) thick. Divide into four and roll each into a log. Wrap them in cling film and refrigerate for 10–20 minutes. Slice each log into 2.5cm (1in) sections. Place each section on its side and roll into a flat circle. At the end you should have 15 circles with a diameter of around 10cm (4in). Place on baking trays, cover and refrigerate.

4. Whisk the cornflour and ¼ cup milk in a large heatproof glass bowl until smooth.

5. Heat the water, sugar, cinnamon and lemon peel to dissolve the sugar. Bring to the boil without stirring to make a clear syrup. Remove from the heat and leave to stand for 30 minutes.

6. Warm the remaining ¾ cup milk and the double cream in a separate pan (do not let it boil). Whisk this into the cornflour mixture until smooth.

7. Remove the cinnamon stick and lemon peel from the syrup. Slowly whisk it and vanilla into the milk mixture, then gradually whisk the egg yolks in, one at a time.

8. Preheat the oven to 250°C (480°F).

9. Place the heatproof glass bowl over a pan of simmering water, stirring constantly, until the mixture thickens.

10. Place the pastry circles into a muffin or tart tin and fill them two-thirds full with the custard mixture. Bake for 10–15 minutes, until the pastry edges are browned but not burnt.

11. Remove from the oven and transfer to a wire rack to cool. Dust with icing sugar and ground cinnamon.

MAKES 15 TARTS

* Pets de Soeurs *

ACADIAN COAST, CANADA

You'll give your guests a laugh when you serve these crisp, sugary cinnamon rolls – a traditional, home-style treat from Canada's French-speaking Acadian communities – and translate their irreverent name.

What is it?

Pets de soeurs are sweet baked pastries, with a swirl of brown sugar, cinnamon, and butter inside – similar to a Chelsea bun but without the dried fruit or icing. The delectably scented bun makes a wonderful brunch served with freshly brewed coffee, but they are also fabulous served with tea for a snack.

Origin

No one knows for sure how *pets de soeurs* got their quirky name. One oft-repeated legend plays on the French word *pet* (meaning 'fart') and the French-Canadian idiom *'c'est un pet'*, which translates as 'it's easy to do'. As the story goes, a priest asked *une soeur* (a nun) what they were having for dessert. She replied, 'Just a little sweet that was *un pet* to prepare. The pun-making priest then declared, 'Ah, our dessert is a *pet de soeur* – a nun's fart!'

Tasting

Filled with brown sugar and aromatic cinnamon, then baked until golden, *pets de soeurs* are crisper and more cookie-like than a traditional sweet roll. The pastry is similar to a pie crust. In fact, Acadian cooks often use leftover pie dough they have to hand. If you're lucky enough to find *pets de soeurs* fresh from the oven at a local Acadian bakery, you can take in their sweet cinnamon fragrance before biting into the warm pastry. In each mouthful, you get both the cookie crust and the rich interior. The brown-sugar filling will often ooze out on to the bottom of the dough, making a sticky, almost caramel glaze, so keep a napkin handy!

Finding it

Pets de soeurs cost C$2–3 (US$1.80–2.70) at the Dieppe Market held every Saturday morning in the Moncton area, New Brunswick.

* WHO ARE CANADA'S ACADIANS? * Descended from French immigrants who settled in eastern Canada in the 1600s, and related to the Louisiana Cajuns in the United States, these francophone communities are concentrated in coastal New Brunswick, Nova Scotia, and Prince Edward Island. Their language and culture differ slightly from French-speaking Québécois, and this dish is unique to their culinary past.

* By Carolyn B. Heller *

Recipe Pets de Soeurs

INGREDIENTS

For the dough

3 cups all-purpose (plain) flour

2 tbs baking powder

1 tsp salt

1 tsp sugar

½ cup butter

1 cup milk

For the filling

1 cup soft light brown sugar

2 tsp cinnamon

2 tbs butter, softened

METHOD

1. Preheat the oven to 190°C (375°F).

2. Generously butter a baking sheet.

3. In a large bowl, sift together the flour, baking powder, salt and sugar. Cut in the butter until the mixture resembles coarse meal or breadcrumbs. Gradually add the milk until a soft dough forms.

4. Pat the dough into a ball. Wrap it in cling film or waxed paper and chill while you prepare the filling.

5. For the filling, mix together the brown sugar and cinnamon in a small bowl. Blend in the butter.

6. Turn out the dough on to a lightly floured surface. Roll out the dough to form a rectangle measuring about 45cm x 35cm (18in x 14in). The dough should be fairly thin – about 3mm (⅛in) thick – but thicker than a pie crust.

7. Sprinkle the filling over the dough to cover it evenly.

8. Starting on one long side, roll up the dough like a jelly roll (Swiss roll).

9. Brush the seam with a small amount of water to seal. Slice the roll into rounds about 15mm (½in) thick.

10. Arrange the rounds on the greased baking sheet, placing them about 5cm (2in) apart. The rolls will spread slightly as they bake.

11. Bake the rolls for 15–20 minutes or until the *pets de soeurs* are golden brown. Remove the baking sheet from the oven and leave to rest for 2 minutes.

12. Transfer the *pets de soeurs* to a wire rack to cool. Enjoy them warm or cold.

MAKES 22–24

* Phở *

VIETNAM

Remember the old desert island cliché about picking something that would be the one thing you eat for the rest of your life? Heads up: *phở* is actually that dish.

What is it?

Why is *phở* so perfect? Because it has everything. Broth, for rehydration. Meat, generally in the form of beef, but sometimes chicken, for protein. It can go vegetarian for herbivores in a pinch, by the way. Starch, in the form of thin, never-too-heavy rice noodles. Greens, in the form of sprouts and herbs that garnish the entire affair.

Tasting

The broth, the base of any *phở*, ranges from clean and crisp to the heavy liquid distillation of *umami*; either way, it rehydrates the body in the morning, when the dish is typically served (*phở* is available at all hours in the West, but in Vietnam it's often off the menu by late morning). Rice noodles provide a comforting, starchy counterpoint to the delicate fragrance of herbs – a bit of cooling *yin* – which itself stands in opposition to the in-your-face flavours of the beef – some full-forced *yang*. *Phở*, especially the southern-style version popularised by the Vietnamese diaspora, is a far more adaptable dish than most Western meals. You're given a dish of herbs and garnish that you can add to, or subtract from, to suit your individual tastes before you add your selection to the broth.

Origin

Vietnam's national dish is, like Vietnam itself, a product of colonialism and deep indigenous currents. The French connection derives from *phở*'s use of beef; like all Southeast Asian nations, Vietnam has a go-to noodle soup dish, but *phở* is the only one in the region that relies on beef and beef stock. Historically, Vietnamese cows were used for ploughing and as beasts of burden rather than for meat, but French colonialists brought their taste for beef to the country, and this was subsequently married with Asian herbs and spices in the late 19th century.

Finding it

Phở Lệ in Ho Chi Minh City serves wonderful *phở* for VND40,000–60,000 (US$1.90–2.90).

* VARIATIONS * The Vietnamese diaspora is largely made up of southern Vietnamese, and the dish described here is primarily southern-style *phở nam*. This tends to be big and bold and looked down upon by Vietnamese from the north. Their *phở* – the original *phở*, they'll have you know – is called *phở bắc and* eschews heavy garnishes for an elegant, almost austere presentation that is anchored by the intense beef broth.

* By Adam Karlin *

Recipe Phở Nam

Phở lives or dies by its stock, which should simmer for *at least* half a day.

INGREDIENTS

2.25kg (5lb) beef bones

3 onions, unpeeled and halved

4 ginger slices

¾ cup fish sauce

1 tbs salt

3 star anise pods

6L (5¼qt) water

340g (12oz) rice noodles

450g (1lb) sirloin steak, finely sliced

For the garnish (all optional)

½ cup coriander

2 tbs chopped green onion

1 bunch Thai basil, separated into leaves

1 cup bean sprout

1 lime, cut into wedges

3 Thai bird or jalapeño chillies, cut into thin rings

ground black pepper, to taste

METHOD

1. Roast the beef bones in a large roasting dish at 220°C (425°F) for 1 hour.

2. Place the onions cut side up in a roasting dish.

3. After the bones have been cooking for 1 hour, put the onions in the oven and roast for 30 minutes, until blackened and tender.

4. Transfer the roasted bones and onions to a very large stock pan. Add the ginger, fish sauce, salt, star anise and water.

5. Bring to the boil, then simmer over a low heat for 6–9 hours, or until the stock reduces by half. This is the broth.

6. Meanwhile, soak the rice noodles for 1 hour. Bring a large pan of water to the boil and cook the noodles in it for 1 minute.

7. Bring the broth to a rolling boil.

8. Divide the noodles between four bowls. Top each portion of noodles with raw sirloin and pour hot stock over the top.

9. Serve along with small bowls containing coriander, green onion, basil, bean sprouts, lime, chilli and ground black pepper, so diners can choose their own garnishes.

SERVES 4

* Pickled Herring *

SWEDEN

Simultaneously salty, sweet and spicy, *inlagd sill* (pickled herring) is a dish that encapsulates Sweden's pristine coastal waters and seafaring traditions, and is a mainstay of any Swedish *smörgåsbord* (buffet).

What is it?

Pickled herring is first cured with salt to extract excess water. The salt is then removed and the fish is pickled in a solution of vinegar, sugar and salt along with ingredients added for flavour, including bay leaves, onions and horseradish. It's traditionally accompanied by fiery *snaps* (schnapps), typically *brännvin* (herb- and spice-infused akvavit).

Origin

Herring is ubiquitous throughout Northern Europe but with the Baltic Sea teeming with these fish, Swedes have pickled herring since medieval times, originally as a preservation. On Sweden's west coast, just north of Göteborg (Gothenburg), the tiny island of Klädesholmen is the country's 'herring capital'. This centuries-old fishing community's heyday was during *den stora sillperioden* (the 'great herring period'), around 1748–1808. Today, it's home to pickled herring company Klädesholmen Sill, where herring is still cut by hand, and there is even a herring museum.

Tasting

Pickled herring's intricate sweet and sour flavours and silky and supple textures mean that this Swedish staple works with simple accompaniments such as boiled potatoes, hard-boiled eggs, cheese such as a Cheddar-style *Prästost* or sharper, crumblier *Västerbottensost*, and sour cream. The luxuriant oiliness of the fish is a perfect match for dark rye crisp bread – another dish invented as a means of preservation.

Herring is an exceptionally healthy fish, containing essential fatty acids, antioxidants, vitamins and minerals, as well as being low in saturated fat and calories (and it is environmentally sustainable too).

Variations on pickling styles include a smothering of mustard marinade. Just don't mistake pickled herring for *surströmming* (fermented Baltic herring), which is soaked in brine and continues fermenting after it's been canned – its overpowering smell has caused buildings to be evacuated (seriously).

Finding it

On herring-famed Klädesholmen, floating restaurant Salt & Sill has sparkling sea views and stunning 'herring boards', costing about SEK159 (US$22).

* TIP * You can safely store pickled herring for at least three months. Sterilise a glass jar with a screw-top lid by boiling both jar and lid for 15 minutes. Drain upside down on a wire rack until dry. Alternatively, you can put the jars in the dishwasher on a hot cycle. Fill with pickled herring, ensuring the pickling mixture completely covers the fish, and seal.

* By Catherine Le Nevez *

Recipe Pickled Herring

INGREDIENTS

340g (12oz) salted herring fillets

½ cup Swedish spirit vinegar or white wine vinegar

1 cup water

⅔ cup fine white sugar

12 whole peppercorns

10 juniper berries, sliced

10 whole cloves

1 bay leaf

1 small red onion, diced

2 small horseradishes, diced

2 medium carrots, thinly sliced

¼ cup dill, roughly chopped, to garnish

METHOD

1. Cover the salted herring fillets in cold water and leave overnight, changing the water once (late at night or early in the morning).

2. Put the vinegar and water in a pan with the sugar.

3. Heat over a medium heat until the sugar has dissolved.

4. Add the peppercorns, juniper berries, cloves, bay leaf, onion, horseradish and carrot and remove from the heat.

5. Leave the pickling mixture to cool, then transfer it to a non-reactive (non-metal) bowl.

6. Drain the herring fillets and add them to the pickling mixture.

7. Cover the bowl with cling film and refrigerate for 72 hours, stirring occasionally.

8. Remove the herring from the pickling mixture and pat dry with kitchen paper.

9. Cut the herring into 1.25cm (½in) slices.

10. Place the herring on a serving platter and ladle over some of the pickling mixture.

11. Garnish with dill and serve.

SERVES 4–6

* Polish Easter Ham with Beetroot Salad *

POLAND

This fortifying brunch, comprising Polish classics pork and gherkins served with a salad of beans, eggs and root vegetables, will power you through the toughest hike in the Tatra Mountains.

What is it?

Polish cuisine is best known as being carnivorous, simple and hearty. A traditional Polish Easter brunch combines some of the country's best-loved ingredients into a delightfully colourful dish: *wędliny* (cold cuts of pork) served with a magenta-stained and very nutritious salad of cooked beetroot, carrot and potato topped with halved boiled eggs.

Origin

Poland is legendary for its hospitality (and appetite). So Easter Sunday, a time of great rejoicing in devoutly Catholic Poland, wouldn't be complete without a feast. Ham and beetroot salad is variously described as being Polish, Ukrainian or Russian in origin. Some swear by mixing chicken or ham into the salad, and recipes vary by household (everyone's grandmother makes the best). The main ingredients are farmhouse fare, and the result tastes surprisingly indulgent. One thing is certain, the festivities will be rounded off with vodka, *śliwowica* (plum brandy) or perhaps both. *Na zdrowie!* (Cheers!)

Tasting

After Mass on Easter Sunday, an enormous brunch brings the whole family (and maybe the local priest) to the table. Family members share boiled eggs and exchange greetings, before snapping *kiełbasa* (dried sausage), slurping *barszcz* (beetroot soup), ploughing through mountains of rye bread, with a *bułka* (brioche-style cake) lying in wait for dessert. Boiled ham is the main event, with a dash of horseradish and gherkin to cut through the saltiness. On the side is an unctuous blend of cubed vegetables, eggs and mayonnaise.

Eggs aren't merely an ingredient at this time of year, but a decoration too. Many Polish households boil them with a drop of food dye (or onion skins to give a rusty-brown hue) and present a rainbow of eggs as the table's centrepiece. For a longer-lasting decoration, you'll find marble, wooden and beaded egg ornaments on sale across Eastern Europe.

Finding it

If you can't score an invitation to a home, grab a brunch for 14zł (US$4) from Krakow's Milkbar Tomasza.

* TIPS * Steam or boil the beetroots in their skins and wear washing-up gloves when you peel them – unless you want fingertips as mauve as your salad. A little lemon juice should remove any stains from your skin. If you use pre-cooked beetroot, don't choose the pickled kind.

* By Anita Isalska *

Recipe Polish Easter Ham with Beetroot Salad

INGREDIENTS

150g (5oz) beetroot

2 medium carrots, peeled

2 large potatoes, peeled

3 eggs

½ onion

½ cup cooked peas

260g (8oz) tinned white haricot or cannellini beans, drained and rinsed

3 heaped tbs mayonnaise

1 small dill sprig

6–8 thick slices cooked ham or ham sausage

pickled gherkins, to serve (optional)

horseradish sauce, to serve (optional)

METHOD

1. Trim the beetroots (but don't top and tail them).

2. Boil the beetroots in their skins in a pan of water for about 40 minutes, until tender.

3. Remove the beetroots from the water and leave them to cool.

4. Wearing gloves, peel off the beetroots' skins.

5. Dice the beetroots into 1cm (⅓in) cubes.

6. Dice the carrots and potatoes into 1cm (⅓in) cubes.

7. Bring a pan of water to the boil.

8. Add the diced potato and carrot and cook for about 5 minutes, or until *al dente*.

9. Immediately drain and then rinse the vegetables in cold water to prevent them from overcooking.

10. Hard-boil the eggs in a pan of boiling water for 4–6 minutes.

11. Remove the eggs from the pan with a slotted spoon and place them straight into a bowl of cool water.

12. Allow the eggs to cool slightly, then peel off the shells.

13. Slice the hard-boiled eggs in half.

14. Finely chop the onion.

15. Mix the diced carrot, potato and onion, peas and beans in a large bowl.

16. Gently fold in the beetroot and mayonnaise.

17. Serve the salad immediately, topped with halved boiled eggs and a sprinkling of dill, alongside slices of ham, gherkins and (for those who like it hot) a little horseradish sauce.

SERVES 4–6

* Potato Farls *

NORTHERN IRELAND

A cross between a thin scone and a pancake, a farl is a soft potato bread with a creamy, melt-in-the-mouth texture that goes perfectly with golden Irish butter.

What is it?

Potato farls are made from mashed potatoes combined with flour or oatmeal and butter to form a circular bread. Cut into quarters (farl means 'fourth') and fried on a pan or griddle, they are an essential part of the Ulster Fry (cooked breakfast).

Origin

Essentially devised a way to use up leftover spuds, the best potato farls are cooked just after the breakfast bacon and sausages, soaking up their juices to give a salty, meaty flavour to what is a relatively plain bread. This blandness gives farls their versatility: they taste just as good with butter and jam as they do beside a fiery curry. They are especially popular in Ulster, where they are called 'fadge' and, fried on both sides, they are a key component of the local cooked breakfast.

Tasting

There's something about a potato farl that just wraps you up like a warm blanket. Its soft, smooth texture, understated flavour and its incredibly forgiving nature (it's almost impossible for even novice bakers to get wrong) make it a classic comfort food. Combined with some crispy bacon, slathered in smoked salmon or used to soak up the oozing yolk of a fried egg, it reveals its willingness to be paired off with any number of gastronomic partners. Eaten the morning after the night before, farls give the impression that you stand some chance of recovering from your pounding head and blood-shot eyes; nibbled by an open fire on a wintry afternoon they suggest that nothing need be hurried; and toasted and spread with a little jam and butter they make the perfect prescription for a good night's sleep.

Finding it

Cafe Conor in Belfast is known for its Big Breakfast, costing £7.25 ($12), and the constituent potato farls won't disappoint.

* VARIATIONS * Farls are very adaptable so experiment with ingredients and proportions until you find your perfect combination. Use less flour and baking powder for a denser, moister texture, or more for a lighter, drier bread. Swap fine oatmeal for the flour to impart a nuttier flavour or add cumin, caraway, sesame or poppy seeds or even grated apple to ring the changes.

* By Etain O'Carroll *

Recipe Potato Farls

INGREDIENTS

6 medium floury potatoes

1 tbs butter

⅓ cup plain flour

¼ tsp baking powder

salt and ground black pepper, to taste

METHOD

1. Peel the potatoes and cut them into quarters.

2. Put the potatoes in a large pan and cover with boiling water.

3. Simmer the potatoes for about 15 minutes or until tender.

4. Melt the butter and add it to the potatoes. Mash together until smooth.

5. Sift in the flour and baking powder and season to taste with salt and pepper.

6. Pull the dough together with your hand. It should come away easily from the sides of the bowl.

7. Divide the dough into two equal portions.

8. Roll out one portion into a circle about 10mm (0.4in) deep.

9. Cut the circle into quarters.

10. Dust a frying pan with flour and place it over a medium heat.

11. Once the frying pan is hot, add the dough.

12. Fry the bread for about 3 minutes on each side, until golden brown.

13. Repeat steps 8 to 12 with the second half of the dough.

14. Serve warm.

MAKES 8 SMALL FARLS

* Quiche Lorraine *

FRANCE

The Lorraine region's signature dish is a scrumptious concoction of egg-thickened savoury custard and choice ingredients, all baked in a pastry-dough shell. Easy as open-faced pie. Literally.

What is it?

Classic quiches combine soft flavourful fillings – traditionally involving egg, milk or cream, sometimes cheese and other select ingredients – with crunchy crusts. Time-honoured quiche Lorraine features lardons (thick-sliced bacon cubes). Previously quiche was typically an autumn or winter dish served warm, but today the dish is an anytime, anyplace, anyone treat that is eaten hot or cold.

Origin

Quiche credit goes to Lorraine, which, while now a region of France, was Germanic for most of its nearly 1200-year history. In its original form – an open tart baked on a bread-dough base – the quiche was called *Lothringer Speckkuchen* (and its onion-heavy Alsatian ally, *Zwiebelkuchen*). *Lothringer* refers to Lotharingia, the kingdom-then-duchy from which the name Lorraine is derived; the German word *Kuchen*, meaning 'cake', morphed into 'quiche'. Like many modern gourmet specialities, quiche was once simple country fare – satisfying, portable and easy to prepare. Nowadays, it's a multi-faceted dish enhanced by pastry dough and an unlimited flavour choice.

Tasting

Julia Child was no stranger to quiche chic, calling the hot wedge served with a salad and a glass of dry white wine the 'perfect light meal'. If anything, this is more true today than ever, given the variety of ingredients used in the quiche's filling (meat, vegetables and even seafood), the trend toward deep-dish crumblier crusts and an emphasis on well-fluffed fillings. Whether eaten oven-hot or as a cold leftover, quiche is a quintessential craving-killer of contrasting tastes and textures. The soft, smooth custard – by turns earthy, tangy, smoky, sweet – remains a delightful counterpoint to the salty, crunchy outer shell, which can easily be knocked up at home by blind-baking some shortcrust pastry or, for speed and ease, bought from any reputable food store.

Finding it

A delectable individual portion of quiche Lorraine costs about €4.40 (US5.50) in *boulangeries* such as Paul, which has branches worldwide.

* VARIATIONS * Tradition notwithstanding, almost anything can go into a quiche so long as the flavour combinations work for you. As a rule of thumb, though, three ingredients are usually more than enough, and it is best to avoid using very wet foods. Many recipes include shredded cheese – Gruyère or Emmental – which, while yummy, is not true to quiche origins.

* By Ethan Gelber *

Recipe Quiche Lorraine

You can follow this basic recipe for any quiche, substituting step 2 below with the preparation of whatever special ingredients you choose. The use of store-bought pastry shells, as in this recipe, makes quiche preparation especially easy these days. However, be sure to follow the packet instructions: some require preheating. Pastry dough made from scratch is still the best, but requires a bit more effort.

INGREDIENTS

230g (8oz) lardons or 6–8 pieces thick-sliced bacon cut into 65mm (¼in) cubes

20cm (8in) pastry shell

3 eggs

1½ cups double cream or milk

pinch of salt

pinch of pepper

pinch of nutmeg

2 tbs butter, cut into small pieces

METHOD

1. Preheat oven to 190°C (375°F) and place a baking sheet on the middle shelf.

2. Lightly fry the lardons or cubes of bacon in a frying pan over a medium-high heat without oil.

3. Place the lardons or bacon in the bottom of the pastry shell.

4. Combine the eggs, cream, salt, pepper and nutmeg in a bowl, mixing well to combine. To reduce the fat content of the quiche, you could replace half (or even all) the cream with milk.

5. Pour the egg mixture into the pastry shell. Be sure not to fill it to the very top; leave a gap of about 3mm (⅛in) as the quiche will puff up slightly as it cooks.

6. Sprinkle the pieces of butter over the top of the mixture.

7. Carefully put the quiche on the preheated baking sheet, taking care not to slop any of the filling over the side.

8. Bake the quiche for 25–30 minutes or until it has browned and puffed up on top. The end result should be firm in the middle and golden brown on the surface. Check the middle by inserting a toothpick or knife; it should come out clean.

9. Remove the quiche from the oven and leave it to cool for 10 minutes or so if you want to eat it hot, or leave it to cool and then chill it if you prefer to eat it cold.

SERVES 4–6

* Roti Canai *

MALAYSIA

Any time is the right time for *roti canai* – a soft, buttery flatbread served with a curry dipping sauce that slips down like the sun sinking into the Malay Straits.

What is it?

Basically, *roti canai* is fried unleavened bread served with a spicy lentil dipping sauce, but no flatbread ever tasted so rich and creamy. You can thank the addition of lashings of melted butter for this, which transforms this humble street snack into a cardiologist's bad dream but a diner's delight.

Origin

The South Indian *parotta* is the obvious precursor of the Malay *roti*, and indentured workers from the Chennai region of India are thought to have carried the recipe for *roti* and *dalcha* – the tangy curry dipping sauce that it is invariably served with – across the Andaman Sea to Malaysia. One popular theory for the origin of the word *canai* for describing the curry is that it is a mispronunciation of Chennai, but it may in fact refer to the bread, since the Malay word *canai* means 'to roll out' or 'spreading out'.

Tasting

As with so many things in the Malay Straits, the preparation of *roti canai* is almost as exciting as eating it. Every *roti* chef keeps an arsenal of balls of oiled dough close at hand, and the second an order is placed the conjuring trick commences. Within seconds, the inch-wide ball of dough is spun, slapped and stretched to the size of a dustbin lid, before being folded into a parcel and puffed on the hotplate. There's something of a matador waving a flag for a bull about the whole affair, and a skilled cook can pull the dough out until it is almost as thin as sheer stockings. As soon as the outside is browned, the *roti* is transferred to the table with that tastebud-tingling lentil and tamarind curry sauce. Then it's tear and dip until the dish is gone as quickly as it was made.

Finding it

For wonderful *roti canai* costing RM1 (US$0.30) head to Nasi Kandar Pelita on Jalan Ampang in Kuala Lumpur.

---

* VARIATIONS * In Sumatra in Indonesia, *roti canai* is reinvented as *roti cane*, which sees the same bread served with a generous side of *kari kambing* (mutton curry), a culinary homage to the Tamil Muslims who introduced the dish to Aceh province in the 17th century.

By Joe Bindloss

Recipe Roti Canai

INGREDIENTS

For the *roti*

3 cups plain (all-purpose) flour

pinch of salt

pinch of sugar

4 tbs melted butter

½ cup milk

¼ cup water

vegetable oil or melted butter, for greasing the surface

For the dipping sauce

1 cup *chana dal* (yellow split peas)

½ tsp ground turmeric

1 tsp vegetable oil

1–2 cups water

1 tbs melted butter

1 tsp mustard seeds

1 small onion, finely chopped

2 garlic cloves, finely chopped and crushed

1 dried red chilli, finely chopped

2.5cm (1in) piece of ginger, grated

1 small piece cinnamon stick

1 star anise

handful of curry leaves

½ tsp garam masala

1 skinned tomato, cut into segments

salt, to taste

METHOD

1. Soak the *chana dal* (yellow split peas) in cold water overnight.

2. Put the flour in a large bowl with a pinch of salt and sugar. Add 2 tbs of the melted butter. Slowly mix in the water, kneading to create a soft, elastic dough that pulls away from the bowl.

3. Divide the dough into six neat balls. Rub with the remaining melted butter and place on a plate, covering with cling film. Set aside for several hours in a warm place.

4. Drain the *chana dal* (yellow split peas). Place in a pan with the turmeric, 1 tsp vegetable oil and enough water to cover.

5. Place the pan over a medium heat and simmer the mixture gently for about 30 minutes, until the lentils are soft.

6. In a frying pan, heat the melted butter. Add the mustard seeds and fry for about 1 minute, until they pop. Add the onion, garlic, chilli, ginger, cinnamon, star anise and curry leaves. Cook, stirring frequently, for about 10 minutes, until the onions are starting to turn golden. Add the garam masala and tomato segments and cook for a few more minutes.

7. Combine the onion mixture with the softened lentils. Add a pinch of salt and simmer for another 5 minutes to thicken.

8. To make the *roti*, pour a little oil or melted butter on to a clean, flat surface. Press out the dough ball to make a flat sheet that is about the size of a dinner plate. With oiled or buttered hands, pick up this sheet and slap it back on to the surface, pulling the dough thinner as you lift it.

9. Repeat this slapping process several times until you end up with a paper-thin sheet of dough. Fold in the sides to form a rectangle. Fry on an oiled baking tray on the stove over a high heat. Turn over when the underside turns golden.

10. Before you transfer it to a plate, squash the *roti* together so it starts to fall apart.

11. Keep the *roti* warm and prepare and cook the remaining balls of dough. Serve with a bowl of the curry sauce for dipping.

MAKES 6 *ROTI*; SERVES 4–6

* Sabich *

ISRAEL

Sabich, much like David facing Goliath, is an unassuming hero. This sandwich, a Jewish immigrant from Iraq, is blue-collar food at its best – fast, filling and fun to eat.

What is it?

Sabich is a Middle Eastern sandwich of hard-boiled eggs (usually browned overnight in a low oven – see the method below), fried aubergine and tahini stuffed in pita with chopped parsley, onion, potato and salad. Often served with *amba*, a spicy Indian mango pickle, it has become an institution in Israel, where stalls selling only *sabich* appear nationwide.

Origin

Derived from the word *sabah* ('morning' in Arabic), *sabich* originated in Iraq among the Jews of Baghdad, one of the world's oldest Jewish communities, who ate it on *Shabbat* (Saturday) mornings. Jewish Kashrut laws prohibit cooking on *Shabbat*, so the Iraqi Jews adopted foods that could be cooked the day before and left on a low heat overnight. For decades, this simple but ingenious meal was passed down through generations. *Sabich* was brought to Israel in the 1940s and 1950s, when 120,000 people (around 75 per cent) of Baghdadi Jews fled a hostile Iraq ruled by the then-Prime Minister Nuri al-Said.

Tasting

Wherever you're from, taking your first bite of *sabich* is always comforting. The familiar softness of the eggs, mushed with the thick tahini sauce, sharp onion, fresh parsley and finely chopped salad all complement *sabich*'s centrepiece – the greasy (in a good way) fried aubergine. The exotic kick to the tastebuds comes from its tangy orange sauce called *amba* (meaning 'mango' in Sanskrit). Eating *sabich* is a messy business, occasionally requiring strategic bites of the pita bread to hold it all together. The busy streets of Tel Aviv are now the undisputed home of this classic, where it provides some healthy competition to the ubiquitous felafel, although anyone with Iraqi roots would say that nobody makes *sabich* better than their grandma. What is certain, however, is that no Saturday morning is complete without it.

Finding it

The king of *sabich* is Oved in Givatayim, Tel Aviv, whose restaurant has cult status. Portions cost 16 NIS (US$4.35).

* TIP * To eat *sabich* like a local, the pita bread must be stuffed with as much filling as possible and washed down with fresh mint tea. But heed this important health warning: due to its heaviness, *sabich* must be followed by a mid-morning nap on the sofa.

* By Dan Savery Raz *

Recipe Sabich

INGREDIENTS

1 red onion

4 eggs

1 aubergine

2 tsp salt

1–2 cups canola oil, for frying

4 pita breads

4 tomatoes, finely chopped

2 cucumbers, finely chopped

4 tsp *amba* or mango chutney (optional)

4 tbs chopped parsley

For the tahini

1 cup tahini

1 cup cold water

juice of ½ lemon

1 tsp salt

METHOD

1. Peel the red onion. Reserve half the peeled onion to use as a filling later.

2. Place the onion skin in a pan of boiling water, add the eggs and boil for 25 minutes.

3. Place the pan on a hot plate or in a low oven (50°C (122°F)) overnight, or until the eggs turn brown.

4. Cut the aubergine in half and then into thin slices from top to bottom. Sprinkle each slice with salt (to absorb the bitterness).

5. Place the aubergine slices in a colander and leave to stand for 2 hours. Then rinse off the salt with cold water and pat the aubergine slices dry with kitchen paper.

6. Pour the oil into a deep-frying pan and heat until it reaches 170°C (340°F) on a thermometer.

7. Carefully lower in a few aubergine slices at a time using a slotted spoon and fry for a few minutes, until they have a crispy golden texture. You will need to do this in several batches. Remove the fried aubergines using a slotted spoon to a plate lined with kitchen paper, interleaving each slice with more kitchen paper.

8. Peel the eggs.

9. For the tahini sauce, place the tahini in a bowl, then slowly pour in the water and lemon juice, stirring.

10. Add salt to the tahini mixture and keep stirring until the sauce becomes creamy in texture.

11. Last but not least, build your *sabich*. Rip open the top of a pita bread, stuff it with two or three slices of fried aubergine, one brown egg, chopped tomato and cucumber and a tiny bit of finely chopped raw onion.

12. Drizzle the *sabich* with tahini sauce, *amba* or chutney, if using, and garnish with parsley on top.

13. Serve immediately, with plenty of napkins!

SERVES 4

* Salteña *

BOLIVIA

Imagine waking up at an altitude of more than 3000m (9842ft): it's cold and you're starving. For Bolivians *salteñas* – the region's ubiquitous pies – are the perfect antidote to the conditions outside.

What is it?

The complex sauce that oozes through this tastier version of the empanada is a mixture of meat (usually chicken or beef), potatoes, peas, onions and a medley of herbs and spices, blended together the night before with gelatine and then refrigerated. The sauce starts melting when it's baked in pastry cases the next morning, creating the *salteñas'* especially succulent filling.

Tasting

The best *salteñas* are vended by indigenous women on street-side stalls, and locations seem to change daily. So the thrill of the chase exacerbates that craving for crusty pastry and sensationally-seasoned meat sauce, and savvy *salteña* buyers get two, minimum – more likely three. No one knows how quickly they'll be gone, right?

   With a couple warming your pockets, grab the third by the pastry seam. *Salteñas* resemble bloated half-moons and have two obvious corners: bite into one of them. The pastry is thick, but you'll need this doughy wall to stop the sauce (*jugote*) spilling out. The pastry's crumbliness combined with the sauce's sweet, *picante* gooiness is just the type of morning pleasure the mouth needs. And another surprise awaits within. Bakers often add signature ingredients: perhaps an egg, olives or dried fruit.

Origin

A variation on the empanada (which has different pastry and a less generous, less juicy filling), *salteñas* originated in Argentina, from where one Juana Manuela Gorriti, a woman from the city of Salta (aka a *Salteñas* in Spanish), was exiled with her family during the country's Juan Manuel de Rosas dictatorship. Having sought refuge across the border in Tarija, Bolivia, the cash-strapped family sold snacks to earn money. Juana's take on the empanada was particularly popular and *salteñas* – with their richer flavours – took off and still reign supreme.

Finding it

Look for the women in felt hats around Plaza San Francisco in La Paz. Their *salteñas* cost BOB 5 (US$0.70) each.

* TIP * Think the breakfast-end of brunch when you go *salteña*-bagging: they're often sold out by midday. The earlier you go, the fresher they are.

Recipe Salteña

INGREDIENTS

For the filling (*jugote*)

3 chicken breasts, skinned (or substitute with a similar weight of another meat)

1 potato, peeled and roughly chopped

4 tbs butter

yellow pepper paste or *ajis amarillos* (yellow chillies), to taste

½ tsp cumin

½ tsp oregano

½ tsp cayenne pepper

1 tbs chopped parsley

salt and ground black pepper, to taste

1 small red onion, finely chopped

1 small white onion, finely chopped

40g (1½oz) peas

1 tbs sugar

¼ tsp vinegar

½ hard-boiled egg, sliced

1–2 green olives, pitted and chopped

3–4 cups chicken stock

14g (½oz) gelatine

For the pastry

4 cups all-purpose (plain) flour

½ tsp salt

5 tbs sugar

½ cup butter, melted

2 eggs, lightly beaten

about 1 cup warm water

METHOD

1. Simmer the chicken breasts in a pan of water for 20–25 minutes, until cooked through. Lift out the chicken breasts with a slotted spoon, reserving the water. Finely chop the chicken until it has an almost shredded consistency.

2. Boil the chopped potato for a few minutes in the reserved chicken cooking water, until soft but still firm.

3. Melt the butter in a large pan over a medium heat with some of the yellow pepper paste (1 tbs initially) or ½ *aji amarillo*, chopped (you can add more to taste at the end if desired).

4. Reduce the heat to low and add the cumin, oregano, cayenne pepper, chopped parsley, salt and pepper.

5. Add the onions, potatoes, peas, sugar, vinegar, hard-boiled egg and green olives to the mixture.

6. Add the chicken and the chicken broth. Let it all cook together for about 10 minutes, until the mixture heat through.

7. Stir in the gelatine and transfer everything to a large bowl and refrigerate for a minimum of 2 hours. Near the end of the chilling time, preheat the oven to 250°C (480°F).

8. Make the pastry. Mix together the flour, salt and sugar in a large bowl. Add the melted butter and most of the beaten egg (reserve a little for brushing the pastry) to the mixture.

9. Add enough warm water to bring it together and mix to form a dough. Roll out the dough on a lightly floured surface to a thickness of 25mm (1in). Stamp out circles with a diameter of 12–15cm (4½–5in).

10. Divide the chilled mixture between the pastry circles, leaving a clear pastry rim of 1cm (⅓in) around the edge of each.

11. Seal each pie by dampening the edges of the pastry with a little water and pinching the edges shut. It is important to seal the edges well so that when the *salteñas* cook the filling does not spill out.

12. Place the *salteñas* on a greased baking tray and brush with a little beaten egg. Bake for about 15 minutes or until the pastry turns golden brown.

MAKES 15–20

* Scones *

UNITED KINGDOM

A cup of tea served with a plate of scones is a quintessential British pastime. Traditionally, an afternoon tea delight, they are equally as scrumptious as a brunch-time snack.

What is it?

In its most traditional form, a scone is a humble small 'cake', made of flour, butter and a bit of milk. This can be served with butter or a dollop of jam and cream. (Note: Confusingly, in the USA a similar, though crumblier, version of the scone is called a 'biscuit' – while what Brits call biscuits are known as cookies in the USA.)

Origin

The origin of the lowly scone is hotly contested. There are, however, several clues to its genealogy: *sgonn* in Gaelic means a 'mass', which could refer to the Roman tradition of baking oat cakes on hot stones; and Dutch white bread is known as *schoonbrot*. However, it's the Scots who have the last (literal) word: reference to 'flour scone' appears in the 16th-century translation of Virgil's *Aeneid*, by Scottish poet Gavin Douglas. This is believed to have been a wedge cut from a bannock, a loaf of unleavened bread baked on a *girdle* (griddle).

Tasting

If you're really going to do the scone thing properly, pull out your best vintage china, a tray, doilies and napkins. Now, imagine you're with the Queen. Halve your warm, freshly baked scone and allow the steam to waft into your face. Breathe in the aroma: a mix of a bakery and a jam factory. Add lashings of butter, or top with clotted or whipped cream and fruit jam. Sink your teeth in. While the scone might look like a cumulous cloud, it should softly hold its form, without being like plaster of Paris. If you don't have cream on your nose, jam on the side of your mouth and a few crumbs down your front, you're clearly not enjoying them. Try again – have another one. Oh, and while you're at it, one for Her Majesty, too.

Finding it

Cafe Portrait is a hidden gem within Edinburgh's Scottish National Portrait Gallery where you can enjoys scones for £2.00 (US$3.20).

* VARIATIONS *

Scone mixes differ enormously: lemonade, soda water or cream are sometimes used and recipes may be sweet or savoury, with raisins, currants and dates, cheese or pumpkin (popular in Australia) added to the mixture.

* By Kate Armstrong *

Recipe Scones

INGREDIENTS

4 cups self-raising flour

3 tbs unsalted butter, chilled and cubed, plus extra for greasing the baking tray

1¼ cups milk, plus extra for brushing the tops of the scones

½ cup single cream

jam and clotted or whipped cream, to serve

METHOD

1. Preheat the oven to 230°C (450°F).

2. Lightly butter a baking tray.

3. Place the flour in a large bowl.

4. Gently rub in the cold, cubed butter using your fingertips, lightly 'lifting' the mixture as you go.

5. Make a well in the centre of the mixture.

6. Pour in the milk and cream.

7. Mix everything together with a flat-bladed knife, cutting the mixture to incorporate air, until it just comes together in a ball. Do not over-work the mixture.

8. Turn the dough out on to a lightly floured surface.

9. Gently flatten the dough with the heel of your hand until it is about 3cm (1¼in) thick, handling the dough as little as possible.

10. Use a 6cm (2.5in) scone cutter (or glass) to cut out 12 scones.

11. Place the scones close together on the prepared baking tray.

12. Brush the tops of the scones with a little milk.

13. Bake the scones for 12–15 minutes (they are ready when they appear 'pinched' in the middle and are slightly golden on top).

14. Remove the scones to a wire rack to cool slightly.

15. Serve warm with jam and clotted or whipped cream.

MAKES 12

* Scotch Eggs *

ENGLAND

Comprising the key ingredients of an entire full English breakfast wrapped into one glorious, ready-to-eat, cricket ball-sized package, the Scotch egg is the ultimate brunch item.

What is it?

A boiled egg is at the heart of this little universe, wrapped in the arms of a rasher of bacon and then embraced by a layer of sausage meat before being rolled in breadcrumbs and fried. You can eat them warm from the pan for brunch, then pack up any leftovers for a picnic another day.

Tasting

Scotch eggs were once the tucker of toffs on the turf – consumed by the dozen at posh picnics and racing meets. Somewhere along the line, however, this spherical snack rolled right down the social ladder until it ended up in the fridge of every motorway petrol station in the United Kingdom, mass produced and largely taste-free.
Recently, however, there has been a Scotch egg renaissance and now many pubs (beer is the best accompaniment) are making gourmet versions of them, perhaps with additional ingredients such as bacon and black pudding. The original is still often the best, though, and biting through the crisp golden shell of a traditional Scotch egg to discover the succulent, savoury sausage meat and the tender heart of yielding hard-boiled egg is pure brunch-time bliss.

Origin

Possibly inspired by the intriguingly named Moghul dish *nargisi kofta* (Narcissus meatballs), which sees hard-boiled eggs wrapped in spicy *kofta* meat, the recipe for Scotch eggs as we know them today was invented by London department store Fortnum & Mason in 1738 (or so they claim). It began to feature in household cookbooks by the early 19th century, and is now an icon of British cuisine, with a particular association with picnics. There appears to be no direct link with Scotland, and the name probably started out as 'scotched eggs' (basically 'eggs that have been tampered with').

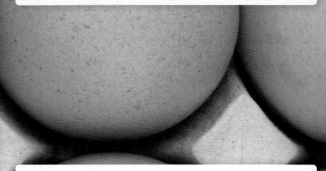

Finding it

Pick up a Scotch egg at its birthplace – Fortnum & Mason in Piccadilly, London – for around £3 (US$4.80).

* **VARIATIONS** * The Manchester egg sees a pickled egg encased in pork mince and Lancashire black pudding, while makers of Worcester eggs marinade them in Worcestershire sauce and then coat them in white pudding. In the northern and eastern regions of the Netherlands, try the Dutch version, *eierbal*, featuring an egg wrapped in ragout.

* By Patrick Kinsella *

Recipe Scotch Eggs

INGREDIENTS

11 free-range eggs

800g (1lb 12oz) good-quality pork sausages (such as Lincolnshire or Cumberland), skinned

2 tsp Worcestershire sauce

2 tsp sage, finely chopped

2 tsp English mustard powder

2 tsp ground mace

salt and ground black pepper, to taste

9 rashers smoked streaky bacon

5 tbs curly parsley, finely diced

3–4 cups dried breadcrumbs

5 tbs plain (all-purpose) flour

sunflower or vegetable oil, for deep-frying

METHOD

1. Boil 9 of the eggs in a pan of boiling water for exactly 5 minutes. Immediately remove the eggs from the hot water with a slotted spoon and place them in a bowl of cold water.

2. In a large mixing bowl, combine the sausage meat, Worcestershire sauce, sage, mustard powder and mace. Season the mixture to taste with salt and ground black pepper. Be aware that the sausage meat already contains a fair amount of seasoning, so you won't need to add much. Add one egg to the bowl. Combine everything thoroughly.

3. Place the breadcrumbs on a large plate. Place the flour on another large plate.

4. Crack the remaining 2 eggs into a large, shallow dish and lightly whisk.

5. Cook the rashers of bacon in a pan of boiling water for 1 minute. Remove the bacon to a piece of kitchen paper to dry.

6. Peel the cooling eggs. Roll the eggs in the flour. Wrap a rasher of bacon around each egg.

7. Form a ball that is bigger than the bacon-wrapped egg from the meat mixture. Create a cavity in the meat ball using your fingers. Drop the bacon-wrapped egg into the cavity.

8. Patch up the top of the ball so the egg is completely encased in meat. Repeat with each of the bacon-wrapped eggs.

9. Roll one of the covered eggs in the flour, then in the beaten egg. Then roll the covered egg in breadcrumbs and place it on a plate. Repeat with the remaining eggs, in the same way. Refrigerate the eggs for a few hours, or overnight.

10. When you are ready to cook, pour the oil into a heavy pan suitable for deep-frying until the oil is about 8cm (3in) deep. Heat the oil to 170°C (340°F), or until a cube of bread dropped in the oil browns in 1 minute.

11. Carefully lower in a couple of Scotch eggs at a time using a slotted spoon. Fry the eggs for 5 minutes, or until the exterior is golden brown and crispy. Carefully remove the cooked Scotch eggs to kitchen paper to drain. Consume hot or cold.

MAKES 9

* Shakshouka *

ISRAEL; NORTH AFRICA

**Gorgeously rich and smoky, this breakfast of eggs
and tomato sauce gives you a warm glow in your belly
and soul that will last the rest of the day.**

What is it?

The recipe consists of eggs baked in a thick sauce of peppers, tomatoes and spices, but that's just the beginning. Throw in some chopped sausage, crumbled feta cheese, chillies or other ingredients to customise it at home. Restaurants in Israel often serve it in the pan it's cooked in, with bread, salad and homemade pesto or garlic butter.

Origin

Shakshouka is eaten in many North African countries, with Morocco, Libya and Tunisia all claiming it as their own. But these assertions are hotly disputed in Israel, where *shakshouka* is so popular it's practically considered a national dish and it's rare to find a breakfast menu that doesn't feature it. Even the name is up for debate: it could be an evolution of *chakchouka*, the Berber word for 'ragout'; derived from *leshakshej* meaning 'to shake' in Hebrew; or adopted from *shakshouka*, which is Arabic slang for 'all mixed up.'

Tasting

The quintessential Tel Aviv brunch takes place on a sunny Friday morning, outdoors at a leafy cafe. The frying pan arrives at the table, still sizzling from the oven, and almost always with a word of warning from the waiter – 'Careful, it's hot'. A perfect *shakshouka*'s egg yolks are still soft and bright yellow, just ready to be split and spilled into the rest of the ingredients. It's the deep flavours of the tomato sauce that are really the making of this dish, that warm smell of paprika, cayenne pepper and cumin spurring you on to soak up every last smear. Normally one order of *shakshouka* is considered big enough for two to share, but done right it's so moreish one person could easily demolish the lot.

Finding it

Dr Shakshouka in Tel Aviv is dependably delicious, and offers nine varieties of the dish for NIS36–42 (US$9.75–11.37).

* TIP * This dish stands up to a lot of experimentation with both flavours and texture, so try it extra spicy or with any additional veggies, cheese or meat you fancy. Adding 1 tsp fennel seeds gives the dish a sweet and earthy aroma.

* By Helen Elfer *

Recipe Shakshouka

INGREDIENTS

1½ tbs olive oil

1 small onion, sliced

1 large red bell pepper, seeded and thinly sliced

2 garlic cloves, thinly sliced

½ tsp ground cumin

½ tsp paprika

cayenne pepper, to taste

400g (14oz) canned whole plum tomatoes with juice, roughly chopped

salt and ground black pepper, to taste

4 eggs

chopped coriander, to garnish

fresh bread, to serve (optional)

METHOD

1. Preheat the oven to 190°C (375°F).

2. Heat the oil in a large ovenproof frying pan over a medium heat.

3. Add the onion and bell pepper.

4. Reduce the heat to low and cook the onion and pepper, stirring occasionally, for about 20 minutes, until soft.

5. Add the garlic and cook for a further 3–4 minutes, until softened.

6. Stir in the cumin, paprika and cayenne pepper and cook for 1 minute.

7. Pour the tomatoes into the frying pan.

8. Season the mixture with salt and pepper.

9. Simmer the mixture for about 10 minutes, until the sauce has thickened.

10. Using the back of a spoon, create four hollows in the sauce for the eggs to sit in.

11. Gently crack the eggs into the frying pan over the tomatoes.

12. Add more salt and pepper to taste.

13. Transfer the frying pan to the oven.

14. Bake for 7–10 minutes, until the eggs are set.

15. Sprinkle with coriander and serve immediately, with fresh bread if you like.

SERVES 2

* Singapore Kaya Toast *

SINGAPORE; MALAYSIA

It's deceptively simple: crisp warm bread, slathered with a creamy, fragrant coconut jam and a hunk of butter that melts and brings everything together to create an oozing sugary delight.

What is it?

This dish begins and ends with its rich jam, which also gives the dish its name '*kaya*'. Made from caramelised sugar, egg and coconut, usually infused with the delicate flavour of pandan leaves, it's traditionally slow-cooked over a low flame until the mixture thickens into a smooth, pale green or dark brown spread that is lavishly applied to toast.

Origin

This dish dates back to the British Empire and is generally attributed to the Hainanese who worked as kitchen hands on British ships. Once they settled in the then British colonies of Singapore and Malaysia, they carried on the tradition of a British breakfast, except with one essential twist: they replaced British jams with their own. Today most jams are a mix or variation of two distinctive types. One originates with the Hainanese, and is a deep reddish-brown because of its brown sugar content; the other belongs to the Nyonya, and is typically green due to the addition of pandan.

Finding it

Chin Mee Chin Confectionery, Singapore, is an original *kopitiam*. A *kaya* bun costs S$1 (US$0.80).

Tasting

There are few things as satisfying to the senses as a good *kaya* toast. The smell is sweet and fragrant. The first bite yields a crunch (some places even double-toast the bread to achieve a greater level of crispness). This is followed by a warm explosion of creamy, almost custard-like jam, which, if done well, should be thick and smooth. The second bite offers you a taste of the melting salted butter. Suddenly it all comes together: the nutty coconut, the vanilla-like hint of pandan, the butter and the smoky charcoal-toasted bread. It will transport you to a bustling *kopitiam* (coffeehouse), where both young and old jostle over tables, and the staff of old aunties admonish you for taking too long to order.

* TIP * If you want to experience this dish the local way, order it with a sweet and bitter *kopi* (Malaysian-style coffee) and a portion of half-boiled eggs drizzled with soy sauce and pepper. Roughly mix the eggs into a yellow slurry, then dunk the *kaya* toast in it to create a sweet-savoury combo.

* By Stephanie Ong *

Recipe Singapore Kaya Toast

This recipe is for a traditional style of *kaya* toast, as it most commonly appears in *kopitiams* in Malaysia and Singapore.

INGREDIENTS

For the *kaya*

3 pandan leaves (fresh or frozen)

3–4 eggs

150g (5½oz) brown sugar

1 cup coconut milk

For the toast

2 slices thick white bread (crusts removed)

1 thick slice salted butter (refrigerated)

METHOD

1. First make the *kaya*. Wash the pandan leaves and cut off the ends. Tie the pandan leaves in knots and set to one side.

2. Whisk the eggs in a large heatproof bowl.

3. Add the sugar to the eggs. Whisk until the sugar has dissolved.

4. Whisk in the coconut milk.

5. Stir in the pandan leaves.

6. Pour water to a depth of about 4cm (1½in) into a pan and bring it to a simmer over a medium heat.

7. Place the heatproof bowl over the pan and reduce the heat to its lowest setting.

8. Stir the *kaya* mixture until the mixture thickens to a spreadable consistency. This may take up to 2 hours. Note: Don't be tempted to speed things up by increasing the heat of the water (which should never reach boiling point) and don't look away for more than a couple of minutes, as the mixture can easily curdle.

9. Once the mixture is thick and smooth (it's said the way to tell a good batch of *kaya* is if when you put a spoon in it, it doesn't move), remove it from the heat immediately.

10. Discard the pandan leaves.

11. Leave the *kaya* to cool.

12. Covered, the *kaya* will keep in the refrigerator for up to a week.

13. When you are ready to eat *kaya* toast, grill two pieces of white bread on both sides until they turn a golden brown.

14. Spread one slice of toast evenly with ample amounts of *kaya*.

15. Put the slice of butter on the other piece of toast.

16. Sandwich the two slices of toast together and cut in two.

17. Serve immediately.

MAKES ROUGHLY 1 CUP OF KAYA; WITH THE TOAST IT SERVES 1

* Soda Bread *

IRELAND

A classic Irish wholemeal bread with a nutty flavour, soda bread is quick and easy to make and tastes fabulous with butter and jam or soft cheese and smoked salmon.

What is it?

Soda bread is a moist, crumbly yeast-free bread with a thick crust. It is made from coarse wholemeal flour and mixed by hand without any proving or kneading required. A staple in Irish homes, it is served year round, at all times of day and, thanks to its versatile nature, is equally wonderful with sweet or savoury toppings.

Origin

The American Indians were the first to use soda ash in bread-making, but the Irish appropriated the idea as their soft wheat was not suitable for making yeasted breads. Wholemeal flour and buttermilk (the residue from butter-making) were readily available and a loaf could be in the oven in minutes. Slashed into quarters, the dough was 'blessed' and the fairies allowed to escape. This deep scoring of the surface also let the bread cook through and made it easy to divide to be taken into the fields.

Tasting

For many Irish people soda bread is simply the taste of 'home', its warm, earthy nature a kind of wholesome comfort that envelops you as soon as you walk into your mother's kitchen. Toasted and slathered with salty Irish butter and blackberry jam nothing could be finer. It's a very humble bread though, and best enjoyed at the kitchen table with the smell of washing drying over a turf fire or stove, a clatter of children and a shaggy dog rolling about on the floor, and a pot of strong tea on the table with which to wash it all down. Being so quick to make and cook, it is perfect for those crisis days when you discover you have run out of standard bread.

Finding it

The finest soda bread is served with breakfast at Ballymaloe House, Cork. The cost is included in the overnight stay.

* VARIATIONS * A white version of soda bread also exists, but this was traditionally reserved for special occasions and was simply known as 'cake'. To adapt the recipe substitute additional plain flour for the wholemeal, and add 1 tsp caster sugar and a handful of raisins.

* By Etain O'Carroll *

Recipe Soda Bread

Soda bread stales very quickly, so is best eaten fresh. If some is left over, it is best eaten the next day as toast or warmed in the oven to accompany soup or stew.

INGREDIENTS

2 cups plain flour

2 cups wholemeal flour

1 tsp bicarb soda (baking soda)

1 tsp salt

2 cups buttermilk

METHOD

1. Preheat oven to 200°C (400°F).

2. Sift the flours, bicarb soda and salt into a large bowl and mix together.

3. Make a well in the centre and pour in the buttermilk little by little, mixing as you go to create a soft dough that just comes away from the edge of the bowl.

4. Tip the dough on to a floured surface and pull it into a ball. Try not to handle it too much.

5. Place the ball on a floured baking sheet.

6. Using a large sharp knife, slash a deep cross into the centre, cutting about two thirds of the way through the dough.

6. Bake for about 40 minutes or until the loaf sounds hollow when tapped underneath.

7. Remove from the oven and wrap in a clean dish towel to stop the crust getting too hard.

8. Serve warm.

MAKES 1 MEDIUM LOAF

* Spanish Omelette *

SPAIN

It's so simple, just eggs and potato, yet here is a dish that will transport you to tapas heaven, rekindling your love affair with Spain, or making one inevitable.

What is it?

Also known as *tortilla espagnola*, this omelette is really a potato *frittata* or 'egg-cake'. So, to be clear: gently sauteed sliced potatoes are bound together in the pan with a pour of seasoned, beaten egg. Cooked until firm, flipped (gently!), then hey presto, your egg-cake is ready to delight.

Origin

What would an origin story be without apocrypha? Is it the genius of a Basque general during the siege of Bilbao, hitting on a cheap, hearty meal for the troops? Is it instead the same general ending up in a peasant woman's house and being served the simple dish? Or is it just solid peasant fare hailing from Pamplona? You know what – it tastes so good, the true origins of the Spanish omelette really don't actually matter…

Tasting

There might be a few ways to enjoy Spanish omelette (served warm from the pan, or stashed in the fridge overnight and packed up for a picnic), but there's one setting that you just know is the right one in which to experience it: a bar, somewhere in Spain. It's midnight and the party is just starting. A glass of Rioja, or a beer, maybe both. Music, laughter… and tapas. And the quintessential tapas dish, Spanish omelette, appears in front of you, small cubes pierced with toothpicks, ready to fortify your stomach for a night of revelry. It's such a satisfying bite, firm and hearty in texture, honest and familiar in flavour, with the almost spongy eggs being the perfect carrier for the tender potatoes. Your challenge for the evening will be resisting the temptation to gorge. Eating's cheating, remember.

Finding it

Head to the home of tortilla, Mesón de la Tortilla in Pamplona, where a wonderful omelette costs about €7 (US$9).

* VARIATIONS * Even the very common addition of onions to Spanish omelette can be considered non-standard. But the reality is you'll find versions that are spiked with spicy chorizo, brightened by capsicum and seasoned with olives. The common characteristic is moreishness. Indulge whenever, however you can.

* By Ben Handicott *

Recipe Spanish Omelette

INGREDIENTS

3 potatoes, peeled

¼ cup olive oil

4 eggs

¼ tsp salt

METHOD

1. Slice the peeled potatoes into 5mm (¼in) rounds.
2. Pour the olive oil into a pre-heated heavy frying pan.
3. Add the potatoes to the hot oil.
4. Sauté the potatoes for about 10 minutes, until soft.
5. Remove the potatoes from the frying pan and set aside on kitchen paper.
6. Whisk the eggs and salt in a bowl until thoroughly combined.
7. Add the potatoes to the egg mixture in the bowl.
8. Pour the mixture into the still-hot frying pan.
9. Cover the frying pan with a lid or heatproof plate.
10. Cook the omelette over a medium heat until the top is dry to the touch and firm.
11. Turn out the omelette on to a plate.
12. Slide the omelette back into the frying pan, top side down.
13. Cook the omelette for another 1–2 minutes.
14. Turn off the heat and leave the omelette to cool slightly in the pan.
15. Slide the omelette on to a board and cut it into bitesize cubes.
16. Spear each cube with a toothpick.
17. Serve the Spanish omelette warm or cold, with your favourite beverage on the side.

MAKES 1

Ⓜ ✋ * Sri Lankan Pan Rolls *

SRI LANKA

**This recipe loads an innocuous-looking pancake
with the signature tastes of Sri Lanka – a squeeze of citrus,
a pinch of spice – which explode in your mouth.**

What is it?

Sri Lankan pan rolls look like simplicity itself – stuffed pancakes, rolled in breadcrumbs, lightly fried – but they're a highly versatile short dish, and a vehicle for an astonishing array of flavours. Perfect for brunch or party fingerfood, you can pack them with myriad creative fillings to suit tastes, moods and dietary preferences. Vegetarians can substitute meat for additional vegetables.

Origin

Sri Lanka's cuisine has been shaped by generations of contact with other cultures – Arabic, Dutch, Malaysian, Indian, British – and pan rolls are the perfect conduit for showcasing all these influences. You'll see them being sold by roadside hawkers to locals as a street snack, and presented to guests by well-heeled hosts on social occasions. They're Sri Lanka's equivalent of a sandwich or a sushi roll – the complexity of the taste and the sophistication of the dish is all in the filling. The common denominator is spice – Sri Lankans like their food hot.

Tasting

In antiquity, Arab traders called Sri Lanka 'Serendib', which travelled into the English language as the noun 'serendipity' – the gift of making surprisingly good discoveries by chance. Sri Lankan pan rolls are serendipity incarnate, with many sensational tastes and textures hidden within their plain packaging. The pancake exterior should be crisp to the bite, offering token resistance before giving up its bounty. Eaten at street level on Sri Lanka's surf coast, you'll experience fantastic fish varieties of the dish, while in the breeze-cooled highlands of the island you might find your rolls stuffed with an egg or curried mutton, generously spiced and delicately laced with vibrant flavours from locally grown produce in a country that enjoys a delightfully diverse climate. Master the art of this dish at home and you'll create an instant portal back to the streets of Colombo or hills of Ella.

Finding it

Wander the busy but beautiful streets of Kandy, feasting on freshly made pan rolls. A selection costs Rp100–150 (US$1).

* TIP * Always eat pan rolls rolls with your hands. Dip them, if you will, in some *sambol* (chilli sauce), but don't overpower the taste of the filling. When cooking them at home, don't make the pancakes too big, and avoid overfilling them.

* By Patrick Kinsella *

Recipe Pan Rolls with Lamb

INGREDIENTS

For the filling

1 tbs vegetable oil

450g (1lb) minced lamb

1 medium onion, finely chopped

2 tbs garlic, grated

5cm (2in) piece of fresh ginger, grated

10–15 curry leaves, torn

1 small stick of cinnamon

1 carrot, finely grated

2 green chillies, seeded and chopped

1 tbs curry powder

½ tsp turmeric

½ tsp chilli flakes or powder

1 tbs vinegar

2–4 tbs soy sauce

1 tbs finely chopped fresh mint leaves

salt and ground black pepper, to taste

juice of 1 lime

3 potatoes, peeled, cooked and roughly mashed

2 cups breadcrumbs

2 cups vegetable oil

For the pancakes

1 cup plain (all-purpose) flour

1 cup self-raising flour

1 tsp salt

1 egg, lightly beaten

2 cups cold water

1 cup milk

1 tbs vegetable oil, for cooking

vegetable oil, for deep-frying

salad and *sambol*, to serve

METHOD

1. To make the pancakes, mix together the flours and salt in a large bowl and make a well in the middle. Pour in the egg, water and milk, whisking constantly, to form a smooth batter. Set aside.

2. To make the filling, heat the oil in a large frying pan. Add the lamb, along with the onion, garlic, ginger, curry leaves, cinnamon stick and carrot.

3. Cook the mixture over a medium heat for about 10 minutes, until the meat is browned. Stir in the chopped chilli, curry powder, turmeric and chilli powder or flakes.

4. Continue cooking for 3 minutes, then stir in the vinegar, soy sauce, mint leaves and seasoning to taste. After 1 minute, take the frying pan off the heat and pour in the lime juice. Allow the mixture to cool. Stir in the roughly mashed potato.

5. To make the pancakes, heat the oil in a pancake pan. Add a ladleful of batter and swirl it round so it coats the surface of the pan. Cook the pancake for 2–3 minutes, until it is just set. Do not flip over the pancake.

6. Place one-quarter of the filling mixture in a line down the middle of the pancake. Fold in the sides and wrap each pancake to form a roll while the pancake is still hot.

7. Transfer the roll to a plate and repeat with enough of the pancake batter to make three more pancakes, using all of the filling mixture.

8. Dip each pan roll in the remaining batter and then roll it in breadcrumbs.

9. Pour the oil for deep-frying into a heavy pan until the oil is about 8cm (3in) deep. Heat the oil to 170°C (340°F) or until a cube of bread dropped in the oil browns in 1 minute.

10. Carefully lower in the pan rolls using a slotted spoon and deep-fry them for 1 minute, or until the exterior is golden brown and crispy.

11. Using a slotted spoon, remove the cooked pan rolls to kitchen paper to drain. Serve immediately with salad and *sambol*.

SERVES 4

* St Louis Slinger *

ST LOUIS, MISSOURI, USA

This diner classic from St Louis, Missouri, features a wonderful blend of ingredients — eggs, meat, chili con carne and potatoes. It looks a mess, but the taste is unbeatable.

What is it?

Although there are variations on the Slinger, the classic recipe features a base of hash browns, covered by a hamburger patty or sausage and topped with eggs. Chili con carne is then slathered over the mixture, along with grated cheese and chopped onions. Every self-respecting diner in St Louis serves Slingers, and plenty of upmarket restaurants do 'classier' variations.

Origin

No eatery or cook has ever laid claim to being the originator of the St Louis Slinger. In fact, the dish may have been inspired by a concoction from Rochester, New York, known as the Garbage Plate. There, in 1918 a restaurateur named Alexander Tahou opened an eatery called Hots and Potatoes. One item on the menu contained a medley of ingredients including meat, potatoes, beans and more, all on one plate. When one diner later asked for the dish 'with all that garbage on it', the name caught on, and today it's known (and trademarked) as the Garbage Plate.

Tasting

It's best to fast and/or exercise before indulging in this very calorific dish. With a now empty belly, head down to the diner, take a seat and watch the cooks in action. Amid the sound of frying eggs and the clatter of forks, diners banter with the easy-going wait staff, while the scent of fresh-brewed coffee and the sizzling grill tinges the air. Then the food arrives and it's down to business. The dish isn't usually pretty, but put aside aesthetic concerns and simply dive in. The flavours and textures complement one another brilliantly: creamy eggs, juicy burger, crispy potatoes and the rich tang of meaty chili binding it all together. Afterwards take a long walk along the riverside, admire the arch and after an hour or three, you'll be making plans for your next Slinger.

Finding it

Chili Mac's Diner (510 Pine St, St Louis, Missouri), where mains cost US$5–10. Wash it down with strong coffee.

---

* VARIATIONS * For an even richer flavour, substitute sausage or bacon for the hamburger patty. Purists order eggs 'over easy', but scrambled or poached ones are good options. You can also swap meat for a veggie pattie and try using oven-roasted potatoes instead of hash browns.

* By Regis St Louis *

Recipe St Louis Slinger

INGREDIENTS

2 tbs unsalted butter

½ cup shredded or coarsely grated potatoes

1 cup prepared chilli con carne

400g (14oz) hamburger patty

2 eggs

1 tbs oil

¼ cup grated Cheddar cheese

2 tbs diced onions

salt and ground black pepper, to taste

METHOD

1. Melt the butter in a large frying pan over a medium heat.

2. Add the shredded potatoes and cook for about 4 minutes on one side.

3. Flip over the potatoes and cook for 2–3 minutes, until golden brown all over.

4. Meanwhile, put the chilli con carne in a pan and leave it over a low heat to warm through while you cook the rest of the dish.

5. Cook the hamburger patty in a separate frying pan to your personal preference.

6. When the hamburger is halfway done, heat the oil in another pan and fry or scramble the eggs.

7. Place the potatoes on a plate, lay the hamburger over the potatoes and put the eggs over the hamburger.

8. Cover everything with chilli con carne.

9. Sprinkle with the grated cheese and diced onions and serve immediately.

SERVES 1

* Steak and Eggs *

USA; UK; AUSTRALIA; CANADA

If it's a high-calorie brunch you're after, look no further. This combination pulls no punches, offering the fat and flavour favoured by athletes, cowboys and lovers of culinary excess.

What is it?

The ultimate pairing of two high-protein foods, steak and eggs, is a carnivore's delight. While advocates of low-fat, high-fibre breakfasts flee in terror at the sight of this dish, the combination of tender meat and yolky fried eggs is actually considered a healthy meal by bodybuilders, protein aficionados and advocates of the 'caveman' (aka Paleo) diet.

Origin

Allied soldiers fighting in World War II knew they were about to be sent on an important mission if that morning's first meal was steak and eggs. Boxers in training order double portions, and steak and eggs has been a traditional pre-launch breakfast since the early Apollo missions. What do these professionals (along with cowboys and farmhands) have in common? Demanding, high-energy jobs requiring lots of calories and sustaining, slow-burning protein. It'd be hard to get more calories (or flavour, when prepared well) per forkful than you do with a plate of steak and eggs.

Tasting

Buttery and rich, steak and eggs is a bold choice of brunch not for the weak of heart. (Seriously, if you've got a weak heart, stick to oatmeal and fruit.) There are as many variations of steak and eggs as there are of, well… steak (New York strip, rib-eye, thin-cut or thick) and eggs (scrambled, over-easy, sunny-side up). The one common denominator is always sheer indulgence. The meal should be served with the fat from the steak still sizzling, the eggs (whether next to or on top of the meat) piping hot. Side orders of home-made fries, toast, and sometimes (for health reasons?) fruit often accompany this dish. For maximum indulgence, order your eggs sunny-side up so the liquid yolk and warm beef fat can be mopped up with buttered toast.

Finding it

Oregon's Columbia Gorge Hotel pairs an excellent steak and egg breakfast for US$13 with an exceptional ambiance and breathtaking views.

* VARIATIONS * This recipe should produce two beautifully cooked medium-done 2.5cm-thick (1in-thick) thick steaks. You can adjust the cooking time upwards or downwards depending on how well done you like your meat. Lovers of the extremely rare (from 'still squealing' to 'warm and pink') can skip the oven stage (steps 8–9) entirely and instead increase the searing time to between 90 seconds and 2 minutes per side.

* By Joshua Samuel Brown *

Recipe Cast-iron Pan Steak & Eggs

Though some restaurants serve their breakfast steaks flame-broiled (flame-grilled), others use the single pan (usually cast-iron) technique. This method is about the best there is for producing a delicious steak without a flame grill, but a good cast-iron pan is absolutely essential!

INGREDIENTS

two 2.5cm-thick (1in-thick) 8oz (230g) ribeye steaks

pinch of salt

pinch of ground black pepper

4 extra-large eggs

4 tsp grapeseed or canola oil, for frying

1 tbs butter (optional)

METHOD

1. Prepare the meat by patting it dry with kitchen paper. This removes excess water on the meat that would interfere with the searing process.

2. Season the steaks with salt and pepper.

3. Leave the steaks to sit at room temperature for about 20 minutes.

4. Preheat the oven to 200°C (400°F) and heat an ungreased cast-iron pan on the stove over a medium-high heat.

5. Crack the eggs into a large bowl, taking care not to break the yolks. (If you do break a yolk, whisk the eggs and just pretend you wanted scrambled eggs all along.)

6. Rub each steak on both sides with about 1 tsp of the oil.

7. Sear the steaks in the hot pan for 60 seconds on each side. You may need to do this in batches, depending on the size of the pan, removing cooked ones to a plate once they are done.

8. After searing all the steaks, place them all back in the pan (if necessary). Put the pan in the oven for 2 minutes.

9. Flip the steaks over and return the pan to the oven for 2 minutes more.

10. Place the steaks in a serving pan, and cover with foil.

11. Return the cast-iron pan to the stove over a medium-high heat.

12. There should be enough fat left in the pan to make butter superfluous. If not (or if you just love butter), add it now.

13. Cook your eggs how you like them. The heat from the pan should make it a quick process, and the leftover beef fat will make the eggs taste divine.

14. Serve the two ingredients together. *Voilà*, steak and eggs!

15. Following the meal, train for a Tyson-esque fight, invade Normandy or find a similar activity to burn off the excess fat and calories before your heart seizes up.

SERVES 2

* Tapsilog *

THE PHILIPPINES

The hangover breakfast (or brunch, or lunch) of champions – fried beef, fried rice, fried egg and enough calories and carbs to absorb all the excesses of the night before.

What is it?

Tapsilog is the Filipino equivalent of the Western world's cooked breakfast, done Asian-style. It consists of a fried egg, salty garlic-fried rice and fried beef strips, served with a handful of fresh-tasting shredded spring onions, cucumber slices, tomatoes and *atchara* (pickled papaya) to balance out the fried flavours and cut through the oil.

Origin

The Filipinos were preparing *tapa* – cured beef strips, salted and spiced and grilled or fried with a dash of soy sauce – before the first Spanish galleons arrived off the coast of Cebu, but *tapsilog* is a modern creation, invented in the 1980s by fast-food restaurateur Vivian del Rosario in Marikina City in Metro Manila. The name is a portmanteau word, combining *tapa* (fried beef strips), *sinangag* (garlic-fried rice) and *itlog* (egg) – very appropriate for this fusion dish.

Tasting

Filipinos like to work hard and play hard, and nothing hits the spot after an evening of San Miguel beer and *balut* (boiled fertilised duck eggs) quite like *tapsilog*. It could be the reassuringly strong flavours and saltiness. It could be the abundant protein and starch. Or it could just be the prodigious volume of calories, perfect for restoring equilibrium after a smidgeon too much Tanduay rum on a big night out. Machismo is a big part of the Filipino national psyche, and *tapsilog* is feted as a 'man's breakfast', though plenty of Filipinas can match their menfolk fork for fork. For travellers to these island shores, *tapsilog* slots perfectly in place as a substitute for steak and eggs or the Full English Breakfast.

Finding it

Seek out *tapsilog* at its source – the Tapsi ni Vivian restaurant in Marikina. Expect to pay ₱80 ($1.80).

* VARIATIONS * Tapsilog has spawned a legion of imitators – all based around the foundation of fried rice and a fried egg. If you love tapsilog, you might also enjoy bangsilog (fried milkfish, rice and egg), longsilog (local longanisa sausage, rice and egg) or cornsilog (fried corned beef, rice and egg).

Recipe Tapsilog

INGREDIENTS

For the *tapa*

800g (1lb 12oz) beef steak

½ cup lemon juice

⅓ cup soy sauce

2 tbs sugar

¼ tsp ground black pepper

1 tbs minced garlic

1 tbs vegetable oil, for frying

For the garlic-fried rice

2 tbs vegetable oil, for frying

10 cloves garlic, minced

8 cups boiled rice

1 tbs soy sauce

For the fried eggs

1 tbs vegetable oil, for frying

4 eggs

cucumber, tomato and sliced spring onions, to garnish

METHOD

1. First prepare the *tapa*. Cut the beef steak into thin strips.
2. Mix together the ingredients for the marinade in a bowl.
3. Add the beef to the bowl and massage the marinade into the meat. Cover the bowl and leave the meat in the fridge to marinate overnight.
4. When you are ready to cook, drain the marinade from the meat.
5. Heat the vegetable oil in a wok or frying pan over a medium heat. Once the oil is hot, add the beef strips.
6. Stir-fry the beef strips until they are just cooked through.
7. Meanwhile, start making the rice. Heat half the oil for the rice in a separate pan over a medium heat.
8. Add the minced garlic to the hot oil.
9. Fry the garlic, stirring constantly to prevent it from sticking, until it is crisp and golden.
10. Scoop out the garlic and set it to one side on a piece of kitchen paper.
11. Add the remaining oil to the pan and stir in the rice.
12. Stir-fry the rice until it is heated through and just starting to brown.
13. Stir in the soy sauce and the fried garlic.
14. Heat the oil for the eggs in a separate frying pan.
15. Crack in the eggs and fry until the whites are cooked but the yolks remains runny.
16. Now it's time to arrange the *tapsilog*. For each serving, pack a small bowl with garlic-fried rice.
17. Invert the bowl on to a plate to create a neat dome.
18. Arrange a portion of the *tapa* around the rice.
19. Top each portion of rice with a fried egg.
20. Arrange the various garnishes on the sides of the plates, and serve.

SERVES 4

* Tsampa *

TIBET; NEPAL; BHUTAN; INDIA

A million Buddhist monks can't be wrong: *tsampa* – roasted barley porridge mixed with butter tea – is the fuel of the Himalaya and makes a wonderful brunch wherever you are.

What is it?

Tsampa is simplicity itself – just roasted barley flour, transformed into porridge with salty Tibetan butter tea and rolled into neat balls with the studied precision of a Buddhist master. Outside of the monasteries, Tibetans sometimes mix *tsampa* with more 'exotic' and 'luxurious' ingredients, such as milk powder and beer.

Origin

Although it forms the dietary mainstay for millions of Tibetan Buddhist monks, *tsampa* actually predates Buddhism, Bon, and most other belief systems in the Himalaya. The ritual of offering handfuls of roasted flour to animist deities dates back millennia, perhaps all the way back to the first nomads who settled in the high valleys of the Himalaya and turned from hunting and gathering to cultivating crops such as the barley that forms the basis of this recipe.

Tasting

With only one ingredient, *tsampa* is not a dish for people who crave complicated flavours. 'Nutty' would be the best way to describe its taste, with a hint of salt and butter from the Tibetan tea. Yet this rudimentary mixture of ground roasted barley has the almost supernatural power to warm you from the inside. This is a dish to be sampled in a remote Buddhist monastery, as novice monks chant passages from the scriptures to the clashing of cymbals and the honking of Tibetan horns. At some point, an elder monk will come around and pour a bowl of steaming Tibetan tea, to be mixed with the *tsampa* to make a malleable porridge. With a little practice, you'll be mixing *tsampa* into bitesize balls with the dexterity of a monk creating a sand mandala.

Finding it

Head to Woeser Zedroe Restaurant near the Jokhang in Lhasa, where you'll pay less than RMB5 ($0.80) for a bowl.

* TIP * Rolling *tsampa* into a ball takes practice and training. The key is to mix tea and *tsampa* in perfect proportions. Too much tea and the porridge will be a sticky mess, too little and your *tsampa* balls will crumble before you get them into your mouth.

* By Joe Bindloss *

Recipe Tsampa with Tibetan Tea

Preparing *tsampa* takes a lot of work for a dish with just one ingredient, but the results are well worth the effort.

INGREDIENTS

For the *tsampa*

1kg (2lb 2oz) hulled barley

For the tea

4 cups water

2 heaped tsp loose black tea

¼ tsp salt

½ cup milk

2 tbs butter

METHOD

1. Wash the hulled barley with cold water in a bowl.

2. Wash the barley again with boiling water in a strainer.

3. As soon as the water drains, cover the barley with a damp cloth.

4. Leave the barley to cook slightly in its own steam for 10 minutes or so.

5. Spread out the barley on a second cloth to dry for another 10 minutes.

6. Meanwhile, heat a dry wok over a low heat.

7. Roast the barley in the wok, keeping the grains moving constantly, until they start to brown very slightly. The aim is to drive all of the moisture from the barley and generate that distinctive nutty flavour.

8. Remove the wok from the heat and allow the mixture to cool.

9. Before grinding, the barley is known as *yoe* – transforming this to *tsampa* is a simple case of grinding the grains to a fine flour in a food processor or with a mortar and pestle.

10. Once the *tsampa* is ready, it's time to prepare the Tibetan tea.

11. Unless you have a Tibetan tea churn to hand, you'll need a large, watertight, heatproof vessel to churn the tea ingredients together. Start by combining the water, black tea, salt and milk in a metal pan.

12. Bring the liquid to the boil.

13. Transfer the boiling liquid to the improvised churn with the butter.

14. Shake the tea vigorously for 3–5 minutes.

15. Serve the *tsampa* in small ceramic bowls with a cup of salty butter tea. Your guests will have to work out the tricky part – judging the right amount of tea and *tsampa* to mix to create malleable porridge balls – for themselves.

SERVES 2–3

✳ Waffles ✳

USA; EUROPE; CANADA

The deliciously sweet aroma of waffles has thrilled foodies on two continents for centuries. Though especially loved by children, waffles are the perfect brunch for anyone who's young at heart.

What is it?

A waffle is leavened dough cooked between two hot plates to produce a distinctive cake with a crisp exterior and a soft, moist interior. Waffles vary in size, shape and grid pattern, but most North American waffles are almost the size of a dinner plate, making them an excellent platform for fruit, ice cream and, of course, maple syrup.

Origin

Waffles date back to medieval times, when European chefs first began cooking batter made with eggs, flour and salt between two heated (often ornately designed) irons. Waffles became popular in the 17th and 18th century as increased commerce made spices and sugar more readily available throughout Europe. Though it's likely that Dutch settlers were enjoying waffles in New Amsterdam before it was New York, the person who gets credit for introducing them to North America is Thomas Jefferson, said to have returned from a trip to Europe with a waffle iron and a passion for the treats.

Tasting

The cheerful sign on the 24-hour diner's door reads 'breakfast served all day', telling you it's waffle time no matter what the hour. Basking in the diner's warm camaraderie, you slide into your booth, where a smiling waitress offers coffee and a menu. As for which waffle to order, let the road be your guide. If you're in Baltimore, the local soul-food favourite is 'chicken and waffles', a savoury pairing of crisp-fried chicken with thick waffles. Elsewhere, sweeter variations are always a safe bet, and a waffle served with warm fruit (or ice cream, if you've got a serious sweet tooth) never fails to offer both sustenance and comfort. If you find yourself along North America's maple belt (specifically Vermont or Québec), anything not incorporating local maple syrup would be an insult to the locals.

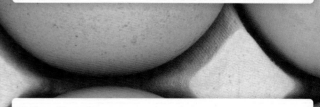

Finding it

Try the Waffle Breakfast (served with eggs, fries and maple syrup) at Sneakers Cafe in Winooski, Vermont, for US$10.85.

✳ TIP ✳ As soon as you remove your last waffles, unplug the waffle iron and stick a couple of very damp pieces of kitchen paper in between the still-hot plates. While you're eating, the dying heat will steam the kitchen paper, softening tenacious bits of batter and chocolate chips, making the post-meal clean-up vastly easier.

By Joshua Samuel Brown ✳

Recipe Waffles with Maple Syrup

As when making buttermilk pancakes or muffins, the secret to a great waffle lies in not over-mixing the batter. Grease the waffle iron according to the instructions that came with it, as some non-stick models require no grease. When in doubt, butter is generally a good choice.

INGREDIENTS

1¾ cups all-purpose (plain) flour

2 tsp baking powder

½ tbs sugar

½ tsp salt

3 egg yolks

1¾ cups full-fat milk

½ cup vegetable oil

3 egg whites, stiffly beaten

fruit, ice cream or maple syrup, to serve

METHOD

1. Preheat the waffle iron, following the manufacturer's instructions.

2. Mix together the flour, baking powder, sugar and salt in a large bowl.

3. Lightly whisk together the egg yolks and milk in a small bowl.

4. Pour the liquid mixture into the dry mixture in the large bowl.

5. Add the oil.

6. Gently stir to combine all the ingredients.

7. Using a large metal spoon, fold in one-quarter of the egg whites to slacken the batter slightly.

8. Carefully fold in the remaining egg whites, taking care not to over-mix the batter.

9. Pour the batter on the middle of the waffle iron, until it almost fills the iron.

10. Close the waffle iron.

11. Cook the waffle for about 5 minutes or until it is golden brown and fragrant.

12. Remove the cooked waffle from the iron and place it on a warm plate while you repeat the cooking process with any remaining batter.

13. Serve with fruit, ice cream or, for maximum authenticity, maple syrup.

SERVES 2–4

* Whitebait Patties *

NEW ZEALAND

When it comes to the world's seafood delicacies, New Zealand whitebait is up there with the best and shown off in all its glory in this simple pattie.

What is it?

This easy dish consists of fresh whitebait, egg and seasoning, all mixed together and formed into a golden fried pattie. Traditional accompaniments are a squeeze of lemon juice and some sliced white bread, but that's where it ends. No messing around, no parsley garnish and certainly no tomato ketchup.

Origin

Although the juvenile fish known as whitebait surface in cuisines throughout the world, native New Zealand whitebait originate from a species of fish known as *Galaxiidae*, which have no scales. They are around 5cm (2in) long, translucent with a speckle of silver, and have an elegant, eel-like form. Come spring, these fish swim upriver from the sea in shoals. Patiently waiting are the whitebaiters, otherwise ordinary people who transform into some of the most obsessive and guarded fisherfolk on the planet. There's a reason for this: whitebait are precious, pricey and seasonal, with whitebaiting only permitted from mid August to mid–late November.

Tasting

In season, whitebait pop up in fishmongers in New Zealand at around NZ$100 per kg – not exactly cheap but still more affordable than those served at fancy restaurants where they may sacrilegiously be turned into haute cuisine. The fresh fish are best cooked yourself. Whitebaiters often sell their catch direct or supply local shops at a respectable going rate, so its worth making a special trip to find the freshest catch. Look out for free-range eggs and organic lemons, often available at roadside stalls, to accompany this premium product. Cook the patties outside on a barbecue hotplate or camp stove, as fresh air will make them taste even better. The key is to go light on the egg and let the whitebait shine – tender, with a delicate fishy flavour.

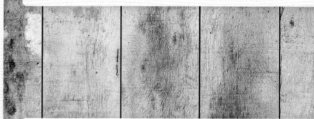

Finding it

Superlative whitebait patties are sold for NZ$9 (US$7) at the Curly Tree Whitebait Company on South Island's West Coast.

* VARIATIONS * While most New Zealanders agree that the pattie is the best way to enjoy whitebait, there is some debate around the best sauce to accompany it. While the masses favour the acidity of lemon juice, 'Coasters' are inclined to favour mint sauce for its king hit of malt vinegar.

* By Sarah Bennett and Lee Slater *

Recipe Whitebait Patties

While some cooks adulterate the venerable pattie with the addition of flour, purists use only egg. Its purpose is simply to bind the whitebait together, not add texture or flavour.

INGREDIENTS

2 eggs

500g (1lb 1oz) fresh whitebait, drained

salt and ground black pepper, to taste

1 tbs butter or oil, for frying

lemon wedge, to serve

thinly sliced white bread, to serve (optional)

METHOD

1. Lightly whisk the eggs in a large bowl.

2. Add the well-drained whitebait, along with salt and pepper.

3. Heat the butter or oil in a frying pan until it reaches sizzling temperature.

4. Spoon in the whitebait mixture to form patties of around 10–12cm (4–4¾in) in diameter.

5. Fry for around 2 minutes on each side, until golden brown.

6. Serve immediately with a squeeze of lemon, sandwiched between thinly sliced white bread should you desire a more substantial repast.

MAKES 4–6 PATTIES; SERVES 2–3

* Xôi Mặn *

VIETNAM

It's the perfect mouthful! Sticky rice, crisp onions, fresh herbs, savoury sausage – texture and taste contrasts are what Vietnamese cuisine is all about, and *xôi mặn* embodies both of these.

What is it?

Xôi mặn is a simple dish: a steaming plate (or sometimes banana leaf) of sticky rice loaded up with a variety of meats – from Chinese sausage to barbecued pork – as well as fried onions, pickled carrot and daikon, cucumber and finally a topping of herbs and a sprinkling of light soy sauce.

Origin

Sticky rice (also known as glutinous rice) has been around for a good 2000 years and is ubiquitous throughout Asia. *Xôi mặn*'s roots are, like so many Asian dishes, found in Chinese cuisine, with a number of southern Chinese variants of savoury sticky rice out there. But as you'll see (and taste!), the Southeast Asian fascination with fresh herbs and cucumber brings a brightness that elevates an otherwise pretty stodgy offering.

Tasting

Xôi mặn can be found in larger markets, in specialist canteens, from carts (often near parks) and, around breakfast time, on almost every street corner of every city in Vietnam. Morning streets resound with the calls of the local *xôi* vendor, peddling his or her particular variation (there are many). It's also a popular brunch snack for school kids whose day can end around 11am. From a cart by a park is a great way to experience *xôi*. Your order comes in a flash, usually on a small plastic plate, and you sit down on tiny plastic chairs with your fellow diners. It's a filling, immensely satisfying dish. Every mouthful is different as you travel through the combinations of herbs and meat and rice. It's a little sweet, a little salty, the rice is soft and squishy, and the extras are crunchy and vibrant.

Finding it

Great *xôi* is served at Xôi Chè Bùi Thị Xuân, 111 Bùi Thị Xuân, Saigon, for about đ25000 (US$1.20).

---

* **VARIATIONS** * *Xôi mặn* is pronounced 'soy mun'. There are so many *xôi* variations to be found, you could probably eat a different version every day of a holiday in Vietnam. Try *xôi gấc* to change it up – a sweet variety dyed a vivid orange by bitter melon, served with coconut cream and desiccated coconut. For the mixed meat variety, ask for *xôi mặn thập cẩm* ('soy mun tup gum').

* By Ben Handicott *

Recipe Xôi Mặn

The secret here is the overnight soaking of the rice, meaning a little advance planning is required.

INGREDIENTS

2 cups glutinous rice

2 tsp light soy sauce, plus extra to serve

1 tbs vegetable oil

2 pork chops or chicken thighs

2 Chinese sausages, thinly sliced

3 tbs small dried shrimp, soaked in water for about 30 minutes, then drained

3 spring onions, sliced

fried shallots

½ cup julienned cucumber

½ cup julienned carrot

1 tbs chopped fresh coriander, to garnish

INGREDIENTS

1. Rinse the rice, then soak it in a bowl of water overnight.

2. Drain the rice.

3. Return the drained rice to the bowl.

4. Stir the soy sauce through the rice.

5. Line a vegetable steamer with some muslin cloth and add the rice. Cover with a lid.

6. Steam the rice for about 15 minutes, until it is cooked; it should be soft to the tooth.

7. While the rice is cooking, heat the oil in a frying pan.

8. Add the pork chop or chicken thigh to the pan and fry until cooked through.

9. Transfer the meat to a plate and let it rest.

10. In the same frying pan, sauté the Chinese sausage, dried shrimp and spring onions for 3 minutes.

11. Shred the rested chicken or pork and add it back to the pan to heat through.

12. Take a small bowl and pack it with the cooked sticky rice.

13. Upend the bowl on to a serving plate, so there is a neat mound of rice in the centre.

14. Garnish the rice with the Chinese sausage, meat and vegetables.

15. Add a sprinkling of the fried shallots, carrot and cucumber.

16. Garnish the dish with a little chopped coriander.

17. Serve with light soy sauce on the side to season to taste.

SERVES 4

* Youtiao *

CHINA

Whether it is called a Chinese cruller, a fried breadstick or just a Song-dynasty doughnut, the *youtiao* is the perfect brunch snack for travellers on the go.

What is it?

A Chinese doughnut, *youtiao* is made from two joined strips of dough that has been proved overnight and then deep-fried, before being lightly salted. It is usually served with hot soy milk, green tea, coffee or *congee* (rice porridge). Don't be misled by the simplicity of the dish – once dipped, the *youtiao* becomes incredibly more-ish and satisfying.

Origin

One popular legend links the invention of *youtiao* to the Chinese folk hero, Yue Fei, a Song-dynasty general who was betrayed by the cowardly prime minister, Qin Hui. In protest, a local baker made two strips of dough to represent Qin Hui and his wife, and fried them in boiling oil, one of the punishments reserved for evil-doers in Buddhist hell.

Tasting

Youtiao is comfort food, so the times you remember it with the most affection are the times when it offers the most comfort – for example, when exploring the Great Wall of China in the perishing depths of winter. Nothing unfreezes the fingers and defrosts the lips quite like tearing chunks of fresh-from-the-oil *youtiao* and dipping them into hot soy milk or coffee. Pleasing through it is, the flavour of *youtiao* – slightly salty, slightly sweet – takes second place to the texture – crisp on the outside, and full of soft bubbles on the inside because of the action of bicarb soda (baking soda) (and alum, in traditional Chinese recipes). *Youtiao* are also served in a huge variety of Asian dishes – stuffed into sandwiches, rolled into rice balls, or snipped into strips on top of bowls of soup.

Finding it

Whenever you sit and order tea, expect *youtiao* to follow close behind. Each pair of doughnuts will cost around RMB2 (US$0.33).

* VARIATIONS * Many Chinese people like to layer the carbs by stuffing *youtiao* inside a *shaobing* – a fat, layered flatbread, baked in the oven. As *shaobing* can be stuffed with anything from fried mung beans to sesame paste, this opens up a whole world of sweet and savoury brunches! In Shanghai, look out for *cifantuan*, *youtiao* steamed inside glutinous rice.

* By Joe Bindloss *

Recipe Youtiao

Although the ingredients are simple, preparing the dough for *youtiao* requires a little finesse.
The dough should be just dry enough to roll out, but still soft, light and pliable.

INGREDIENTS

4 cups plain (all-purpose) flour

½ tsp salt

¼ tsp bicarb soda (baking soda)

1 tsp sugar

½ tsp dried yeast

1 cup water

vegetable oil, for deep-frying

hot soy milk, tea, coffee, hot
chocolate or melted chocolate
spread, to serve

METHOD

1. Sift together the flour, salt and bicarb soda (baking soda)
    in a large bowl.

2. Dissolve the sugar and yeast in a little of the water in a
    separate bowl.

3. Add the yeast mixture to the dry ingredients.

4. Add the water a little at a time, kneading everything together,
    until you achieve a soft dough that isn't too sticky to roll.

5. Oil the bowl and return the dough to it.

6. Cover the bowl with cling film and leave the dough to ferment
    for 20 minutes at room temperature. Place the bowl in the
    fridge and leave the dough to prove overnight.

7. When you are ready to use the dough, bring it up to room
    temperature. Roll out the dough on a lightly floured surface
    into a wide 1cm-thick (⅓in-thick) strip. Slice this strip
    crossways into thick slices.

8. To make the distinctive pairing of Qin Hui and his wife, score
    down the middle of each strip with a moistened chopstick,
    taking take not to cut right through the dough.

9. Pour enough oil in a deep-frying pan or wok to come about
    halfway up the sides. Heat the oil over a medium-high heat
    until the surface shimmers.

10. Pull each dough strip out to about the length of your forearm.

11. Carefully lower each dough strip into the hot oil.

12. As soon as the dough puffs up and floats to the surface, roll
    it over to brown it on both sides.

13. Remove the *youtiao* using a slotted spoon and leave it to
    drain on a piece of kitchen paper.

14. Repeat the cooking process until all the dough is cooked.

15. Serve the warm *youtiao* with hot soy milk, tea, coffee or, for
    a European twist, hot chocolate or melted chocolate spread.

MAKES 12

* Zongzi *

MALAYSIA; INDONESIA

A soft rice parcel with a mystery filling, China's *zongzi* is the perfect portable brunch; grab a few before you leap on the train and munch as the countryside flashes by.

What is it?

Zongzi is a soft, sticky pyramid of glutinous rice, stuffed with a wonderful variety of Asian fillings and then steamed inside a tidy packet of bamboo leaves. What you find inside could be anything from salted duck eggs to chestnuts, stewed pork, or sweet red beans – so unwrap the leaves and delve into the depths of the rice...

Origin

The dish was first served as part of the celebrations for the Duanwu Dragon Boat Festival, but people soon cottoned on to its suitability as a portable feast, and *zongzi* became a year-round staple. According to legend, the dish was invented when the poet Qu Yuan drowned himself in a lake in sadness because of the Qin takeover of Chu and locals threw parcels of rice into the lake to keep his body safe from nibbling fish.

Tasting

If *zongzi* were a different shape, and didn't come wrapped in a bamboo leaf, they probably wouldn't have quite the same appeal. There's something about a snack you unwrap that appeals to the child in all of us, and the frisson of anticipation as you take the first bite and discover what is inside just adds to the magic. The best place to hunt them down is a bustling Chinese market, where porters and traders have just enough time to munch down a couple of *zongzi* before the next pallet of century eggs rolls off the truck. Eating *zongzi* is a bit of a lucky dip – unless you are competent in Mandarin or Cantonese – but the filling is always delicious.

Finding it

Experience *zongzi* for RMB3 (US$0.50) at the boat races held every May or June along the Miluo River, Hunan.

* **VARIATIONS** * The sticky rice dumpling tradition spreads right across Asia. In Thailand and Laos, seek out *bachang*; in Cambodia, ask for *nom chang*; in Myanmar, hunt down *pya htote*; and in Indonesia and the Malay Straits, search for *bak chang*.

* By Joe Bindloss *

Recipe Zongzi

INGREDIENTS

For the rice

1kg (2lb 2oz) glutinous rice

pinch of salt

For the filling

10 salted duck yolks

300g (11oz) split mung beans

pinch of salt

500g (1lb 1oz) boneless pork belly

3 tbs light soy sauce

2 tbs dark soy sauce

2 tbs rice wine

¼ tsp cinnamon powder

1 tsp Chinese five-spice powder

To serve

35–40 bamboo leaves (if unavailable, you can use corn cob leaves or parchment paper)

METHOD

1. If you plan to add salted duck yolks, you'll need to buy some duck eggs, separate the yolks and steep them in salt water in a cool, dark place for at least 3 weeks.

2. The day before you make the *zongzi*, prepare the glutinous rice, mung beans and pork belly. Soak the rice overnight in a bowl of water with a pinch of salt. Soak the mung beans overnight in a bowl of water with a pinch of salt.

3. Cut the pork belly into strips. Mix together the soy sauces, rice wine, cinnamon and Chinese five-spice powder in a bowl. Add the pork belly strips and stir to combine. Cover the bowl and leave the meat to marinate overnight.

4. Soak 30–45 bamboo leaves in water overnight.

5. When you are ready to cook, drain the water from the rice, mung beans and bamboo leaves and prepare yourself mentally for the difficult part – folding the bamboo leaves to create a tidy pyramid that can be stuffed with the ingredients you prepared overnight.

6. To make your leaf wrapping, hold two leaves together and fold them to the centre. Fold back a strip at the back to create a hollow 'cup'. Line this 'cup' with a third leaf to seal any holes, and you are ready to start filling.

7. Start by adding a generous spoonful of rice to the 'cup'. Add some mung beans, half a salted duck yolk and a strip of marinated belly pork. Top the filling with more rice.

8. Fold over the leaf parcel, and wrap it tightly with food-safe string to create a secure bundle. Repeat the process until all the bamboo leaves and filling mixture have been used.

9. When all the *zongzi* are prepared, fill a stockpot with boiling water. Gently lower in the *zongzi* bundles with a spoon and cover the pan.

10. Boil the *zongzi* for 2–3 hours, checking regularly to make sure there is enough water to keep them all submerged (if necessary, add more water). When the *zongzi* are done, the rice should be melded together in a dough-like shell. Remove the *zongzi* from the water, unwrap and enjoy.

MAKES 10–15

Drinks & Condiments

Legend

(E) **Easy** - A very basic recipe, eg, putting together a sandwich or tossing salad ingredients.

(M) **Medium** - Suitable for the average home cook.

(C) **Complex** - Several parts to make, or lots of ingredients to prepare, or a specific technique involved that may take some practice.

(🥕) **Vegetarian**

(🥤) **Drink**

(✕) **Knife and fork**

(🥄) **Spoon**

(✋) **Hands**

(❤) **Healthy**

(🔥) **Indulgent**

* Bloody Mary *

PARIS, FRANCE

A feisty Bloody Mary is guaranteed to give your senses a wake-up call and this classic cocktail is a brunch-time fixture the world over thanks to its reputation as a hangover cure.

What is it?

In essence, a Bloody Mary consists of tomato juice laced with vodka, but its real flavour kick comes from the zing of the lemon juice, the spiciness of the Worcestershire sauce (an unlikely combination of fermented tamarinds and anchovies), and a liberal seasoning of salt and fiery pepper, all of which is swizzled together with a crisp stick of celery.

Origin

The Bloody Mary was born in 1920s Paris at Harry's New York Bar, when Parisian barman Fernand 'Pete' Petiot experimented with recently available Russian vodka (distilled by enterprising immigrants who had fled the Russian Revolution) and newly invented canned tomato juice imported from America – like the entire mahogany bar itself, which was dismantled and shipped piece by piece from Manhattan, and became a refuge for Americans abroad during the Prohibition era. Petiot's creation was christened by one of Harry's first customers to try it, American singer/pianist Roy Barton, after the Chicago nightclub Bucket of Blood and its waitress, Mary.

Tasting

Sharp, piquant, and refreshingly savoury, a Bloody Mary is ideal for brunch at any time of year, whether enjoyed alfresco on a scorching hot summer's morning or by a crackling fire in winter, with the spicy heat balanced by the cooling tomato juice. The absence of an alcoholic taste makes it much more palatable – and stomachable – than other spirits would be at an early hour. (Whether it actually cures hangovers is another matter.) The Bloody Mary is often described as 'the world's most complex cocktail' and crimes witnessed in bars around the world include the quantity of Worcestershire sauce outweighing the amount of tomato juice in the glass, and the unforgivable sin of substituting tomato juice for dry, powdered tomato soup mix. Much more successful variations involve swapping vodka for gin, adding horseradish, or garnishing with olives.

Finding it

History-steeped Harry's New York Bar remains a Bloody Mary lover's Holy Grail, where the drink costs €15 (US$20).

* TIP * Use as large a block of ice as the cocktail shaker or glass jar will allow; smaller cubes tend to melt and dilute the Bloody Mary. For the smoothest finish, use Tabasco sauce rather than cayenne.

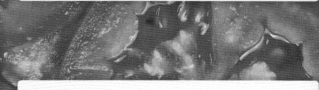

* By Catherine Le Nevez *

Recipe **Bloody Mary**

INGREDIENTS

60mL (2fl oz) vodka

120mL (4fl oz) tomato juice

1 tbs freshly squeezed lemon juice

pinch of salt

pinch of finely ground black pepper

1 tsp Tabasco sauce (or a pinch of finely ground cayenne pepper)

3 tsp Worcestershire sauce

1 large ice cube

1 celery stick, to garnish

1 lemon wedge, to garnish

METHOD

1. Place all of the ingredients except the garnishes in a cocktail shaker or a tightly sealed screw-top jar.

2. Shake vigorously for 10–15 seconds.

3. Strain into a 240mL (8fl oz) highball glass.

4. Garnish with the celery stick and lemon wedge.

5. Enjoy!

MAKES 1 COCKTAIL

* Bramble Jelly *

UNITED KINGDOM

Wild, seasonal and local, this homemade jelly captures the essence of the late summer/early autumn hedgerow bounty and makes a fruity companion to toast or a bowl of steaming porridge.

What is it?

Most places have their own version of a jam or jelly that makes use of the late-summer glut of berries foraged from hedgerows and forests. In Scandinavia, it's made from lingonberries, while in Britain blackberries are the most abundant ingredient. The berries are stewed, the juice strained for pips and then set into an intoxicatingly deep purple jelly.

Origin

Primitive people may well have cooked the annual bounty of autumn berries that appear in temperate parts of the world, but it wasn't until the 19th century that French confectioner Nicolas Appert discovered that he had the necessary technology – glass containers sealed with corks and wax – to preserve food without it decaying. Known as the 'father of canning', Appert published the first book on modern food preservation in 1810. The technique – sealing cooked foods in a sterile, airtight container remains the same today – and means that late-summer's harvest of berries can be enjoyed throughout the winter.

Tasting

Bramble jelly is a taste of the British countryside. Specifically, it's the taste of Britain's richest season, a few weeks across late August and September when battalions of berries ripen from green to maroon to black in waves. You get your first taste of them standing at a hedgerow, gingerly picking them from between the prickly stems of the bramble and the inevitable stinging nettles; robust long sleeves are recommended for foraging, though gloves will limit your fingers' nimbleness. Some are sharp, some sweet. Satiated, you start collecting them in a bag, hauling your loot home to cook up. Months later, when the hedgerows are coated in snow, you open a jar and, via the jelly's deep, sweet, tart taste, are transported back to the day the blackberries were picked. And remembering the pain you went through doing it adds a little frisson to the experience...

Finding it

The World Jampionships – the perfect competition for the sticky-fingered and sweet-toothed – takes place annually in Blairgowrie, Perthshire, Scotland. But the best place to buy jam is at a village fete where you can expect to pay around £3 (US$4.80).

* VARIATIONS * Blackcurrants, elderberries (those hanging clumps of small black berries) and berries from rowan trees also make good jellies. In North America wild berries include blueberries and cranberries. All lift a piece of toast from the ordinary to the sublime.

* By Robin Barton *

Recipe Bramble Jelly

Warming the sugar before adding it to the juice will speed up the dissolving time.

INGREDIENTS

lots of blackberries – 1.5kg (3lb 5oz) produces around 2½ cups of juice

water – about 1½ cups per 1.5kg (3lb 5oz) blackberries

juice of 2 lemons

preserving sugar (2½ cups per 2½ cups blackberry juice)

METHOD

1. Pick through the fruit, removing any spiky hulls and bits of bramble, leaves, cobwebs or other hedgerow detritus.

2. Simmer the berries in a large steel-bottomed pan (jam-making pans are larger than conventional pans) with the water and the lemon juice.

3. Set up a jelly bag, if you have one. If not you can use a large piece of muslin, corners tied together and suspended from a cupboard handle above a large measuring jug.

4. After 10–15 minutes, when the fruit is soft, strain the mixture through the jelly bag or muslin into a measuring jug. Let it drip for a few hours; if you squeeze it you'll get more juice out but the jelly will be cloudy (it will taste the same).

5. Meanwhile, thoroughly wash a large number of jam jars and their lids, dry them and then leave them to warm and dry in a very low oven. Alternatively, put the jars and their lids in the dishwasher and run a hot cycle.

6. Return the strained juice to the rinsed-out large pan. Add 2½ cups preserving sugar for every 2½ cups of juice. For a sharper flavour, reduce the sugar, but ensure that the ratio of sugar to liquid does not drop below 2:3 or it may not set.

7. Stir until the sugar has dissolved, then bring the mixture to the boil – this can take anywhere from 5 to 20 minutes.

8. Check the temperature of the mixture using a sugar thermometer. When it has reached 105°C (221°F) the jelly is ready. Another way of checking whether the jelly will set is to put a few drops on to a chilled saucer. Wait a few seconds, then push the jelly with your finger. It should have formed a skin that wrinkles when you push it if it is set. If not, boil the jelly until this does happen, testing every couple of minutes.

9. Ladle the jelly into jars using a funnel. Fill the jars to within 1cm (⅓in) of the top. Screw the lids on tightly while the jelly is hot; as it cools it will cause the lids to seal tightly.

10. Allow the jelly to cool, then label the jars and store in a cool, dry place.

* Breakfast Martini *

UNITED KINDGOM; USA

A martini for breakfast is clearly an outrageous thing to suggest. Of course, it's wrong. But this zesty jolt to the system on a certain kind of morning can feel oh-so-right...

What is it?

A gin-based martini, mixed with orange liqueur, lemon juice and a spoonful of top-quality marmalade, this decadent drink must be served ice cold. The best kind come garnished with a small, elegantly cut triangle of toast balanced on the rim of the glass, otherwise a twist of orange peel will do.

Origin

A version of this drink, the Marmalade Cocktail, appeared in the 1930s' *The Savoy Cocktail Book*, but the most recent incarnation, upon which the recipe given here is based, was invented by bartender Salvatore Calabrese in the 1990s. An Italian, he was used to having just an espresso for breakfast until his English wife persuaded him to sit down to eat toast and marmalade one morning. He enjoyed the fruity spread so much he took the jar to work with him at London's Library Bar in the Lanesborough Hotel, and used it to create this cocktail.

Tasting

First of all, the occasion needs to be just right. Otherwise you're really just drinking gin at breakfast – and that isn't normally a good thing. So the setting must be decadent, the company wild (and non-judgemental) and the day ahead blissfully responsibility-free. Madcap city breaks, glamorous weekends away, stag or hen dos gone awry – all qualify, as does any time you wake up in the kind of hotel that will serve you one of these before noon. When the drink is served, the refreshing citrus scent at first overpowers the booze, and it smells delightfully healthy. The first sip puts paid to that lie, as the sweet, complex tang of the marmalade, zing of the lemon juice and burn of the alcohol hit your palette all at once – and if that doesn't perk you up pretty sharpish, nothing will.

Finding it

London's Anchor and Hope pub in Waterloo does a Breakfast Martini for £4.80 (US$7.67), or order it off-menu at upscale bars.

* TIP * Despite its name, there's no reason not to order this drink during more conventional drinking hours too – it's one of the best citrus cocktails out there. If you must have it in the morning, we highly recommend that you order it with, well, breakfast. You'll need to be made of stern stuff to manage one on an empty stomach.

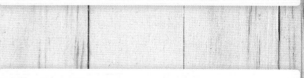

* By Helen Elfer *

Recipe **Breakfast Martini**

INGREDIENTS

1 heaped tsp finely cut marmalade

50mL (1.7fl oz) gin

1 tbs Cointreau or any triple sec

1 tbs lemon juice

ice

orange zest

a small triangle of plain toast

METHOD

1. Stir the gin and marmalade together in the bottom of a cocktail shaker until the marmalade dissolves.

2. Add the lemon juice and triple sec to the cocktail shaker.

3. Add the ice to the cocktail shaker.

4. Shake the mixture well.

5. Strain the drink into a chilled glass.

6. Twist the orange zest over the glass so the essential oils go in the drink.

7. Add the orange twist to the glass.

8. Cut a small slit in the edge of the toast.

9. Balance the toast triangle on the rim of the glass.

SERVES 1

* Buck's Fizz *

UNITED KINGDOM

Fresh, sassy orange juice and chilled champagne – this sparkling cocktail hints at luxury, yet it's so easy to make. Who doesn't love an excuse to drink champagne for breakfast?

What is it?

Buck's Fizz is a refreshing cocktail comprising one-third fresh orange juice mixed with two-thirds champagne, served in champagne flutes with a simple fresh orange twist. It's often served at an indulgent brunch or as a light daytime cocktail. If you're mixing your own, add more or less champagne depending on just how wicked you want to be.

Origin

London, 1921. While frivolity and jazz swirl all around, it's in the exclusive setting of a private club in Mayfair that the first Buck's Fizz was mixed. It's said that Mr McGarry, the barman at the Buck's Club, concocted the drink as a something to offer to members at breakfast to take the edge off their hangovers, or as an excuse to begin drinking early in the day. To add a little mystery to the tale, a true Buck's Fizz contains secret extra ingredients, the identity of which are known only by the barmen of the Buck's Club.

Tasting

Brunch oozes languor and luxury and, quite simply, Buck's Fizz is what turns breakfast into brunch. It is decadent yet elegant, a refreshing cocktail to be sipped in the sunshine. It's the bubbles that make it so special. Take a sip and feel the sparkle of the wine popping gently against the top of your mouth while tangy orange juice peps up your taste buds. You may be brunching in a swanky hotel, a funky little cafe or in your own backyard, but once the Buck Fizz turns up you know that it's time to chill. Yes, you could have tea or coffee, or even a Bloody Mary for the determined drinkers, but ordering a Buck's Fizz says, 'Relax, what's the hurry, we've got all day...'

Finding it

For the best, go to the Buck's Club, Mayfair, London, where you can expect to pay £10 (US$16) a glass.

* VARIATIONS * Just vary the proportion of champagne and juice to one-third champagne to two-thirds orange juice and – ta-dah! – you have a brand-new cocktail, a Mimosa. Alternatively, try squeezing different varieties of oranges for your juice – you could use navel oranges for a hint more sweetness or blood oranges for a ravishing ruby colour.

* By Tracy Whitmey *

Recipe Buck's Fizz

INGREDIENTS

375mL (about 13fl oz) freshly squeezed, unsweetened orange juice, chilled

750mL (about 1.6 pints) champagne, chilled

orange slices, to garnish

METHOD

1. Pour the orange juice into six champagne flutes so each flute is about one-third full.

2. Top up each glass with champagne.

3. Stir gently.

4. Garnish with a twist of orange and serve immediately.

SERVES 6

* Chai *

Leave breakfast tea to the English. In India, *chai* – that marvellous combination of milk, tea leaves, sugar and spices – is something to be savoured at any time of day.

What is it?

At its simplest level, this is a good-old fashioned cuppa – built on solid foundations of tea leaves, milk and sugar. But the unique combination of spices (cardamom, cloves, cinnamon, ginger, pepper) added by each *chai-wallah* transforms *chai* from breakfast beverage to all-day magic potion that is simultaneously warming and refreshing.

Origin

Chai has been part of Indian life for millennia, but the British played a key role in making the drink available to people other than just the ruling classes. During the early years of the Raj, black tea was mainly produced for export, but in the early 20th century, the Indian Tea Association launched a massive campaign to promote tea-drinking within the subcontinent, using the conduit of the rapidly expanding Indian rail service.

Tasting

The glory of *chai* comes partly from the ritual of preparation: the call of the *chai-wallah* echoing around the train station platform; the waft of kerosene as the stove is primed; the bubble and churn of frothing milk and tea leaves in a battered tin pan; the sly pinch of secret-recipe spices that marks each vendor out from the vendor next door; then the glorious long pour, as the *chai* is tipped from on high into tiny glasses or flimsy paper cups. The first sip is all sweetness and cream (low-fat milk has yet to make inroads in the subcontinent), then the spices creep in, exotic and complex. It might be 30°C (86°F) outside, but that tiny cup of *chai* will be as refreshing as a cold beer after a marathon run along the Equator.

Finding it

Chai-wallahs congregate at every bus and taxi stand, train station and marketplace in the subcontinent. A cuppa costs ₹8 (US$0.15).

* TIP * *Chai* by itself is amazing; *chai* with biscuits is something else. Most vendors have a jar of *mathri* (sweet Rajasthani biscuits scented with cumin seeds) on hand to bulk up your brunch order.

* By Joe Bindloss *

Recipe Chai

INGREDIENTS

For the *chai masala*

4 tbs ground black pepper

3 tbs ginger powder

1½ tbs cinnamon powder

1½ tbs ground cardamom

½ tsp clove powder

½ tsp nutmeg powder

For the tea

½ cup full-fat milk

½ cup water

1 tbs sugar

1 tsp broken black tea leaves

METHOD

1. First, prepare the *chai masala*: combine all the dry spices.

2. For each cup of *chai*, stir together the milk, water, sugar, loose tea leaves and a pinch of the *chai masala* powder in a metal pan.

3. Bring the *chai* to the boil.

4. Remove the pan quickly from the heat and stir the *chai*.

5. Return the pan to the heat.

6. Bring the mixture back to the boil.

7. Remove the pan quickly from the heat and stir the *chai* again.

8. Repeat steps 3–5 several times to draw the maximum flavour from the ingredients.

9. To serve, pour the *chai* through a strainer into a small glass or cup and let the aromas transport you back to the subcontinent!

SERVES 1; MAKES ENOUGH *CHAI MASALA*
FOR NUMEROUS CUPS

* Dulce de Leche *

ARGENTINA

If there were ever an award for the world's creamiest, stickiest and most sugary treat, dulce de leche ('milk sweet') would surely win. Dentists love it (or hate it) depending which way you look at it.

What is it?

South America's sublime saccharine snack, this is – pure and simple – a sweet-lover's comfort spread; a sinfully sweet milky caramel goo that can be slathered on bread or pancakes, used as a filling in baked goods or furtively consumed neat with a teaspoon. It's what peanut butter is to Americans, or Vegemite to Australians. Only it's far more wicked.

Tasting

The texture is one thing – smooth, rich and sticky, slowly melting away on your tongue. Its flavour is another – think caramel with a twist. Grab a spoon, dig into a jar and get your tongue working. The less sinful among you can spread it on bread. Or you can get your fill by munching on an *alfajor*, a shortbread biscuit sandwiched with a layer of this decadent delight.

Origin

The origins of *dulce de leche* are fiercely claimed by both Uruguay and Argentina, with Argentina appealing to UNESCO to recognise the beloved delicacy as belonging to them. A popular version of the Argentinian tale is that it was invented by accident in 1829 by a maid of General Juan Manuel de Rosas while the country was at war. While preparing *la lechada* (a milk and sugar drink), she was distracted by the enemy, General Juan Lavalle who, unbeknown to her, had come to the camp to sign a peace treaty. (Some versions have him asleep on her boss' bed; nothing gets in the way of an Argentinian and his siesta. Or a good story.) Not knowing of the impending agreement, she ran for help, leaving the milk preparation on the heat. She returned to find a caramelised sweet substance and the rest is happy history (for a dentist, anyway).

Finding it

Torre de panqueques con dulce de leche (a pancake tower layered with caramel) costs a few dollars at Malvón in Buenos Aires.

---

* VARIATIONS * Similar spreads (sometimes prepared slightly differently) include: *arequipe* (Columbia and Venezuela); *cajeta* (Mexico); *doce de leite* (Brazil); *manjar* (Chile and Ecuador); and *manjar blanco* (Bolivia, Colombia, Costa Rica, Ecuador, Panama, Peru).

* By Kate Armstrong *

Recipe Dulce de Leche

INGREDIENTS

300mL (10fl oz) condensed milk in a can (or whatever size can is available)

METHOD 1

1. Carefully pierce two holes on opposite sides of the lid with a can opener. Note: this step is vital – without these holes, there is a danger of the can exploding.

2. Place the can in a pan that is just taller than the can is high.

3. Add enough water to come most of the way up the sides of the can, to within 10cm (4in) of the top of the can.

4. Boil for 3–4 hours, topping up the water as required with boiling water from the kettle.

5. Remove the can from the pan and leave it to cool.

6. Remove the lid with a can opener.

7. Transfer the caramel to a serving bowl and stir it well.

METHOD 2

1. Pour the condensed milk into a double boiler (bain-marie).

2. Simmer the milk for around 1½ hours, or until it is toffee-brown and thick.

3. Beat the caramel until it is smooth.

4. Leave the caramel to cool, then serve.

* Hagelslag *

THE NETHERLANDS

Imagine people of all ages boldly dumping chocolate sprinkles on their bread each morning. So it goes in the Netherlands, where a prodigious topping of *hagelslag* jumpstarts the day.

What is it?

Hagelslag are candy sprinkles. Entire Dutch supermarket shelves are dedicated to the sugar flecks, which come in dark chocolate, milk chocolate, white chocolate and fruity flavours. You buy them by the box and pour a healthy dose on to buttered bread or toast. The butter is key to adhere the sprinkles to the surface of the bread.

Origin

A liquorice-factory owner supposedly concocted anise-flavoured sprinkles in 1919 to cheer up Amsterdammers during a bout of cold, wet weather. He called them *hagelslag*, meaning 'hailstorm', and they were a hit. Chocolate sprinkles came on the scene in 1936 after a young boy sent repeated letters to the chocolate company Venz asking for a topping to make his bread less boring. Venz created chocolate *hagelslag*, and the industry boomed.

Tasting

You're in your hotel's breakfast room or maybe a cafe. A cup of rich coffee wafts its scents from the table beside a plate of bread slices – plain white or coarse brown, your choice. A crock of butter sits alongside, as well as something unexpected: a small bowl of chocolate sprinkles. You look around, thinking perhaps you've received a child's order by mistake. But then you notice everyone – young *and* old – putting a whopping spoonful of sprinkles on to his or her bread. What the heck: you try it. First a slathering of butter, then enough sprinkles to cover the slice. You bite, and there's a mild crunch. And then a sweet flavour-burst that transforms the bread into a light version of cake. It's simple. It's genius. It's addictive. Heck, it's so delicious many locals also eat it for lunch.

Finding it

Munch a *broodje de hagelslag* (bread roll with sprinkles) at Amsterdam's waterside Café de Jaren (Nieuwe Doelenstraat 20–22) for €3.50 ($4.40).

* VARIATIONS * *Muisjes* ('little mice') are also a topping for bread, except they are anise-flavoured and shaped as small round dots. They're coloured either blue or pink, and the Dutch eat them on biscuits to celebrate a baby's birth.

* By Karla Zimmerman *

Recipe Chocolate Hagelslag

INGREDIENTS

1¼ cup icing sugar

7 tbs cocoa (either Dutch or natural)

2 tbs water

2 tbs vanilla extract

¼ tsp salt

¼ tsp instant coffee powder (optional)

METHOD

1. Combine all the ingredients in a bowl using a hand-held mixer on medium-low speed until a homogenous paste forms.

2. Use a rubber spatula to scrape the bowl and beaters, then mix for another minute until the batter is smooth. Make sure no lumps remain, as they will clog the pastry tip.

3. Pour the mixture into a piping bag that has a small plain tip or a multi-opening tip (#42, #89 and #134 all work well). If you don't have a piping bag, pour the mixture into a homemade baking-parchment cone.

4. Line two baking sheets with baking parchment.

5. Pipe the mixture on to the parchment in close parallel lines.

6. Set the baking sheets aside to dry for 24 hours.

7. Gently scrape the sprinkle-lines from the baking parchment; a bench scraper works best for the task.

8. Collect the lines into a bundle, then chop them with a knife into 5mm-long (less than ¼in-long) pieces.

9. Put the sprinkles into an airtight container. They'll keep for several months.

MAKES 1 CUP

* Hibiscus Ginger Punch *

JAMAICA

If the Caribbean came in a cup, it'd taste something like this refreshingly tangy summer cooler, made from hibiscus flowers and toughened up with a liberal splash of rum.

What is it?

This deep-rouge tropical tipple (beware: it will stain like red wine) is a delicious blend of Jamaican sorrel (hibiscus) petal-infused water, ginger, Caribbean rum, and lime, naturally sweetened to perfection with agave syrup and garnished with a sprig of mint. This is then chilled and served with plenty of ice, for the coolest drink in town.

Tasting

There aren't many other blooms that scream summer quite like pink hibiscus. And its flowers really are good enough to eat – when infused in water, it produces a deliciously tart crimson cordial somewhat similar to cranberry juice. It's so refreshingly tasty you could simply pour the cooled infusion over ice and enjoy; indeed this very beverage is commonly served as an *agua fresca* (fresh water) by street vendors and bodegas across Mexico and Central America. It's also a popular tea. But the addition of sugar (which balances out the tartness of the hibiscus), ginger (for extra zing), and a splash of rum (it's Jamaican, after all) takes this summer cooler to the next level. Sweet, tangy and deliciously exotic, it's the ultimate sweaty-day quencher. All that's missing is a plate of jerk chicken – or a cheeky slice of Jamaican fruitcake.

Origin

Rich in antioxidants and vitamin C, the petals of the Jamaican sorrel (not to be confused with the pungent green plant) have been used to make a refreshing herbal infusion in West Africa (where it originates, and the flowers are generally known as roselle or bissap), Latin America (where it is called *agua de Jamaica*) and the Caribbean for centuries – its use in Jamaica alone dates back to the 1700s. As the pretty pink flowers generally reach maturity in December, it comes as little surprise that this festively rouge beverage has been adopted as Jamaica's favourite Christmas drink.

Finding it

Usually served at Christmas time in the family home, this rum punch also graces Jamaican bar menus throughout the year; expect to pay USD$3–5/glass.

* VARIATIONS * **For an extra tropical spice kick, add a dried cinnamon stick to the dried flowers as they are steeping. Prefer your punch with bubbles? Add some soda water or ginger ale to the chilled mixture before serving. And, naturally, a little (or a lot) more rum to balance out the extra liquid.**

* By Sarah Reid *

Recipe Hibiscus Ginger Punch

INGREDIENTS

2 cups dried Jamaican hibiscus (sorrel) flowers

¼ cup minced fresh ginger

8 cups boiling water

2/3 cup agave syrup (or substitute for 1 cup raw sugar)

amber rum to taste (use Appleton Estate for Jamaican authenticity)

2 fresh lemons or limes, cut into wedges

2 cups ice cubes

mint, to garnish

METHOD

1. Place the hibiscus flowers and ginger in a large heatproof bowl.

2. Pour in the boiling water.

3. Cover the bowl and allow the mixture to steep for 1–2 hours.

4. Stir in the agave or sugar.

5. Strain the mixture into a large pitcher.

6. Chill the drink in the fridge.

7. Once the drink is cold and you are ready to serve it, add lightly squeezed lemon or lime wedges to the pitcher, along with ice and rum to taste.

8. Stir to combine everything.

9. Garnish with a sprig of mint and serve.

MAKES 1 LARGE JUG/PITCHER

* Hong Kong Yuan Yang *

HONG KONG

A heady concoction of tea and coffee, with generous lashings of evaporated milk, *yuan yang* is an invigorating mid-morning drink and a bitter-sweet reminder of Hong Kong's colonial past.

What is it?

The golden ratio when making *yuan yang* is three parts black tea and one part coffee. A blend of leaves is used that always includes a bold Ceylon and Pu'er (or Pu'erh), a dark, fermented Chinese tea. The resulting brew is combined with strong coffee made from robusta beans. *Yuan yang* is drunk black, or with evaporated milk and sugar.

Tasting

Yuan yang with milk is tan and opaque – the colour of grandma's tights – with a nose of nuts, smoke and a hint of vanilla. The first sip delivers the morning jolt – the coffee's smoky acidity and bitterness cut through the milk and sugar. *Sans* milk, it could taste harsh, almost like liquid cigarettes – a stark reminder that this was no ladies' drink. Your tastebuds are soon washed over by notes of spice and chocolate – that's the tea, with the rich and bold Ceylon tempered by the deep and woodsy insinuations of the Pu'er. Then comes the sweet aftertaste, subtle and complex, yet distinct from the sugar, and buoyed by the milk's creamy richness. Once sipped, you'll understand why the Chinese say 'one who hasn't tasted bitterness knows not sweetness'.

Origin

The beverage is a marriage between Southeast Asian coffee and 'pantyhose milk tea', the poor man's English tea. The latter, served in street stalls and *cha chaan tengs* (tea cafes), is brewed with eggshells for silkiness, and filtered through a cloth that hangs like a stocking. One day, an operator steeped in Chinese medical wisdom, wondered, 'Tea has cool energy – *yin*; coffee has hot energy – *yang*. Why not combine the two for balance?' Thus *yuan yang* was born. It's doused with creamy calorie-packed milk for the benefit of labourers.

Finding it

Lan Fong Yuen (2 Gage St, Central), where it may have been invented. It costs HK$18 (US$2.30) hot, HK$20 (US$2.60) cold.

* TIP * It's often consumed with evaporated milk and sugar, because the Chinese believe these protect the stomach against the harmful effects of caffeine. Cold *yuan yang* takes the edge off the taste, making it possible to down it between meetings. Accompanied by Hong Kong-style pastries such as egg custard tart or pineapple bun, it makes a sumptuous mid-morning snack.

* By Piera Chen *

Recipe Yuan Yang

If you want to make chilled *yuan yang*, leave the drink to cool, then chill it and serve it over ice.

INGREDIENTS

1½ cups water

1 tbs bold Ceylon tea leaves

1 tbs Pu'er tea leaves

½ cup extra-strong filtered Robusta coffee

just over 1 cup evaporated milk

sugar, to taste

METHOD

1. Boil the water.

2. Put the tea leaves into a teapot.

3. Pour the boiling water over the tea leaves.

4. Leave the tea to steep for 7 minutes. Cover pot with a tea cosy if necessary.

5. (Optional) If you like your beverage very hot, place the milk in a heatproof bowl set over a pan of simmering water.

6. Stir the milk frequently, until bubbles form around the edge and steam begins to rise from the milk.

7. Remove the milk from the heat.

8. Three-fifths fill a cup with tea.

9. Add a fifth of a cup of coffee (so the golden ration of three parts tea and one part coffee is achieved).

10. Fill the rest of the cup with hot or cold evaporated milk. If you don't take milk, adjust the quantities of tea and coffee accordingly, maintaining the golden ratio.

11. Stir in sugar, to taste.

SERVES 4–6

* Hummus *

LEBANON; JORDAN; ISRAEL; PALESTINE

Try not to let the oil drip as you scoop up a dab of smooth hummus with a piece of warm pita and bring the lemony, garlicky morsel to your lips – heaven!

What is it?

Hummus (or houmous) is chickpea paste. Traditionally it is spread across the bottom and along the sides of a shallow bowl, drizzled with olive oil and eaten with pita. Levantine Arabs often top theirs with minced lamb, caramelised onions and pine nuts, while Israelis tend to keep things vegetarian, spicing up their hummus with pickles, onion and/or *s'chug* (Yemenite hot paste).

Origin

Hummus comes from the Middle East, but exactly when and where it developed no one is sure. Chickpeas were cultivated in Neolithic times, and Arab recipes from the Middle Ages mention ways of preparing them but, according to one scholar, the first batch of hummus as we know it was boiled up in 18th-century Damascus. Whatever the case, hummus is hugely popular all over the Levant and is revered among both Jews and Arabs.

Tasting

Hummus inspires passions, and many connoisseurs have ardent views about the right way to prepare and serve it. Some like theirs as smooth and creamy as mousse, others prefer it textured and a little bit rough. Israelis enjoy 'wiping up' hummus with a pita at any time of the day or night, but for Palestinians, Jordanians and Lebanese hummus is commonly eaten for breakfast or brunch, often in little eateries that close by mid-afternoon. If you want to get Arabs and Israelis to agree about something, though, casually suggest making the beloved paste with peanut butter instead of tahini (as one celebrity chef does) – disbelief will quickly be replaced by a united chorus of outrage and disgust! For the best hummus, forget the cloying roasted pepper and coriander versions available in supermarkets and make the real deal for yourself.

Finding it

Hummus Said, deep in the Old City of Akko (Acre), Israel, serves superlative hummus for NIS15 (US$4).

* DID YOU KNOW? * When eaten together with pita, hummus is a 'complete protein' (ie it provides all nine essential amino acids), in addition to being an excellent source of protein and fibre.

* By Daniel Robinson *

Recipe Hummus

INGREDIENTS

250g (9oz) dried chickpeas

5 cups water, for cooking the chickpeas

½ tsp bicarb soda (baking soda) (optional)

½ cup tahini (sesame-seed paste)

¼ cup freshly squeezed lemon juice

2 garlic cloves, crushed

½ tbs salt

Toppings the hummus can be served with:

extra-virgin olive oil

chopped fresh parsley

pickle slices

ground cumin

sweet paprika

ground black pepper

pine nuts

ful medames (broad bean paste, see pages 66–67)

To serve

fresh pita

diced hard-boiled egg (optional)

felafel (optional)

s'chug (Yemenite hot chili paste) (optional)

thick slices of white onion (optional)

METHOD

1. Sort through the chickpeas and remove any damaged, misshapen or discoloured ones. Rinse the chickpeas.

2. Soak the chickpeas in a large bowl of cold water for 24 hours (in hot weather, place the bowl in the fridge so the mixture doesn't ferment). Change the water after 12 hours.

3. Drain and rinse the chickpeas. Put the chickpeas in a large pan with the water over a high heat.

4. If you'd like your hummus to be creamy (rather than textured), add the bicarb soda (baking soda).

5. When the mixture is boiling, skim off any foam that floats to the top. Reduce the heat to medium and cook the chickpeas 2–3 hours (in a pressure cooker, cook them for 45 minutes after the contents start boiling).

6. Make sure the chickpeas remain covered with liquid during the cooking time, adding water if necessary.

7. Stir the chickpeas every 30 minutes so the mixture doesn't stick to the bottom of the pan.

8. The chickpeas are ready when they squash easily between your thumb and index finger. Let the chickpeas cool in the water. Then drain the chickpeas, setting aside 1 cup of the cooking liquid.

9. If you'd like to garnish the hummus with whole chickpeas, set aside ½ cup of the cooked chickpeas.

10. Put the chickpeas, tahini, lemon juice, crushed garlic and salt in a blender and puree for at least 3 minutes (traditionally, this is done using a mortar and pestle). If the mixture is too thick, add cooking liquid as required to achieve your preferred consistency.

11. Using a circular motion, spread the now-creamy hummus in a shallow bowl so that it is evenly distributed along the bottom and sides.

12. Garnish the hummus with your preferred combination of toppings. Serve the hummus with fresh pita (for scooping up the hummus) and, if you'd like, diced hard-boiled egg, felafel, *s'chug* (Yemenite hot chili paste) and/or thick slices of onion.

* Maple Syrup *

CANADA

It doesn't just flow through their beloved trees, it courses through their veins. Maple syrup gives sweet life to Canadian brunches, one glorious drop at a time.

What is it?

Maple syrup is a sweet condiment produced exclusively from the sap of certain maple trees. Typically poured over pancakes, waffles and French toast, it can also be used as a key ingredient in numerous brunch dishes and treats: maple and fennel sausages, maple and blueberry bread pudding, maple syrup-soaked doughnut holes...

Tasting

Silky smooth and mildly fragrant out of the bottle, genuine maple syrup cannot be replicated, though many try. The sap's unique maple flavour, which is heightened by the caramelisation process that occurs during boiling, contains up to 300 different flavour compounds – hints of caramel, vanilla, rum, smoke, coffee, honey and wood are but a few. Much like wine, there is an enormous natural variety. But it's not until the maple syrup hits the steaming pancake or waffle that these flavours and fragrances come into their own. The syrup adds a depth of sweetness, and brings much-needed moisture to dishes. It also complements the savoury notes of bacon and sausages. Brunch is a social event in Canada, so it will always be a lively affair, with plenty of chatter, coffee and perhaps a log fire or two.

Origin

Long before the arrival of Europeans in northeastern parts of North America, aboriginal peoples produced maple syrup. During the spring thaw Algonquians created V-shaped incisions in tree trunks and inserted reeds to funnel the sap into birch bark containers. This was then concentrated into syrup by submerging scalding stones in the vessels or by letting the contents freeze overnight and discarding the layer of ice in the morning. Some tribes developed rituals, celebrating the first full moon of spring (known as the 'sugar moon') with a special dance. The equipment and processes have evolved, but the fundamentals remain unchanged.

Finding it

Havana, Vancouver, offers French toast stuffed with white chocolate, bananas and mascarpone served with genuine maple syrup for C$13.95 (US$12.45).

* DID YOU KNOW? * Québec, which produces 79 per cent of the world's maple syrup, was rocked in 2012 when some C$18 million was discovered to have been stolen from the Global Strategic Maple Syrup Reserve north of Montreal. The 'Great Maple Syrup Heist' is one of the world's largest agricultural thefts of all time.

* By Matt Phillips *

Recipe Maple Syrup

Making your own maple syrup is a unique culinary challenge. Not only will you need some maple trees and patience, but you'll also have to endure a very cold winter. The frigid temperatures are required to cause the trees to store starch in their root tissues – it's this material than turns into sugar. Spring is the maple syrup harvesting season, when nights are below 0°C (32°F) and days are getting warm.

INGREDIENTS

- maple trees with at least a trunk diameter of 25cm (10in) – sugar maples are best, though red maples and black maples work too
- taps (or spiles) – online is the easiest place to buy them
- collection containers – you have the option of a bag, an attached bucket or a ground bucket (a clean milk jug will do the job)
- electric hand drill
- coffee filter
- 20L (171/qt) pot
- sugar thermometer
- cheesecloth

METHOD

1. Use an electric hand drill to make a hole on the side of the maple tree that receives the most light. The hole, located above a large root or under a large branch, 30–120cm (12–48in) above the ground, should be made at a slight downward angle. The hole's diameter should match the size of the tap, but its depth should be 1.25cm (½in) longer.

2. Attach the collection container beneath the tap. It's best to fit a cover to keep rainwater and bugs out.

3. Repeat steps 1 and 2 on more trees. Each tree will produce almost 40L (70 pints) of sap each season, which yields just 1L (1¾ pints) of maple syrup.

4. Check the containers every couple of days and transfer the sap to larger sealed containers for storage until the season ends.

5. Use the coffee filter to remove sediment, twigs or bugs from the collected sap.

6. Fill the pot with 15L (26 pints) or so of filtered sap and bring it to the boil.

7. As the sap level lowers in the pot due to evaporation, continue adding more sap.

8. When all the sap has been added, and the remaining fluid starts to get low, use a sugar thermometer to check the temperature. Remove the pot from the heat when it reaches 103.9°C (219.02°F).

9. Use the cheesecloth to filter the syrup while it is still fairly hot.

10. Pour the syrup into sterilised containers.

11. Remove the tap from each tree (the hole will seal itself).

EACH TREE AND TAP YIELDS APPROXIMATELY 1L (1¾PINTS) OF MAPLE SYRUP

* Michelada *

MEXICO

The Michelada is *the* preferred Mexican brunch drink and for good reason – the refreshing beer cocktail goes down oh-so-nicely with spicy food, and yes, it even calms throbbing hangovers.

What is it?

In its simplest form, a Michelada is a cold Mexican beer with a splash of lime juice served in a glass rimmed with salt and/or chilli powder. But the popular cocktail comes in many different forms: it's often prepared with Clamato juice (tomato juice flavoured with spices and clam broth) and sauces such as Worcestershire, Maggi and Tabasco.

Tasting

When ordering a Michelada at a restaurant or bar in Mexico, the waiter will often ask if you prefer '*clara o oscura*' (light or dark) beer. Don't worry, there's no wrong answer. Mexican beers Bohemia, Negra Modelo and Pacífico work particularly well.
A spicy Michelada is often referred to as a Cubana. Similar to a Bloody Mary, *sans* vodka, the Cubana is the hangover remedy of choice in Mexico – the hot sauce and chilli powder in the cocktail help you sweat out those party toxins, while the chilled beer is just plain refreshing. Nothing beats knocking back Micheladas in a boisterous *cantina*, where you can bond with locals while watching televised *fútbol* matches, get slap-happy playing dominoes or chow down tasty bar grub such as ceviche cocktails and seafood soup.

Origin

No one can say for certain who invented the Michelada, so if anyone claims to have the answer, well, the dude's probably had too many Micheladas. Mi-chel-ada most likely is an abbreviated form of the Spanish phrase '*mi chela helada*' ('my ice-cold brew'). The drink has long been popular along the Pacific coast and in major cities such as Mexico City and Guadalajara, but you can find it pretty much anywhere in Mexico nowadays.

Finding it

Los Aguachiles' Playa del Carmen and Tulum branches prepare a fine '*Clamato preparado*' Michelada for M$53 (US$4) in *cantina*-style settings.

* VARIATIONS * In some places specialising in Pacific coast cuisine, the Michelada is often a meal in itself. Prepared like a seafood cocktail, raw oyster, baby clams or boiled shrimp are served in a glass with beer, Clamato juice, avocado squares, diced tomato and coriander. The seafood Michelada served at Sinaloa-style eatery Mi Gusto Es has many fans.

Recipe Michelada

INGREDIENTS

2 tbs coarse salt

1 tbs chilli powder, preferably Tajín brand

1¼ limes

350mL (12fl oz) Mexican beer (light or dark)

2 dashes Worcestershire sauce

1 dash Maggi sauce

2 dashes hot sauce, preferably Tabasco

3–4 cubes of ice

METHOD

1. Mix the salt and chilli powder seasoning on a plate.

2. Cut the whole lime in half and rub it around the rim of a chilled 475mL (16fl oz) beer mug or large glass.

3. Upend the glass and dip the edge in the salt and chilli powder mixture, so the edge is coated in the powder.

4. Pour cold beer into the glass, taking care not to disturb the prepared rim.

5. Squeeze the whole lime.

6. Add the lime juice, Worcestershire, Maggi and Tabasco sauces to the glass.

7. Stir and add ice if desired.

8. Garnish with the reserved ¼ lime wedge by positioning it on the rim of glass.

SERVES 1

* Oliang *

THAILAND

Forget Starbucks; when it comes to starting the day with a real caffeine kick, the only thing that truly hits the spot is *oliang*, a Thai-Chinese version of iced coffee.

What is it?

Oliang is no normal coffee. Because coffee beans are somewhat scarce in Thailand, locals came up with a plan: they roasted the beans alongside soy beans and corn and created a gorgeous drink with an especially sharp, bitter flavour. *Oliang* is a traditional Thai coffee, drunk almost exclusively before noon.

Origin

Hailing from the Thai-Chinese community, the name *oliang* derives from the Teochew dialect; the o part means 'black' while *liang* means 'iced'. This iced, black breakfast drink has stayed true to its roots and, while there are variations, it is usually found only on roadside stalls or in rustic restaurants, not in fancy coffee shops. Trendy Thai teens may dimiss *oliang* as something their grandparents sip, but its sharp flavour easily beats any espresso or latte.

Tasting

Oliang is like sipping on nostalgia. For decades, it has been the drink of choice for Thais, who love its powerful, cool flavours. Imagine starting your day at a busy Thai restaurant, sitting on a blue plastic stool, surrounded by wooden tables and bare floors. All around, locals are slurping noodles or munching on grilled pork and sticky rice. Your *oliang* arrives in a glass, a glistening all-black combination of ice, roasted coffee and soy beans. Take a sniff first; it's coffee, but not as you know it. As you sip *oliang* through a straw, the coffee flavours flood your senses, but they are quickly overtaken by the bitter notes of the roasted soy beans. The unique aftertaste is wonderfully robust and sharp.

Finding it

Head to the stalls along Yaowarat, in Bangkok's Chinatown, for the best *oliang*. It will cost around 30 baht (US$1).

* TIP * If the original *oliang* packs too much of a punch for your tastes, add some syrup to sweeten the drink. Other options include pouring in milk, or condensed milk (known as *yok-lor*), which has the added bonus of creating swirling, tumbling streaks of white as it blends with the black liquid. The strength of *oliang* depends on how much coffee is used; this can vary significantly in pre-made mixes so check the packet.

* By Mark Beales *

Recipe Oliang

INGREDIENTS

2 tbs dried corn

2 tbs soy beans

1 tsp white sesame seeds

4 tbs coffee beans (robusta is best)

2 cups boiling water

1 tbs sugar

2 cups crushed ice

METHOD

1. Roast the corn and soy beans in a large frying pan on a low heat, shaking them occasionally.

2. After about 5–8 minutes, when they start to brown, turn off the heat and add the sesame seeds.

3. Leave everything to cool completely, then stir in the coffee beans.

4. Transfer the mixture to a coffee grinder and process until it becomes powdery, or pound the mixture using a mortar and pestle if you don't own a coffee grinder.

5. Tip the powder into a large heatproof jug.

6. Add the boiling water and leave to infuse for 1 minute.

7. Strain the liquid through a muslin or coffee filter into four heatproof coffee glasses and leave to stand for 5 minutes. If you only have thick standard glasses, place a metal teaspoon in each before adding the hot liquid, as this will prevent the glass from cracking.

8. Add the sugar and stir to dissolve.

9. Add the crushed ice and serve immediately.

MAKES 4 GLASSES

* Seville Marmalade *

UNITED KINGDOM

Beloved by Paddington Bear and many Britons worldwide, wobbling amber spoonfuls of this bittersweet preserve, spread on to warm buttered toast, make the ideal way to start the day.

What is it?

Come January in Britain, kitchens the length of the country are flooded in a bright citrus aroma as kilo upon kilo of Seville oranges are simmered with sugar on stoves for several hours. The result is marmalade and your first taste may be the start of a life-long love affair conducted over toast and a cup of tea.

Origin

In 1952–3, Sir Edmund Hillary and his team breakfasted on marmalade at the foot of Mt Everest. Forty years previously, marmalade almost made it to the South Pole with Robert Scott. And 2000 years ago, marmalade began its own journey in Southern Europe, probably Spain, as a quince paste (*marmelo* is Portuguese for 'quince'). Using otherwise bitter fruit to create preserves wasn't unusual; but few people would have picked Dundee, Scotland, as the place where marmalade made its transformation from after-dinner delicacy to breakfast staple. By the 19th century several firms were producing dozens of varieties and sending crates of it to Britain's colonies.

Tasting

There's a pop as you crack open the first jar of your homemade marmalade. This is the big moment: has it set? What's the flavour like? Doubts are allayed as a zesty scent of oranges reaches your nose. The colour is golden-bronze, the jelly catching the morning sunlight. You spread a rounded spoonful on a hot, buttered slice of toast and marvel at how a couple of hours' work can uncover the essence of a fruit. Sugar, water and lots of oranges: such a simple way to start the day. However you prefer it – thinly shredded with the spirit-lifting translucence of stained glass, or dark, brooding and chunky – marmalade's secret is the unmistakeable Seville orange and its loose-fitting, knobbly skin. The sharp, pectin-rich Seville is not an orange you'd want to juice, but it creates perfect preserves.

Finding it

The last remaining manufacturer of marmalade in Dundee is Mackays but you don't have to go that far north; The Original Marmalade Festival takes place at Dalemain Mansion in Cumbria, England, every March. Marmalade is a staple of British village fetes, where jars sell for about £3 (US$4.80).

* VARIATIONS * **Marmalade is a chameleon among preserves. Limes in the West Indies, grapefruit in New Zealand, lemons and quinces all find their way into regional recipes where Seville oranges are unavailable.**

* By Robin Barton *

Recipe Seville Marmalade

In Britain, making Seville marmalade is a welcome antidote to the winter weather. This recipe is for a strong, dark, Dundee-style marmalade with hints of the Caribbean.

INGREDIENTS

1.3kg (2lb 14oz) Seville oranges

2 lemons (unwaxed)

2 limes (unwaxed)

2 sweet oranges (unwaxed)

3.4 litres (6 pints) of water

10 cups preserving sugar

splash of dark rum

1 tbs treacle

METHOD

1. Scrub all the fruit under hot water to remove any wax that may be on the skins. Put the whole fruits into a large preserving pan with the water. Bring the water to the boil and simmer over a low heat for up to 2 hours or until the fruit pierces easily with the point of a knife.

2. Meanwhile, thoroughly wash a large number of jam jars and their lids, dry them and then leave them to warm and dry in an oven set to 140°C (275°F). Alternatively, put the jars and their lids in the dishwasher and run a hot cycle.

3. Lift out the fruit using a slotted spoon, reserving the cooking water.

4. When the fruit is cool enough to handle, cut all the fruits in half. Scrape out the flesh and pips and place these in a muslin bag or square. Tie up the muslin tightly and place it in the reserved cooking liquid in the pan.

5. Slice all the orange skins (and some of the lemons and limes according to taste) into strips, according to your preference. Up to 5mm (¼in) is a suitable width. Add the sliced peel to the pan and bring the liquid to the boil.

6. Add the sugar and stir until it is dissolved. Add the treacle.

7. Remove the muslin bag of pith, scraping the outside of the bag and adding any residue to the pan. Continue boiling the mixture until the marmalade reaches a temperature of 105°C (221°F). Stir in a slug of rum.

8. Ladle the marmalade into the prepared jars using a steel funnel, taking care not get any on the lip of the jar (this will prevent the lid from sealing properly).

9. Seal the jars with lids while the marmalade is still hot; as it cools it will cause the lids to seal tightly.

10. Allow the marmalade to cool, then label the jars and store in a cool, dry place.

MAKES ABOUT A DOZEN JARS

* Smashed Avocado *

MELBOURNE, AUSTRALIA

This quintessential Melbourne brunch element elevates avocado on toast to a whole new level, with the city's chefs combining simple ingredients and fresh flavours to create a modern Australian classic.

What is it?

The star ingredient, avocado, is combined with peppery olive oil, lemon juice, salt and pepper, and slathered thickly on toothsome sourdough toast. It's served with two poached eggs, perhaps scattered with goat's cheese, chilli, dukkah, fresh herbs, and often accompanied by beetroot or tomato chutney.

Tasting

'Going out for brunch' has become as ingrained in Melbourne's culture as catching the tram or whiling away a Saturday afternoon at the footy. Every weekend morning you'll find friends catching up over coffees and brunch, with patrons spilling out into cafe courtyards. The high standards Australians have come to expect are reflected in the quality of the food and coffee; dishes come beautifully presented, and chefs offer new takes on menu classics. While creativity is rewarded – expected, even – there are a few essential components of the classic smashed avo: crunchy sourdough; perfectly ripe avocado mixed with good-quality olive oil and seasoned well; salty cheese, preferably a local goat's cheese or Persian feta; and fresh, fragrant herbs, such as mint or parsley. The crowning glory is the perfectly poached eggs.

Origin

Melburnians can hardly lay claim to being the first to mash avocado – surely that honour belongs to the Aztecs – but the city's chefs bring a fresh perspective on how to enjoy the humble fruit. The origins of smashed avocado is unclear; some sources state that Sydney chef Bill Granger created it, while Melbourne newspaper *The Age* credits local cafe Porgie + Mr Jones with being the first to offer the dish.

Finding it

You can buy a great smashed avo with an egg at Industry Beans, 3/62 Rose Street, Melbourne, for A$18.50 (US$16.20).

* TIPS * Over the last decade Melbourne has become renowned throughout the world for the quality of its coffee, giving rise to 'Australian-style' cafes in cities such as London, Paris and New York. Enjoy your smashed avo with the classic Australian coffee, the flat white.

* By Katie O'Connell *

Recipe Smashed Avo on Sourdough

Use this recipe as a starting point; feel free to add your favourite brunch extras, such as smoked salmon, or grilled tomatoes or mushrooms.

INGREDIENTS

1 medium avocado

1 tbs extra-virgin olive oil

squeeze of lemon juice, to taste

salt and ground black pepper, to taste

chilli flakes, to taste (optional)

4 slices thick sourdough, toasted

1–2 tbs white wine vinegar

4 fresh eggs

80g (3oz) goat's cheese or fetta, roughly diced

1 tbs dukkah (Egyptian seed mix)

1 tbs fresh mint (or a herb of your choice), finely chopped

2 tbs tomato or beetroot relish, to serve

METHOD

1. Roughly mash the avocado, olive oil, lemon juice, salt and pepper and chilli flakes (if using) together using a fork.

2. Divide the mixture into four portions and spread each thickly on a slice of toasted sourdough.

3. To poach the eggs, bring about 10cm (4in) of water to a simmer in a pan.

4. Add the white vinegar to the water and stir until a whirlpool forms.

5. Crack an egg into a cup or a ramekin.

6. Slide the egg into the centre of the whirlpool, folding the edges of the whites inwards to keep the egg together and to form a spherical shape.

7. Repeat with the remaining eggs, so they are all in the water.

8. Cook the eggs for 3–4 minutes, until the white are set but the yolks are still runny.

9. Carefully lift out the eggs with a slotted spoon and place them on kitchen paper to dry.

10. Sprinkle the cheese over the avocado mixture on each slice of sourdough toast.

11. Sprinkle with dukkah and chopped fresh herbs.

12. Top each portion with a poached egg.

13. Season with salt and pepper.

14. Serve with relish on the side, and enjoy immediately.

* Smoothie *

Smoothies are not a new treat; for centuries, people around the world have pureed local fruits to create tasty, satisfying beverages and today this trend remains as strong as ever.

What is it?

A smoothie is a dense blended drink made from pureed fresh fruit, often processed with ice, milk, yoghurt or ice cream (or a combination of these) and sweetened (or not) with honey and sugar. There are countless variations and endless possibilities, making the drink one of the most versatile around.

Tasting

Drinking a smoothie is the perfect way to tantalise your mouth. Seriously. Think about it. Whether zesty or zingy, sweet or savoury (it depends on the flavour, after all), the first sip of a smoothie bounces off your taste buds. Then the physical sensation kicks in – the drink's cream-like texture rolls like velvet across your tongue. Even your teeth get some post-taste action – let's be upfront here: we nibble on micro-chunks of strawberry, or small pieces of banana, long after our digestive systems have relished the sweet puree. And hey, you get to do it all over again, at least for as many gulps as it takes to finish this very satisfying and filling 'edible drink'. The best time to enjoy a smoothie is when you're hungry (rather than thirsty); it's a meal in itself.

Origin

While it's generally agreed that the beverage has been around for centuries in various guises, the origin of the term 'smoothie' is another matter. Americans lay claim to first 'naming' it, and some sources state that the Waring Blendor company mentioned the term 'smoothie' in its cookbooks in the 1940s. Others say the word became the norm during the 'hippy sixties', when smoothies were offered as a healthy alternative to the popular milkshake as part of a new wave of macrobiotic vegetarianism. Since then, the term has become widely associated with pureed drinks made in a blender.

Finding it

Some of the best *licuados* (smoothies) are served by apron-clad women in Sucre's *Mercado Central*, Bolivia for $b5.50 (US$0.80).

* DID YOU KNOW? * Slight 'downer': being high in sugar and calories, most smoothies are not as healthy as the health gurus first believed, especially those made with added sugar and the likes of ice cream.

* By Kate Armstrong *

Recipe Banana Smoothie

There are more smoothie recipes than there are cookbooks. Given the never-ending combinations, we've gone for one of the classics – the banana smoothie (with a healthy twist). You can use any blendable fruit in place of bananas and supplement wheat germ with superfoods such as chia seeds.

INGREDIENTS

2 ripe bananas, peeled and roughly chopped

1½ cups skimmed milk, chilled

7¼ cup natural yoghurt (full-fat or low-fat)

1 tbs honey

1 tbs wheat germ

METHOD

1. Place the banana, milk, yoghurt, honey and wheat germ in a blender.

2. Process the mixture until it is well combined and smooth.

3. Pour the smoothie into four glasses.

4. Serve the smoothies immediately.

SERVES 4

* Teh Tarik *

(E) (cup icon)

MALAYSIA; INDONESIA

You haven't arrived in Southeast Asia until you've drunk a mug of *teh tarik* – a strongly steeped colonial cuppa served with a generous spoonful of sticky condensed milk.

What is it?

As *chai* is to India, *teh tarik* is to Southeast Asia. The name literally means 'pulled tea' – a reference to the ritual of preparation, during which the steaming-hot liquid is poured back and forth between two pans to mix in the condensed milk, cool the drink, and churn up a rich, foaming head.

Origin

Before the colonial period, tea in Malaysia and Indonesia was mainly green, but migrant workers from India imported the tradition of black tea served with milk. These indentured nation-builders were only deemed worthy of bitter, low-grade Ceylonese tea but, by lucky happenchance, their arrival coincided with the invention of sweetened condensed milk, transforming second-rate tea into something altogether new and spectacular.

Tasting

This Asian variation on the British cuppa is for people who like their beverages strong and sweet enough to dissolve the enamel from their teeth. *Teh tarik* originated with the Mamak (Indian Tamil) community, and Mamak food stalls are still the best place to enjoy the glorious theatre of its preparation. The 'pulling' of *teh tarik* is an art form – anything less than a metre between the two jugs that the tea is poured between would be considered amateur. Virtuoso tea-makers can pour two cups simultaneously, even sideways, while spinning backwards, sloshing the drink from one vessel to the next to achieve the perfect flavour, sweetness and consistency. Miraculously, not a drop is spilled – imagine Tom Cruise in *Cocktail* but with a Malay-Indian twist.

Finding it

Try the Mamak food stalls around the Central Market in Kuala Lumpur. Expect to pay less than RM2 (US$0.26).

* TIP * *Teh tarik* was born to be served with *roti canai* (see pages 140–141). No matter how exhausted you are by the heat and chaos, the sucker punch of caffeine, tannin and sugar will snap you to your senses, and you are guaranteed to be hungry when it happens. Fortunately, the soothing combination of soft, flaky flatbread and fragrant curry sauce will be close at hand to create the perfect all-day brunch.

* By Joe Bindloss *

Recipe **Teh Tarik**

The ingredients are simple – it's the 'pulling' of the *teh tarik* that takes practice.

INGREDIENTS

4 cups water

4 heaped tbs broken black tea leaves

4 generous tbs condensed milk

METHOD

1. Boil the water.

2. Place a sackcloth strainer in a large heatproof container.

3. Put the tea leaves in the strainer.

4. Pour over the boiling water.

5. Steep the tea leaves for at least 10 minutes, until the tea is dark and strongly brewed.

6. To make the first cup of tea, pour 1 cup of the steeped tea into a metal jug.

7. Stir in 1 generous tbs condensed milk.

8. Start the pulling ritual. You will need another metal jug. The trick is to pour the mixture back and forth between the two jugs to generate the required foam and aeration. Start and end each pour with the two vessels close together but hold them as far apart as you dare for the middle part of each pour. Six pours should be the minimum. This is your chance to be a showman, so don't be afraid to throw in a few stunt moves.

9. When the *teh tarik* is definitely 'pulled', pour it into a pre-warmed glass mug and serve it immediately.

10. Repeat the process with the remaining steeped tea and condensed milk.

SERVES 4

* Tomato Ketchup *

USA

Its name might not be American, but ketchup is *the* hero condiment of American cuisine. Fries, burgers, hot dogs... these are mere shadows of themselves without their partner in crime.

What is it?

Such a straightforward sauce – at its purest, just tomatoes, sugar and salt – but it's a transformation that makes you believe in alchemy: from the simple to the sublime in a couple of hours. The tomatoes are crushed and cooked with sugar and spices, then strained, seasoned with vinegar and salt, and simmered until reduced to a thick sauce.

Origin

The word 'ketchup' comes from the Chinese *kôe-chiap* or *kê-chiap*, a sauce made from fish and spices in the 17th century. This was taken to the Malay states in the early 18th century, where it was called *kecap*, and then brought back to Britain, where it was called 'ketchup' and modified to consist primarily of mushrooms. British colonists took the mushroom condiment with them to the USA, and tomato versions of the sauce started to appear in American publications in the early 19th century.

Tasting

It's all about the sweet salty tang when it comes to good ketchup. Smooth and almost creamy in texture, the mouth-feel is satisfying and reassuring. Now picture this: fresh, soft, long bread roll, split and loaded with a juicy frankfurter. A perfect stream of ketchup runs the length of the sausage. It is the magic ingredient, marrying up the crumb of the roll and the eponymous dog. But what else? In Australia, it's virtually a sin to eat a meat pie without tomato sauce (as ketchup is known Down Under). Bologna sandwich – ketchup! The true joy of it, though, is that everyone has a dish they can't eat without it. It might be eggs, it might be meatloaf, perhaps macaroni, maybe even cheese. Ketchup is irrepressible and universally adored.

Finding it

Try squirting a generous amount of ketchup on a sublime 'single dog' for US$1.95 at Gray's Papaya, 2090 Broadway, New York City.

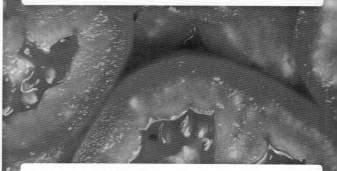

* VARIATIONS * If you're feeling adventurous, why not seek out a recipe for the original ketchup. Not for the faint-hearted, this pungent sauce is made from fermented fish and pickled vegetables. Or look up the traditional mushroom ketchup that was made in Britain.

* By Ben Handicott *

Recipe Tomato Ketchup

INGREDIENTS

2 tbs olive oil

1 large onion, peeled and chopped

1 carrot, peeled and chopped

1 celery stick, chopped

½ cup chopped parsley

1 garlic clove, peeled and sliced

1 tsp ground cumin

1 tsp ground fennel

2 cloves

1 tsp ground black pepper

1kg (2lb 2ozlb) chopped ripe tomatoes

1½ cups water

1 cup red or white wine vinegar

½ cup soft light brown sugar

salt

METHOD

1. Place all the ingredients except the tomatoes, water, vinegar, sugar and salt in a large pan.

2. Bring the mixture to the boil, then simmer over a medium heat for about 15 minutes, stirring occasionally.

3. Stir in the tomatoes and the water.

4. Simmer the mixture, uncovered, for 45 minutes to 1 hour, until it has reduced by half, stirring occasionally to prevent it from sticking.

5. Blend the sauce in a food processor or with a stick blender, until it is as smooth as possible.

6. Push the sauce through a sieve into a clean pan.

7. Stir in the vinegar and sugar.

8. Simmer the sauce again until it has a thick and creamy consistency, stirring often.

9. Add salt to taste.

10. Transfer the ketchup to a bowl, if eating it immediately. Alternatively, decant the hot sauce into clean bottles or jars that have been sterilised by being put through a dishwasher on a hot cycle, or had boiling water poured into them and left for 10 minutes before being tipped away.

MAKES ABOUT 2 CUPS

* Glossary *

açai Grape-like fruit from a palm native to Central and South America, often pulped.

ackee Tropical fruit with a buttery, egg-like consistency, native to West Africa but transplanted to Jamaica.

chana dal Yellow dried split peas used in Indian and Malaysian cuisine.

chicharrón Fried, crispy pork rinds (also sometimes made from chicken, mutton or beef), originating from Spain but popular throughout Latin America.

cotija Dry hard cow's milk cheese from Mexico, similar to Parmesan.

dal Dried pulse which has been split, though the term also refers to a thick stew made from them that is an important part of cuisine on the Indian sub-continent.

dashi Japanese fish stock, the base of miso soup.

ful medames Broad bean paste originally from Egypt but popular throughout the Middle East.

gạ ch cua xào dầu ăn Vietnamese crab paste in soybean oil.

gach tôm xao dau an Vietnamese shrimp paste.

grits Porridge of boiled-down, stone-milled corn of Native American origin.

katsuobuoshi Dried, fermented and smoked skipjack tuna or bonito, often flaked.

kombu Dried seaweed eaten throughout East Asia.

labneh Strained yoghurt cheese made from goats milk from the Eastern Mediterranean.

mirin Japanese rice wine, similar to sake but less alcoholic and with a higher sugar content.

nước mắm Vietnamese fish sauce.

pandan leaves Long green leaves used in Southeast Asian cuisine for their sweet, toasted coconut/pecan/basmati flavour.

pu'er Dark, fermented Chinese tea. Sometimes spelt pu'erh.

sambar Lentil and tamarind stew popular in South India and Sri Lanka.

sambol Sri Lankan chili sauce.

s'chug Yemenite hot chili paste often used in Israel to spice up hummus.

tahini Paste made from ground, hulled sesame seeds used in Eastern Mediterranean cuisine.

urad dal Black lentils from India and Sri Lanka.

* Contributing Authors *

Bill Granger is an Australian chef and food writer. In 1993, at the age of 24, he dropped out of art school and opened his first restaurant, *bills*, in Sydney's Darlinghurst. It quickly became famous for the best scrambled eggs and ricotta hotcakes in town. Since then, he has opened restaurants in London, Tokyo, Seoul and Honolulu. Today, Bill has five TV series, viewed in 30 countries; 11 cookbooks, which have sold over 1 million copies worldwide; and he writes weekly newspaper and magazine columns in both the UK and Australia. You can experience Bill's famous brunches in any of his restaurants, including:

BILLS DARLINGHURST	GRANGER AND CO	GRANGER AND CO
433 Liverpool Street	Clerkenwell	Notting Hill
Darlinghurst	50 Sekforde Street	175 Westbourne Grove
NSW 2010	London EC1R 0HA	London W11 2SB
bills.com.au	grangerandco.com	grangerandco.com

Kate Armstrong Street-food connoisseur and lover of all things sweet. Capable chef. Global taste buds. Stomach of steel. Nothing – except oysters – is off her menu.

Johanna Ashby Food and travel freelance writer and specialist author for Lonely Planet, keen on everything epicurean from street food to fine dining and everything in between. www.thehappydiner.co.uk.

Robin Barton An editor, journalist and award-winning author who covers food, adventure and travel.

Mark Beales Co-author of Lonely Planet's *Thailand*, dedicated foodie and curry connoisseur. Visit markbeales.com.

Sarah Bennett & Lee Slater A New Zealand-based writing duo specialising in food, travel and outdoor adventure.

Joe Bindloss Former food critic for *Time Out*'s restaurant guides, specialising in food from Southeast Asia, China, Korea and the Indian subcontinent, and current Lonely Planet Destination Editor.

Joshua Samuel Brown Purveyor of good eats from Singapore's hawker centres to Taiwan's night markets to Portland's food-truck scene, Joshua is co-author of a dozen-plus Lonely Planet guides and two collections of short stories, *Vignettes of Taiwan* and *How Not to Avoid Jet Lag and Other Tales of Travel Madness*.

Piera Chen Travel addict, sometime poet, author of Lonely Planet books on Hong Kong and China, Piera's idea of the perfect brunch involves Prosecco and dim sum.

Jessica Cole London-based travel fanatic working as a Commissioning Editor at Lonely Planet. Believes a good brunch should be a compulsory component of any day.

Megan Eaves New Mexican travel writer living in London; currently a Destination Editor for Lonely Planet. Will eat anything, but takes a special shine to food in dumpling form and knock-your-head-off spice. Evangelist for New Mexican cuisine.

Helen Elfer Martini fanatic who has written about cocktails (and

travel) in the Middle East, London and Shanghai. Prefers breakfast in the early afternoon.

Ethan Gelber Founder/editor of TheTravelWord.com; Outbounding. org founder; agitator for responsible, sustainable and local travel; voracious consumer of culture, especially of the edible kind.

Ben Handicott Once published travel pictorial and reference books for a living, now dreams about, writes about and sometimes even does, travel. Eats too.

John Hecht Feeds his hopeless street-food habit as a Mexico City-based travel writer. He has authored numerous Lonely Planet *Mexico* books.

Carolyn B. Heller Writes about travel and food for Lonely Planet, Forbes Travel, and other publications, and has eaten her way across five continents.

Anita Isalska Travel editor, freelance writer and gluten-free gourmand. Anita blogs about her life in food at madamefreefrom.blogspot.co.uk.

Adam Karlin A US-based Lonely Planet author who loves to eat, wander and combine the two whenever possible.

Patrick Kinsella An English writer who specialises in exploring the adventurous and edible sides of the world's wilder corners. Most recently he was to be found eating bees in Moldova. @paddy_kinsella

Alex Leviton A travel writer, editorial director and long-time Lonely Planet author, Alex is a Slow Travel and Slow Food enthusiast who once moved to Europe with buttermilk powder specifically for biscuit-baking purposes.

Catherine Le Nevez Lonely Planet author primarily based (wanderlust aside) in foodie mecca Paris; Doctor of Creative Arts in Writing; Bloody Mary devotee.

Shawn Low Singapore-born, Melbourne-based travel editor Shawn lives vicariously through food (and coffee). His mantra? 'Try anything at least once.' Find him on Twitter @shawnlow

MaSovaida Morgan Georgia-born, Texas-raised and currently Nashville-based, MaSovaida is Lonely Planet's South America Destination Editor and believes bacon is its own food group.

Karyn Noble An Australian-born, London-based editor, writer and shameless epicurean who specialises in gourmet and luxury travel content. She can polish off a full English breakfast with ease.

Etain O'Carroll Author of over 20 Lonely Planet guidebooks, Etain loves to bake and writes here about favourite dishes from a childhood in the west of Ireland.

Katie O'Connell A Melbourne-based Lonely Planet editor and writer, keen home cook, cheese and beer connoisseur, and regular sampler of Melbourne's restaurant scene.

Zora O'Neill Co-author of *Forking Fantastic! Put the Party Back in Dinner Party* and blogging at Roving Gastronome (rovinggastronome.com).

Stephanie Ong Writer, editor, relentless traveller and food fanatic (especially when it come to the Malaysian/Singaporean dishes of her youth), Stephanie has lived in four different cities and is currently based in Milan, Italy.

Matt Phillips Born in the 'Great White North', this London-based writer, editor and brunch-lover ensures his homemade pancakes and waffles are never wanting for Canadian maple syrup.

Josephine Quintero A resident of Spain for over 20 years who has enthusiastically embraced the country's cuisine, particularly when it appeals to her sweet tooth… still more so when it involves chocolate.

Kevin Raub An American-born, Brazil-based travel and entertainment journalist who never misses the opportunity to stroll through a grocery store in a foreign country.

Sarah Reid Travel journalist, Lonely Planet editor and eternal globetrotter, Sarah has sampled the classic foodie delights of more than 70 countries, but this book represents her first attempt at recreating some of her favourite dishes at home.

Daniel Robinson Author of food reviews – and Lonely Planet guides – of culinary hot spots such as Israel, Tunisia, Cambodia, Borneo, France and Germany.

Brendan Sainsbury A British Lonely Planet writer based near the gastronomically eclectic city of Vancouver in Canada. He has tasted weird and wonderful food in over 70 countries around the world and lived to tell the tale.

Dan Savery Raz An author based in the culinary capital of Tel Aviv, Dan contributed to Lonely Planet's *Street Food*, *Israel* and BBC Travel. See: www.danscribe.com

Regis St Louis Regis has travelled the globe in search of memorable meals, contributing to dozens of Lonely Planet guides. He lives in Brooklyn, New York.

Steve Waters Melbourne-based author; wasted whole decades travelling to places with unpronounceable names; has been hunting the perfect barra for the last five years.

Luke Waterson Co-author of Lonely Planet's *Peru*, *Ecuador*, *Cuba* and *Mexico* books and food/travel writer for the BBC. Addicted to Oaxaca's chillies.

Tracy Whitmey Lonely Planet editor with a voracious appetite for food and travel, usually found hanging around food markets saying 'What is that? How do you cook it?'

Rob Whyte Writer, teacher-trainer, Busan resident and Korean food aficionado.

Karla Zimmerman A Chicago-based writer who has tested the sausages, beer and chocolates of more than 55 countries. Follow her on Twitter and Instagram at @karlazimmerman.

* Index *

Location

Type of Dish

The World's Best Brunches
Published in March 2015
by Lonely Planet Publications Pty Ltd
ABN 36 005 607 983
www.lonelyplanet.com
ISBN 978 1 74360 746 6
© Lonely Planet 2015
Foreword and recipe on page 21
© William Granger
Photographs on pages 6, 21, 218
© Mikkel Vang
© Photographs as indicated 2015
10 9 8 7 6 5 4 3 2 1

Printed in China

Publishing Director Piers Pickard
Commissioning Editor Jessica Cole
Layout Designer Austin Taylor
Cover Designer Mark Adams
Editors Lucy Doncaster, Sonja Brodie
Image Researcher Shweta Andrews
Pre-press production Tag Publishing
Print production Larissa Frost

Lonely Planet offices
Australia
90 Maribyrnong St, Footscray, Victoria,
3011, Australia
Phone 03 8379 8000
Email talk2us@lonelyplanet.com.au
USA
150 Linden St, Oakland, CA 94607
Phone 510 250 6400 Email info@lonelyplanet.com
United Kingdom
Media Centre, 201 Wood Lane, London W12 7TQ
Phone 020 8433 1333 Email go@lonelyplanet.co.uk

Paper in this book is certified against the
Forest Stewardship Council™ standards.
FSC™ promotes environmentally responsible,
socially beneficial and economically viable
management of the world's forests.